CLYMER®
KAWASAKI
KDX200 • 1983-1988

P.O. Box 12901, Overland Park, Kansas 66282-2901

Copyright ©1990 Prism Business Media Inc.

FIRST EDITION
First Printing June, 1990
Second Printing September, 1995
Third Printing April, 2000
Fourth Printing July, 2006

Printed in U.S.A.

CLYMER and colophon are registered trademarks of Prism Business Media Inc.

ISBN: 0-89287-514-3

Library of Congress: 90-55151

AUTHOR: *Ron Wright.*

TECHNICAL PHOTOGRAPHY: *Ron Wright.*

TECHNICAL ASSISTANCE: *Curt Jordan, Jordan Engineering, Santa Ana, California.*

TECHNICAL ILLUSTRATIONS: *Steve Amos.*

TOOLS AND EQUIPMENT: *K & L Supply Co. at www.klsupply.com.*

COVER: *Photographed by Mark Clifford Photography at www.markclifford.com.*

All rights reserved. Reproduction or use, without express permission, of editorial or pictorial content, in any manner, is prohibited. No patent liability is assumed with respect to the use of the information contained herein. While every precaution has been taken in the preparation of this book, the publisher assumes no responsibility for errors or omissions. Neither is any liability assumed for damages resulting from use of the information contained herein. Publication of the servicing information in this manual does not imply approval of the manufacturers of the products covered.

All instructions and diagrams have been checked for accuracy and ease of application; however, success and safety in working with tools depend to a great extent upon individual accuracy, skill and caution. For this reason, the publishers are not able to guarantee the result of any procedure contained herein. Nor can they assume responsibility for any damage to property or injury to persons occasioned from the procedures. Persons engaging in the procedure do so entirely at their own risk.

Chapter One
General Information **1**

Chapter Two
Troubleshooting **2**

Chapter Three
Lubrication, Maintenance and Tune-up **3**

Chapter Four
Engine Top End **4**

Chapter Five
Engine Lower End **5**

Chapter Six
Clutch, Kickstarter and External Shift Mechanism **6**

Chapter Seven
Transmission and Internal Shift Mechanism **7**

Chapter Eight
Fuel and Exhaust Systems **8**

Chapter Nine
Electrical System **9**

Chapter Ten
Front Suspension and Steering **10**

Chapter Eleven
Rear Suspension **11**

Chapter Twelve
Brakes **12**

Index **13**

Wiring Diagrams **14**

CLYMER®

Publisher Shawn Etheridge

EDITORIAL

Managing Editor
James Grooms

Associate Editors
Richard Arens
Steven Thomas

Technical Writers
Jay Bogart
Jon Engleman
Michael Morlan
George Parise
Mark Rolling
Ed Scott
Ron Wright

Group Production Manager
Dylan Goodwin

Senior Production Editors
Greg Araujo
Darin Watson

Production Editors
Julie Jantzer-Ward
Justin Marciniak
Holly Messinger

Associate Production Editor
Susan Hartington

Technical Illustrators
Steve Amos
Errol McCarthy
Mitzi McCarthy
Bob Meyer

MARKETING/SALES AND ADMINISTRATION

Sales Channel & Brand Marketing Coordinator
Melissa Abbott Mudd

Art Director
Chris Paxton

Sales Managers
Justin Henton
Dutch Sadler
Matt Tusken

Business Manager
Ron Rogers

Customer Service Manager
Terri Cannon

Customer Service Representatives
Felicia Dickerson
Courtney Hollars
April LeBlond

Warehouse & Inventory Manager
Leah Hicks

PRiSM BUSINESS MEDIA™

P.O. Box 12901, Overland Park, KS 66282-2901 • 800-262-1954 • 913-967-1719

The following books and guides are published by Prism Business Media

More information available at *clymer.com*

CONTENTS

QUICK REFERENCE DATA IX

CHAPTER ONE
GENERAL INFORMATION 1

    Manual organization
    Notes, cautions and warnings
    Safety first
    Service hints
    Washing the bike
    Torque specifications
    Fasteners
    Lubricants
    Parts replacements
    Basic hand tools
    Test equipment
    Mechanic's tips

CHAPTER TWO
TROUBLESHOOTING 21

    Operating requirements
    Troubleshooting instruments
    Starting the engine
    Starting difficulties
    Engine starting troubles
    Engine performance
    Engine noises
    Excessive vibration
    Two-stroke pressure testing
    Clutch
    Transmission
    Ignition system
    Front suspension and steering
    Brakes

CHAPTER THREE
LUBRICATION, MAINTENANCE AND TUNE-UP 35

    Pre-checks
    Tires and wheels
    Lubricants
    Cleaning solvent
    Engine lubrication
    Periodic lubrication
    Periodic maintenance
    Engine tune-up
    Suspension adjustment
    Storage

CHAPTER FOUR
ENGINE TOP END 73

    Engine principles
    Engine lubrication
    Engine cooling
    Cleanliness
    Servicing engine in frame
    Cylinder head
    Cylinder
    Piston, wrist pin and piston rings
    Break-in procedure
    Reed valve assembly

CHAPTER FIVE
ENGINE LOWER END 96
    Servicing engine in frame
    Engine
    Engine sprocket
    Crankcase and crankshaft

CHAPTER SIX
CLUTCH, KICKSTARTER AND EXTERNAL SHIFT MECHANISM 122
    Clutch cover (1983-1985)
    Clutch cover (1986-on)
    Clutch
    Primary drive gear
    Clutch cable
    Clutch release mechanism
    Kickstarter
    External shift mechanism

CHAPTER SEVEN
TRANSMISSION AND INTERNAL SHIFT MECHANISM 148
    Transmission operation
    Transmission
    Transmission overhaul
    Internal shift mechanism

CHAPTER EIGHT
FUEL AND EXHAUST SYSTEMS 161
    Air cleaner
    Carburetor operation
    Carburetor service (1983-1987)
    Carburetor fuel level adjustment
    Fuel tank
    Fuel shutoff valve
    Exhaust system
    Exhaust system decarbonizing
    Exhaust system repair

CHAPTER NINE
ELECTRICAL SYSTEM 187
    Capacitor discharge ignition
    Magneto
    Capacitor discharge ignition unit
    Ignition coil
    Spark plug
    Engine kill switch
    Lighting system
    Enduro timer case
    Wiring diagrams

CHAPTER TEN
FRONT SUSPENSION AND STEERING 196
    Front wheel
    Front hub
    Tire changing
    Tire repairs
    Handlebar
    Steering head
    Front fork

CHAPTER ELEVEN
REAR SUSPENSION 224
    Rear wheel
    Rear hub
    Drive sprocket
    Drive chain
    Tire changing and tire repairs
    Uni-trax rear suspension
    Uni-trax shock absorber (1983-1985)
    Uni-trax shock absorber (1986-on)
    Uni-trax linkage
    Swing arm
    Swing arm bearing replacement

CHAPTER TWELVE
BRAKES 252
- Drum brakes
- Front brake cable
- Front disc brake (1986-on)
- Front brake pad replacement
- Front caliper
- Front master cylinder
- Front brake hose replacement
- Front brake disc
- Bleeding the system

INDEX 273

WIRING DIAGRAMS ....end of book

QUICK REFERENCE DATA

GENERAL ENGINE SPECIFICATIONS

Bore × stroke	66.0 × 58.0 mm (2.60 × 2.28 in.)
Displacement	198 cc (12.08 cu. in.)
Compression ratio	
1983-1987	7.7:1
1988	7.5:1
Port timing	
1983-1985	
Intake	
Open	—
Close	—
Transfer	
Open	62° BBDC
Close	62° ABDC
Exhaust	
Open	93° BBDC
Close	93° ABDC
1986-on	
Intake	
Open	—
Close	—
Transfer	
Open	60° BBDC
Close	60° ABDC
Exhaust	
Open	89° BBDC
Close	89° ABDC
Lubrication	Fuel/oil premix

SPARK PLUG TYPE AND GAP

Model	Type	Gap mm (in.)
U.S.	B9ES	0.7-0.8 (0.028-0.032)
All other	BR9ES	0.7-0.8 (0.028-0.032)

RECOMMENDED LUBRICANTS AND FUEL

Engine oil	Kawasaki 2-stroke racing oil
Transmission oil	SAE 10W/30 or 10W/40 automotive engine oil
Front fork oil	10 wt fork oil
Air filter	Foam air filter oil
Drive chain	Chain lube
Control cables	Cable lube
Control lever pivots	10W/30 motor oil
Swing arm assembly	Lithium grease base grease
Steering head, wheel bearings	Wheel bearing, waterproof type
Fuel	Premium grade—Research octane 90 or higher
Brake fluid (1986-on)	DOT 3

FUEL/OIL PREMIX RATIO

Model	Premix ratio with Kawasaki Racing Oil
1983	20:1
1984	30:1
1985-on	32:1

MAINTENANCE TORQUE SPECIFICATIONS

Item	N·m	ft.-lb.
Cylinder head nuts	25	18
Cylinder nuts		
1983-1985	34	25
1986-on	25	18
Transmission drain plug	20	14.5
Spark plug	27	20
Front axle nut		
1983-1985	64	47
1986-on	78	58
Fork tube pinch bolts	20	14.5
Handlebar clamp bolts		
1983-1985	14	10
1986-on	21	15
Swing arm pivot shaft nut	78	58
Rear axle nut	98	72

DRIVE CHAIN LENGTH MEASUREMENT

Model	Standard mm (in.)	Wear limit mm (in.)
1983-on	317.5 (12.50)	323 (12.7)

DRIVE CHAIN SLACK

Model	mm	in.
Normal or dry conditions	50-60	1.96-2.36
Muddy conditions	55-65	2.2-2.6

TIRE INFLATION PRESSURE

Front	1.0 kg/cm^2 (14 psi)
Rear	1.0 kg/cm^2 (14 psi)

CLUTCH/TRANSMISSION OIL CAPACITY

Model	cc	qts.
1983-1985	600	0.63
1986-on	700	0.74

FRONT FORK OIL CAPACITY

Model	cc	oz.
1983-1985	441-449	14.91-15.18
1986	631-639	21.3-21.6
1987-on	626-634	21.2-21.4

FRONT FORK OIL LEVEL

Model	Standard range mm	in.	Adjustable range mm	in.
1983-1985	163-167	6.42-6.57	—	—
1986	148-152	5.8-6.0	120-152	4.7-6.0
1987-on	133-137	5.2-5.4	105-160	4.1-6.3

FRONT FORK AIR PRESSURE

Model	kg/cm^2	psi
1983-1985		
Maximum	2.5	36
Operating range	0-2.5	0-36
1986-on		
Maximum	2.5	36
Operating pressure	0.4	6

CLYMER®
KAWASAKI
KDX200 • 1983-1988

CHAPTER ONE

GENERAL INFORMATION

This detailed, comprehensive manual covers all 1983-1988 Kawasaki KDX200 models.

Troubleshooting, tune-up, maintenance and repair are not difficult, if you know what tools and equipment to use and what to do. Anyone of average intelligence and with some mechanical ability can perform most of the procedures in this manual.

The manual is written simply and clearly enough for owners who have never worked on a motorcycle, but is complete enough for use by experienced mechanics.

Some of the procedures require the use of special tools. Using an inferior substitute tool for a special tool is not recommended as it can be dangerous to you and may damage the part.

Table 1 lists model coverage with engine serial numbers.

Metric and U.S. standards are used throughout this manual. U.S. to metric conversion is given in **Table 2**.

Torque specifications for fasteners which do not have specific torque recommendations are listed in **Table 3**.

Tables 1-3 are found at the end of the chapter.

MANUAL ORGANIZATION

This chapter provides general information and discusses equipment and tools useful both for preventive maintenance and troubleshooting.

Chapter Two provides methods and suggestions for quick and accurate diagnosis and repair of problems. Troubleshooting procedures discuss typical symptoms and logical methods to pinpoint the trouble.

Chapter Three explains all periodic lubrication and routine maintenance necessary to keep your Kawasaki running at its best. Chapter Three also includes recommended tune-up procedures, eliminating the need to constantly consult other chapters on the various assemblies.

Subsequent chapters describe specific systems such as the engine top end, engine bottom end, clutch, transmission, fuel, exhaust, electrical, suspension, steering and brakes. Each chapter provides disassembly, repair, and assembly procedures in simple step-by-step form. If a repair is impractical for a home mechanic, it is so indicated. It is usually faster and less expensive to take such repairs to a dealer or competent repair shop. Specifications concerning a particular system are included at the end of the appropriate chapter.

NOTES, CAUTIONS AND WARNINGS

The terms NOTE, CAUTION and WARNING have specific meanings in this manual. A NOTE provides additional information to make a step or procedure easier or clearer. Disregarding a NOTE could cause inconvenience, but would not cause damage or personal injury.

A CAUTION emphasizes areas where equipment damage could occur. Disregarding a CAUTION could cause permanent mechanical damage; however, personal injury is unlikely.

A WARNING emphasizes areas where personal injury or even death could result from negligence. Mechanical damage may also occur. WARNINGS *are to be taken seriously.* In some cases, serious injury and death has resulted from disregarding similar warnings.

SAFETY FIRST

Professional mechanics can work for years and never sustain a serious injury. If you observe a few rules of common sense and safety, you can enjoy many safe hours servicing your own machine. If you ignore these rules you can hurt yourself or damage the equipment.

1. Never use gasoline as a cleaning solvent.

2. Never smoke or use a torch in the vicinity of flammable liquids, such as cleaning solvent, in open containers.

3. If welding or brazing is required on the machine, remove the fuel tank and rear shock to a safe distance, at least 50 feet away.

4. Use the proper sized wrenches to avoid damage to fasteners and injury to yourself.

5. When loosening a tight or stuck nut, be guided by what would happen if the wrench should slip. Be careful; protect yourself accordingly.

6. When replacing a fastener, make sure to use one with the same measurements and strength as the old one. Incorrect or mismatched fasteners can result in damage to the vehicle and possible personal injury. Beware of fastener kits that are filled with cheap and poorly made nuts, bolts, washers and cotter pins. Refer to *Fasteners* in this chapter for additional information.

7. Keep all hand and power tools in good condition. Wipe greasy and oily tools after using them. Slippery tools are difficult to hold and can cause injury. Replace or repair worn or damaged tools.

8. Keep your work area clean and uncluttered.

9. Wear safety goggles during all operations involving drilling, grinding, the use of a cold chisel or anytime you feel unsure about the safety of your eyes. Safety goggles should also be worn anytime compressed air is used to clean a part.

10. Keep an approved fire extinguisher nearby. Be sure it is rated for gasoline (Class B) and electrical (Class C) fires.

11. When drying bearings or other rotating parts with compressed air, never allow the air jet to rotate the bearing or part; the air jet is capable of rotating them at speeds far in excess of those for which they were designed. The bearing or rotating part is very likely to disintegrate and cause serious injury and damage.

SERVICE HINTS

Most of the service procedures covered are straightforward and can be performed by anyone reasonably handy with tools. It is suggested, however, that you consider your own capabilities carefully before attempting any operation involving major disassembly of the engine or transmission.

1. "Front," as used in this manual, refers to the front of the motorcycle; the front of any component is the end closest to the front of the motorcycle. The "left-" and "right-hand" sides refer to the position of the parts as viewed by a rider sitting on the seat facing forward. For example, the throttle control is on the right-hand side. These rules are simple, but confusion can cause a major inconvenience during service.

2. Whenever servicing the engine or clutch, or when removing a suspension component, the bike should be secured in a safe manner. An excellent support for KDX200 models is a motocross workstand, but a sturdy and inexpensive workstand can be made with 3/4 in. plywood that will last a long time.

3. When disassembling any engine or suspension component, mark the parts for location and mark all parts which mate together. Small parts, such as bolts, can be identified by placing them in plastic sandwich bags. Seal the bags and label them with masking tape and a marking pen. When reassembly will take place immediately, an accepted practice is to place nuts and bolts in a cupcake tin or egg carton in the order of disassembly.

4. Finished surfaces should be protected from physical damage or corrosion. Keep gasoline and brake fluid off painted surfaces.

GENERAL INFORMATION

5. Use penetrating oil on frozen or tight bolts, then strike the bolt head a few times with a hammer and punch (use a screwdriver on screws). Avoid the use of heat where possible, as it can warp, melt or affect the temper of parts. Heat also ruins finishes, especially paint and plastics.

6. No parts removed or installed (other than bushings and bearings) in the procedures given in this manual should require unusual force during disassembly or assembly. If a part is difficult to remove or install, find out why before proceeding.

7. Cover all openings after removing parts or components to prevent dirt, small tools, etc. from falling in.

8. Read each procedure *completely* while looking at the actual parts before starting a job. Make sure you *thoroughly* understand what is to be done and then carefully follow the procedure, step by step.

9. Recommendations are occasionally made to refer service or maintenance to a Kawasaki dealer or a specialist in a particular field. In these cases, the work will be done more quickly and economically than if you performed the job yourself.

10. In procedural steps, the term "replace" means to discard a defective part and replace it with a new or exchange unit. "Overhaul" means to remove, disassemble, inspect, measure, repair or replace defective parts, reassemble and install major systems or parts.

11. Some operations require the use of a hydraulic press. It would be wiser to have these operations performed by a shop equipped for such work, rather than to try to do the job yourself with makeshift equipment that may damage your machine.

12. Repairs go much faster and easier if your machine is clean before you begin work. There are many special cleaners on the market, like Bel-Ray Degreaser, for washing the engine and related parts. Follow the manufacturer's directions on the container for the best results. Clean all oily or greasy parts with cleaning solvent as you remove them. See *Washing the Bike* in this chapter.

WARNING
Never use gasoline as a cleaning agent. It presents an extreme fire hazard. Be sure to work in a well-ventilated area when using cleaning solvent. Keep a fire extinguisher, rated for gasoline fires, handy in any case.

CAUTION
If you use a car wash to clean your bike, don't direct the high pressure water hose at fork seals, steering bearings, carburetor hoses, suspension linkage components or wheel bearings. The water will flush grease out of the bearings or damage the seals. After washing your bike, remove the wheels and clean the wheel drums (if so equipped) of all water and dirt.

13. Much of the labor charged for by dealers is for removal, disassembly, assembly, and reinstallation of other parts in order to reach the defective part. It is frequently possible to perform the preliminary operations yourself and then take the defective unit to the dealer for repair at considerable savings.

14. If special tools are required, make arrangements to get them before you start. It is frustrating and time-consuming to get partly into a job and then be unable to complete it.

15. Make diagrams (or take a Polaroid picture) wherever similar-appearing parts are found. For instance, crankcase bolts are often not the same length. You may think you can remember where everything came from—but mistakes are costly. There is also the possibility that you may be sidetracked and not return to work for days or even weeks—in which the time carefully laid out parts may have become disturbed.

16. When assembling parts, be sure all shims and washers are replaced exactly as they came out.

17. Whenever a rotating part butts against a stationary part, look for a shim or washer. Use new gaskets if there is any doubt about the condition of the old ones. A thin coat of oil on non-pressure type gaskets may help them seal more effectively.

18. If it is necessary to make a clutch cover or ignition cover gasket and you do not have a suitable old gasket to use as a guide, you can use the outline of the cover and gasket material to make a new gasket. Apply engine oil to the cover gasket

surface. Then place the cover on the new gasket material and apply pressure with your hands. The oil will leave a very accurate outline on the gasket material that can be cut out.

CAUTION
When purchasing gasket material to make a gasket, measure the thickness of the old gasket and purchase gasket material with the same approximate thickness.

19. Heavy grease can be used to hold small parts in place if they tend to fall out during assembly. However, keep grease and oil away from electrical and brake components.

20. A carburetor is best cleaned by disassembling it and soaking the parts in a commercial carburetor cleaner. Never soak gaskets and rubber parts in these cleaners. Never use wire to clean out jets and air passages. They are easily damaged. Use compressed air to blow out the carburetor only if the float has been removed first.

21. Take your time and do the job right. Do not forget that a newly rebuilt engine must be broken in just like a new one.

WASHING THE BIKE

Dirt bikes get dirty. If you are riding your KDX200 frequently and maintaining it properly, you will spend a good deal of time cleaning it. After each riding session, wash the bike. It will make maintenance and service procedures quick and easy. More important, proper cleaning will prevent dirt from falling into critical areas undetected. Failing to clean the bike or cleaning it incorrectly will add to your maintenance costs and shop time because dirty parts wear out prematurely.

When cleaning your KDX200, you will need a few tools, shop rags, scrub brush, bucket, liquid cleaner and access to water. Many riders use a coin-operated car wash. Coin-operated car washes are convenient and quick, but with improper use, the high water pressures can do your bike more damage than good.

NOTE
A safe biodegradable, non-toxic and non-flammable liquid cleaner that works well for washing your bike as well as removing grease and oil from engine and suspension parts is Simple Green. Simple Green can be purchased through some hardware, garden and discount supply houses. Follow the directions on the container for recommended dilution ratios.

When cleaning your bike, and especially when using a spray type degreaser, remember that what goes on the bike will rinse off and drip onto your driveway or into your yard. If you can, use a degreaser at a coin-operated car wash. If you are cleaning your bike at home, place thick cardboard or newspapers underneath the bike to catch the oil and grease deposits that are rinsed off.

1. Place the bike on a stand.
2. Remove the air filter unit as described in Chapter Three. Insert a dry rag into the carburetor throat to keep water from getting inside the engine.

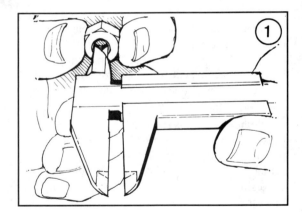

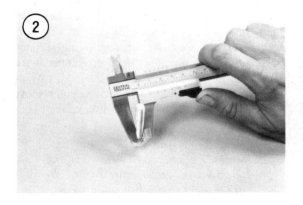

GENERAL INFORMATION

3. Check the following before washing the bike:
   a. Make sure the gas cap is screwed on tightly.
   b. Make sure the oil fill cap is tight.
   c. Plug the silencer opening with a large cork or rag.

4. Wash the bike from top to bottom with soapy water. Use the scrub brush to get excess dirt out of the wheel rims and engine crannies. Concentrate on the upper controls, engine, side panels and gas tank during this wash cycle. Don't forget to wash dirt and mud from underneath the fenders.

5. Remove the gas tank, side panels and seat. Wrap a plastic bag around the ignition coil and CDI unit. Concentrate the second wash cycle on the frame tube members, outer airbox areas, suspension linkage, rear shock and swing arm.

6. Direct the hose underneath the engine and swing arm. Wash this area thoroughly. If this area is extremely dirty, you may want to lay the bike on its side.

7. The final wash is the rinse. Use cold water without soap and spray the whole motorcycle again. Use as much time and care when rinsing the bike as when washing it. Soap deposits can quickly corrode electrical connections and remove the natural oils from tires, causing premature cracks and wear. Make sure you thoroughly rinse the bike off.

8. If you are washing the bike at home, remove the rag from the air filter box and start the engine. Idle the engine to burn off any internal moisture. Idle the bike long enough to use the gas remaining in the float bowl. This will prevent fuel leakage problems when cleaning the carburetor later.

9. Before taking the bike into the garage, wipe it dry with a shop rag. Inspect the machine as you dry it for further signs of dirt and grime. Remove the ignition cover and let any moisture in the ignition dry before reinstalling the cover. Make a quick visual inspection of the frame and other painted pieces. Spray any worn-down spots with WD-40 or Bel-Ray 6-in-1 to prevent rust from building on the bare metal. When the bike is back at your work area you can repaint the bare areas with touch-up paint. A quick shot from a paint can each time you work on the bike will keep it looking sharp and stop rust from starting.

TORQUE SPECIFICATIONS

Torque specifications throughout this manual are given in Newton-meters (N·m) and foot-pounds (ft.-lb.).

Table 3 lists general torque specifications for nuts and bolts that are not listed in the respective chapters. To use the table, first determine the size of the nut or bolt by measuring it with a vernier caliper. **Figure 1** and **Figure 2** show how to do this.

FASTENERS

The materials and designs of the various fasteners used on your Kawasaki are not arrived at by chance or accident. Fastener design determines the type of tool required to work the fastener. Fastener material is carefully selected to decrease the possibility of physical failure.

Nuts, bolts and screws are manufactured in a wide range of thread patterns. To join a nut and bolt, the diameter of the bolt and the diameter of the hole in the nut must be the same. It is just as important that the threads on both be properly matched.

The best way to tell if the threads on 2 fasteners are matched is to turn the nut on the bolt (or the bolt into the threaded hole in a piece of equipment) with fingers only (**Figure 3**). Be sure both pieces are clean. If much force is required, check the thread condition on each fastener. If the thread condition is good but the fasteners jam, the threads are not compatible. A thread pitch gauge can also be used to determine pitch. Kawasaki motorcycles are manufactured with ISO (International Organization for Standardization) metric fasteners. The threads are cut differently than those of American fasteners (**Figure 4**).

Most threads are cut so that the fastener must be turned clockwise to tighten it. These are called right-hand threads. Some fasteners have left-hand threads; they must be turned counterclockwise to be tightened. Left-hand threads are used in locations where normal rotation of the equipment would tend to loosen a right-hand threaded fastener.

ISO Metric Screw Threads

ISO (International Organization for Standardization) metric threads come in 3 standard thread sizes: coarse, fine and constant pitch. The ISO coarse pitch is used for most all common fastener applications. The fine pitch thread is used on certain precision tools and instruments. The constant pitch thread is used mainly on machine parts and not for fasteners. The constant pitch thread, however, is used on all metric thread spark plugs.

ISO metric threads are specified by the capital letter M followed by the diameter in millimeters, the pitch (or the distance between each thread) and the length in millimeters. For example, an M8—1.25 ×

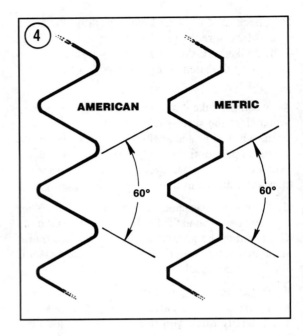

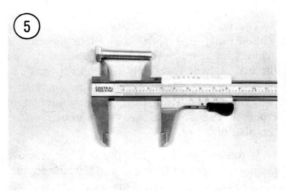

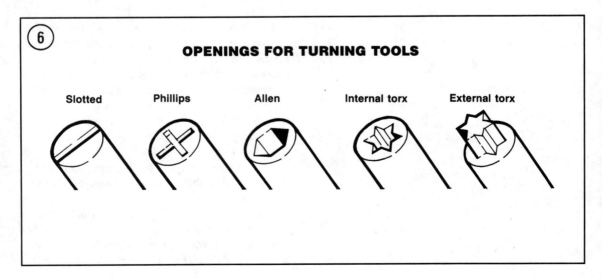

GENERAL INFORMATION

130 bolt is one that has a diameter of 8 millimeters with a distance of 1.25 millimeters between each thread and a length of 130 mm. The measurement across 2 flats on the head of the bolt indicates the proper wrench size to be used. **Figure 2** shows how to determine bolt diameter.

NOTE
*The correct way to measure bolt length is by measuring the length starting from underneath the bolt head to the end of the bolt (**Figure 5**). Always measure the bolt length in this manner to avoid purchasing bolts that are too long.*

Machine Screws

There are many different types of machine screws. **Figure 6** shows a number of screw heads requiring different types of turning tools. Heads are also designed to protrude above the metal (round) or to be slightly recessed in the metal (flat). See **Figure 7**.

Bolts

Commonly called bolts, the technical name for these fasteners is cap screw. Metric bolts are described by the diameter and pitch (or the distance between each thread).

Nuts

Nuts are manufactured in a variety of types and sizes. Most are hexagonal (6-sided) and fit on bolts, screws and studs with the same diameter and pitch.

Figure 8 shows several types of nuts. The common nut is generally used with a lockwasher. Self-locking nuts have a nylon insert which prevents the nut from loosening; no lockwasher is required. Wing nuts are designed for fast removal by hand. Wing nuts are used for convenience in non-critical locations.

To indicate the size of a metric nut, manufacturers specify the diameter of the opening and the thread pitch. This is similar to bolt specifications, but without the length dimension. The measurement across 2 flats on the nut indicates the proper wrench size to be used.

Prevailing Torque Fasteners

Several types of bolts, screws and nuts incorporate a system that develops an interference

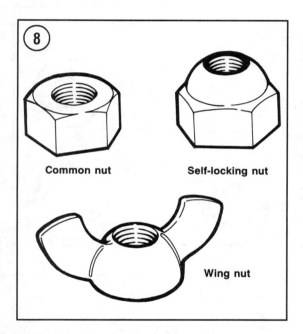

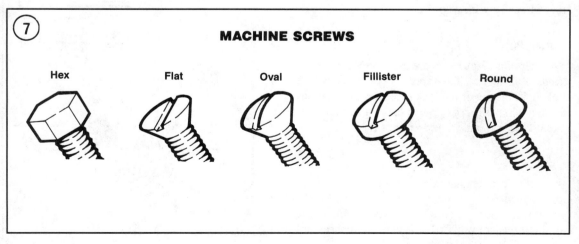

between the bolt, screw, nut or tapped hole threads. Interference is achieved in various ways: by distorting threads, coating threads with dry adhesive or nylon, distorting the top of an all-metal nut, using a nylon insert in the center or at the top of a nut, etc.

Prevailing torque fasteners offer greater holding strength and better vibration resistance. Some prevailing torque fasteners can be reused if in good condition. Others, like the nylon insert nut, form an initial locking condition when the nut is first installed; the nylon forms closely to the bolt thread pattern, thus reducing any tendency for the nut to loosen. When the nut is removed, the locking efficiency is greatly reduced. For greatest safety, it is recommended that you install new prevailing torque fasteners whenever they are removed.

Washers

There are 2 basic types of washers: flat washers and lockwashers. Flat washers are simple discs with a hole to fit a screw or bolt. Lockwashers are designed to prevent a fastener from working loose due to vibration, expansion and contraction. **Figure 9** shows several types of washers. Washers are also used in the following functions:
 a. As spacers.
 b. To prevent galling or damage of the equipment by the fastener.
 c. To help distribute fastener load during torquing.
 d. As seals.

Note that flat washers are often used between a lockwasher and a fastener to provide a smooth bearing surface. This allows the fastener to be turned easily with a tool.

Cotter Pins

Cotter pins (**Figure 10**) are used to secure special kinds of fasteners. The threaded stud must have a hole in it; the nut or nut lock piece has castellations around which the cotter pin ends wrap. Cotter pins should not be reused after removal.

Circlips

Circlips can be internal or external design. They are used to retain items on shafts (external type) or within tubes (internal type). In some applications, circlips of varying thicknesses are used to control the end play of parts assemblies. These are often called selective circlips. Circlips should be replaced during installation, as removal weakens and deforms them.

Two basic styles of circlips are available: machined and stamped circlips. Machined circlips (**Figure 11**) can be installed in either direction (shaft or housing) because both faces are machined, thus creating two sharp edges. Stamped circlips (**Figure 12**) are manufactured with one sharp edge and one rounded edge. When installing stamped circlips in a thrust situation (transmission shafts, fork tubes, etc.), the sharp edge must face

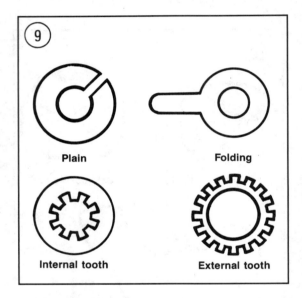

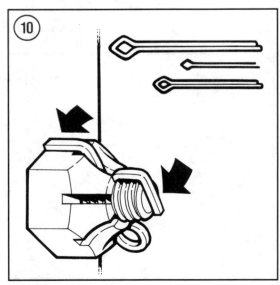

GENERAL INFORMATION

away from the part producing the thrust. When installing circlips, observe the following:
a. Compress or expand circlips only enough to install them.
b. After the circlip is installed, make sure it is completely seated in its groove.

LUBRICANTS

Periodic lubrication assures long life for any type of equipment. The *type* of lubricant used is just as important as the lubrication service itself, although in an emergency the wrong type of lubricant is better than none at all. The following paragraphs describe the types of lubricants most often used on motorcycle equipment. Be sure to follow the manufacturer's recommendations for lubricant types.

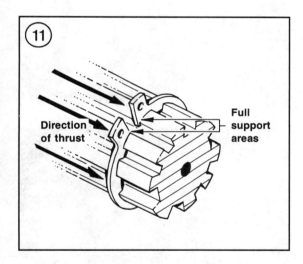

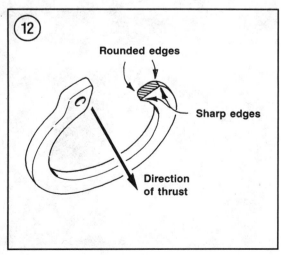

Generally, all liquid lubricants are called "oil." They may be mineral-based (including petroleum bases), natural-based (vegetable and animal bases), synthetic-based or emulsions (mixtures). "Grease" is an oil to which a thickening base has been added so that the end product is semi-solid. Grease is often classified by the type of thickener added; lithium soap is commonly used.

Engine Pre-mix

All Kawasaki KDX200 models require a mixture of oil and gasoline that lubricates the piston, cylinder, crankshaft, connecting rod and all bearings. Always use a two-cycle oil designed for pre-mixing purposes in motorcycle engines. Do not use a two-cycle oil for injectors or outboard motor oil.

Refer to *Lubrication* in Chapter Three for pre-mix ratios and mixing directions.

Clutch/Transmission Oil

Oil for your bike's clutch and transmission and 4-cycle motorcycle and automotive engines is graded by the American Petroleum Institute (API) and the Society of Automotive Engineers (SAE) in several categories. Oil containers display these ratings on the top or label.

API oil grade is indicated by letters; oils for gasoline engines are identified by an "S". The clutch and transmissions used on KDX200 models covered in this manual require SE or SF graded oil.

Viscosity is an indication of the oil's thickness. The SAE uses numbers to indicate viscosity; thin oils have low numbers while thick oils have high numbers. A "W" after the number indicates that the viscosity testing was done at low temperature to simulate cold-weather operation. Engine oils fall into the 5W-30 and 20W-50 range.

Multi-grade oils (for example 10W-40) are less viscous (thinner) at low temperatures and more viscous (thicker) at high temperatures. This allows the oil to perform efficiently across a wide range of engine operating conditions. The lower the number, the better the engine will start in cold climates. Higher numbers are usually recommended for engine running in hot weather conditions.

Grease

Greases are graded by the National Lubricating Grease Institute (NLGI). Greases are graded by number according to the consistency of the grease; these range from No. 000 to No. 6, with No. 6 being the most solid. A typical multipurpose grease is NLGI No. 2. For specific applications, equipment manufacturers may require grease with an additive such as molybdenum disulfide (MOS2).

PARTS REPLACEMENT

Kawasaki makes frequent changes during a model year, some minor, some relatively major. When you order parts from the dealer or other parts distributor, always order by frame and engine numbers. The frame number and the vehicle identification number are stamped on the steering head pipe (**Figure 13**). The engine number on 1983-1985 models is stamped on right-hand side of the crankcase directly underneath the cylinder (**Figure 14**). The engine number on 1986 and later models is stamped on the right-hand crankcase above the engine drain plug (**Figure 15**).
Write the numbers down and carry them with you. Compare new parts to old before purchasing them. If they are not alike, have the parts manager explain the difference to you. **Table 1** lists engine serial numbers for KDX200 models covered in this manual.

NOTE
*If you purchased a used KDX200 model (that should be covered in this manual), and you are not sure of its model or year, use the bike's engine serial number and the information listed in **Table 1**. Check your bike's engine serial number. Then compare the number with the engine and serial numbers listed in **Table 1**. If your bike's serial number is listed in **Table 1**, cross-reference the number with the adjacent model number and year.*

BASIC HAND TOOLS

Many of the procedures in this manual can be carried out with simple hand tools and test equipment familiar to the average home mechanic. Keep your tools clean and in a tool box. Keep them organized with the sockets and related drives together, the open-end combination wrenches together, etc. After using a tool, wipe off dirt and grease with a clean cloth and return the tool to its correct place.

Top quality tools are essential; they are also more economical in the long run. If you are now starting to build your tool collection, stay away from the "advertised specials" featured at some parts houses, discount stores and chain drug stores.

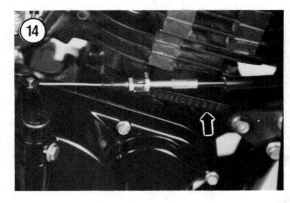

GENERAL INFORMATION

These are usually a poor grade tool that can be sold cheaply and that is exactly what they are—*cheap*. They are usually made of inferior material, and are thick, heavy and clumsy. Their rough finish makes them difficult to clean and they usually don't last very long. If it is ever your misfortune to use such tools, you will probably find out that the wrenches do not fit the heads of bolts and nuts correctly and damage the fastener.

Quality tools are made of alloy steel and are heat treated for greater strength. They are lighter and better balanced than cheap ones. Their surface is smooth, making them a pleasure to work with and easy to clean. The initial cost of good quality tools may be more but they are cheaper in the long run. Don't try to buy everything in all sizes in the beginning; do it a little at a time until you have the necessary tools.

The following tools are required to perform virtually any repair job. Each tool is described and the recommended size given for starting a tool collection. Additional tools and some duplicates may be added as you become familiar with the vehicle. Kawasaki motorcycles are built with metric standard fasteners—so if you are starting your collection now, buy metric sizes.

Screwdrivers

The screwdriver is a very basic tool, but if used improperly it will do more damage than good. The slot on a screw has a definite dimension and shape. A screwdriver must be selected to conform with that shape. Use a small screwdriver for small screws and a large one for large screws or the screw head will be damaged.

Two basic types of screwdriver are required: common (flat-blade) screwdrivers (**Figure 16**) and Phillips screwdrivers (**Figure 17**).

Screwdrivers are available in sets which often include an assortment of common and Phillips blades. If you buy them individually, buy at least the following:

   a. Common screwdriver—5/16 × 6 in. blade.
   b. Common screwdriver—3/8 × 12 in. blade.
   c. Phillips screwdriver—size 2 tip, 6 in. blade.

Use screwdrivers only for driving screws. Never use a screwdriver for prying or chiseling metal. Do not try to remove a Phillips or Allen head screw with a common screwdriver (unless the screw has a combination head that will accept either type); you can damage the head so that the proper tool will be unable to remove it.

Keep screwdrivers in the proper condition and they will last longer and perform better. Always keep the tip of a common screwdriver in good condition. **Figure 18** shows how to grind the tip to the proper shape if it becomes damaged. Note the symmetrical sides of the tip.

Pliers

Pliers come in a wide range of types and sizes. Pliers are useful for cutting, bending and crimping. They should never be used to cut hardened objects or to turn bolts or nuts. **Figure 19** shows several pliers useful in motorcycle repairs.

Each type of pliers has a specialized function. Gas pliers are general purpose pliers and are used mainly for holding things and for bending. Vise Grips are used as pliers or to hold objects very tightly like a vise. Needlenose pliers are used to hold or bend small objects. Channel Lock pliers can be adjusted to hold various sizes of objects; the jaws remain parallel to grip around objects such as pipe or tubing. There are many more types of pliers.

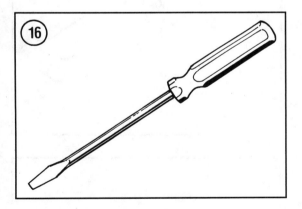

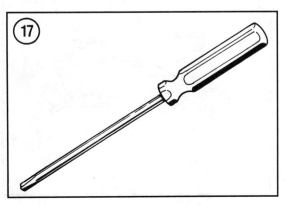

CHAPTER ONE

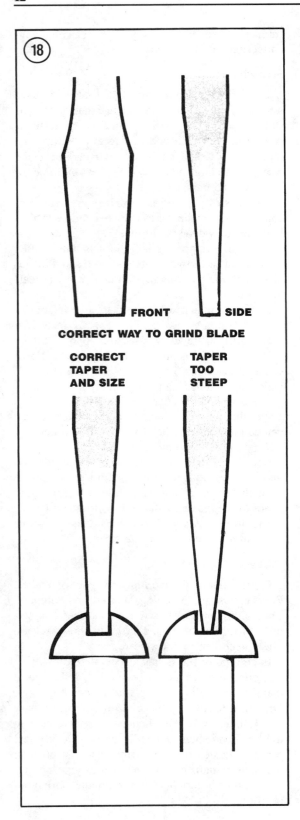

CORRECT WAY TO GRIND BLADE

CORRECT TAPER AND SIZE

TAPER TOO STEEP

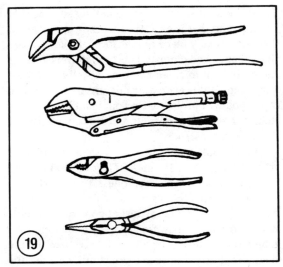

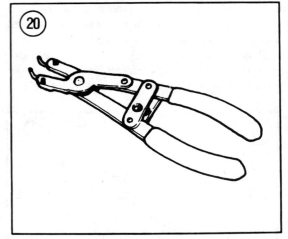

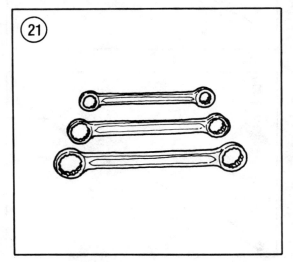

GENERAL INFORMATION

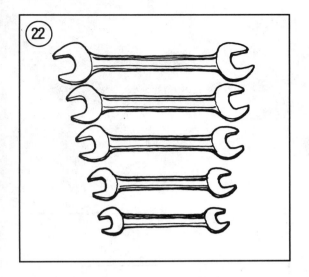

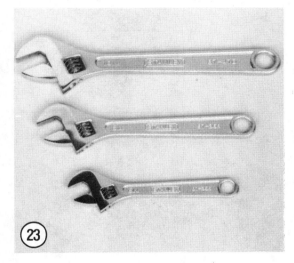

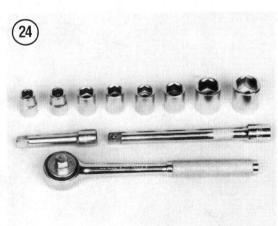

Circlip Pliers

Circlip pliers (**Figure 20**) are special in that they are only used to remove circlips from shafts or within engine or suspension housings. When purchasing circlip pliers, there are two kinds to distinguish from. External pliers (spreading) are used to remove circlips that fit on the outside of a shaft. Internal pliers (squeezing) are used to remove circlips which fit inside a gear or housing.

WARNING
Because circlips can sometime slip and "fly off" during removal and installation, always wear safety glasses.

Box and Open-end Wrenches

Box and open-end wrenches are available in sets or separately in a variety of sizes. The size number stamped near the end refers to the distance between 2 parallel flats on the hex head bolt or nut.

Box wrenches (**Figure 21**) are usually superior to open-end wrenches (**Figure 22**). Open-end wrenches grip the nut on only 2 flats. Unless a wrench fits well, it may slip and round off the points on the nut. The box wrench grips on all 6 flats. Both 6-point and 12-point openings on box wrenches are available. The 6-point gives superior holding power; the 12-point allows a shorter swing.

Combination wrenches which are open on one side and boxed on the other are also available. Both ends are the same size.

Adjustable Wrenches

An adjustable wrench can be adjusted to fit a variety of nuts or bolt heads (**Figure 23**). However, it can loosen and slip, causing damage to the nut and injury to your knuckles. Use an adjustable wrench only when other wrenches are not available.

Adjustable wrenches come in various sizes.

Socket Wrenches

This type is undoubtedly the fastest, safest and most convenient to use. Sockets which attach to a ratchet handle (**Figure 24**) are available with 6-point or 12-point openings and 1/4, 3/8, 1/2 and 3/4 inch drives. The drive size indicates the size of the square hole which mates with the ratchet handle.

Torque Wrench

A torque wrench (**Figure 25**) is used with a socket to measure how tightly a nut or bolt is installed. They come in a wide price range and with either 3/8 or 1/2 in. square drive. The drive size indicates the size of the square drive which mates with the socket.

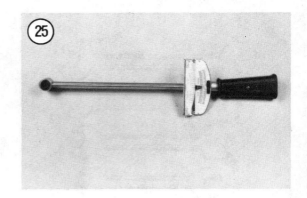

Impact Driver

This tool makes removal of tight fasteners easy and eliminates damage to bolts and screw slots. Impact drivers and interchangeable bits (**Figure 26**) are available at most large hardware and motorcycle dealers. Sockets can also be used with a hand impact driver. However, make sure the socket is designed for impact use. Do not use regular hand type sockets, as they may shatter.

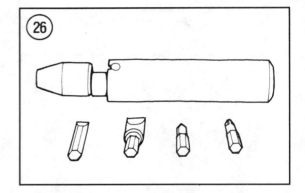

Hammers

The correct hammer is necessary for repairs. Use only a hammer with a face (or head) of rubber or plastic or the soft-faced type that is filled with buckshot. These are sometimes necessary in engine teardowns. *Never* use a metal-faced hammer, as severe damage will result in most cases. You can always produce the same amount of force with a soft-faced hammer.

Feeler Gauge

This tool has both flat and wire measuring gauges and is used to measure spark plug gap. See **Figure 27**. Wire gauges are used to measure spark plug gap; flat gauges are used for all other measurements.

Vernier Caliper

This tool is invaluable when reading inside, outside and depth measurements to within close precision. It can be used to measure clutch spring length and the thickness of clutch plates, shims and thrust washers. The vernier caliper can be purchased from large dealers or mail order houses. See **Figure 28**.

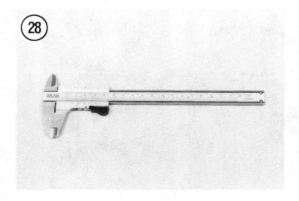

Spoke Wrench

This special wrench is used to tighten wheel spokes (**Figure 29**). Always use the correct size wrench to prevent rounding out and damaging the spoke nipple.

GENERAL INFORMATION

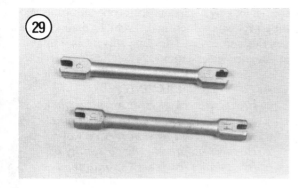

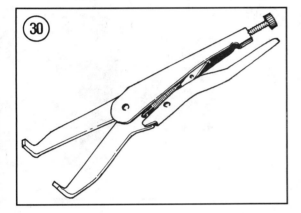

The Grabbit

This is a special tool that is very useful as a holding tool especially in the removal and installing of the clutch nut and the drive sprocket nut. It is called the Grabbit (**Figure 30**) and can be ordered through your Kawasaki dealer.

Tire Levers

When riding and maintaining a dirt bike, get used to changing tires. To prevent pinching tubes during tire changing, purchase a good set of tire levers (**Figure 31**). Never use a screwdriver in place of a tire lever; refer to Chapter Ten for its use. Before using a tire lever, check the working end of the tool and remove any burrs. Don't use a tire lever for prying anything but tires.

Flywheel Puller

A flywheel puller will be required whenever it is necessary to remove the rotor and service the stator plate assembly or when adjusting the ignition timing. In addition, when disassembling the engine, the rotor must be removed before the crankcase can be split. On KDX200 models, a 2-piece flywheel puller (**Figure 32**) will be required. On stock rotors, there are no internal threads cut into the rotor to accept a flywheel puller. Instead, a threaded plate must be bolted onto the outside of the rotor and a separate pressure screw threaded into the plate. There is no satisfactory substitute for this tool. Because the rotor is a taper fit on the crankshaft, makeshift removal tools often result in crankshaft and rotor damage. Don't think about removing the rotor without this tool.

Special Tools

A few special tools may be required for major service. These are described in the appropriate chapters and are available either from Kawasaki dealers or other manufacturers as indicated.

TEST EQUIPMENT

Multimeter or VOM

This instrument (**Figure 33**) is invaluable for electrical system troubleshooting and when adjusting the ignition timing on models with breaker points. Multimeters are available at electronic hobbyist stores and mail order outlets.

Compression Gauge

An engine with low compression cannot be properly tuned and will not develop full power. A compression gauge (**Figure 34**) measures engine compression. The one shown has a flexible stem with an extension that can allow you to hold it while kicking the engine over. Open the throttle all the way when checking engine compression. See Chapter Three.

Dial Indicator

Dial indicators (**Figure 35**) are precision tools used to check dimension variations on machined parts such as transmission shafts and axles and to check crankshaft and axle shaft end play. Dial indicators are available with various dial types for different measuring requirements. For motorcycle repair, select a dial indicator with a continuous dial. This type of dial is required to accurately measure ignition timing.

Strobe Timing Light

This instrument is useful for checking ignition timing. By flashing a light at the precise instant the spark plug fires, the position of the timing mark can be seen. The flashing light makes a moving mark appear to stand still opposite a stationary mark.

Suitable lights range from inexpensive neon bulb types to powerful xenon strobe lights. See **Figure 36**. A light with an inductive pickup is recommended to eliminate any possible damage to ignition wiring.

When using a strobe timing light to check the ignition timing on your KDX200, you will also need a 6-volt battery to connect to the timing light.

Expendable Supplies

Certain expendable supplies are also required. These include grease, oil, gasket cement, shop rags and cleaning solvent. Ask your dealer for the special locking compounds, silicone lubricants and lube products which make vehicle maintenance simpler and easier. Cleaning solvent is available at some service stations.

> *WARNING*
> *Having a stack of clean shop rags on hand is important when performing engine and suspension service work. However, to prevent the possibility of fire damage from spontaneous*

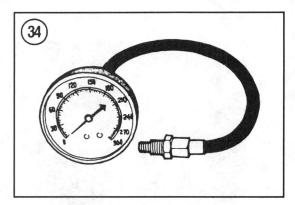

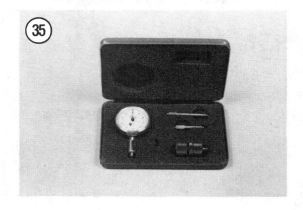

GENERAL INFORMATION

combustion from a pile of solvent soaked rags, store them in a lid sealed metal container until they can be washed or discarded.

NOTE
To prevent from absorbing solvent and other cleaners into your skin while cleaning parts, wear a pair of petroleum-resistant rubber gloves. These can be purchased through industrial supply houses or well-equipped hardware stores.

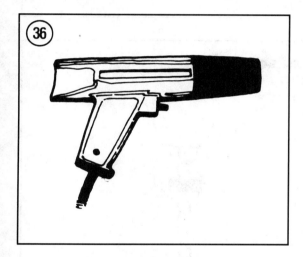

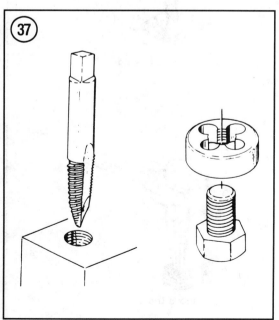

MECHANIC'S TIPS

Removing Frozen Nuts and Screws

When a fastener rusts and cannot be removed, several methods may be used to loosen it. First, apply penetrating oil such as Liquid Wrench or WD-40 (available at hardware or auto supply stores). Apply it liberally and let it penetrate for 10-15 minutes. Rap the fastener several times with a small hammer; do not hit it hard enough to cause damage. Reapply the penetrating oil if necessary.

For frozen screws, apply penetrating oil as described, then insert a screwdriver in the slot and rap the top of the screwdriver with a hammer. This loosens the rust so the screw can be removed in the normal way. If the screw head is too chewed up to use this method, grip the head with Vise Grips pliers and twist the screw out.

Avoid applying heat unless specifically instructed, as it may melt, warp or remove the temper from parts.

Remedying Stripped Threads

Occasionally, threads are stripped through carelessness or impact damage. Often the threads can be cleaned up by running a tap (for internal threads on nuts) or die (for external threads on bolts) through the threads. See **Figure 37**. To clean or repair spark plug threads, a spark plug tap can be used (**Figure 38**).

Removing Broken Screws or Bolts

When the head breaks off a screw or bolt, several methods are available for removing the remaining portion.

If a large portion of the remainder projects out, try gripping it with Vise Grips. If the projecting portion is too small, file it to fit a wrench or cut a slot in it to fit a screwdriver. See **Figure 39**.

If the head breaks off flush, use a screw extractor. To do this, centerpunch the exact center of the remaining portion of the screw or bolt. Drill a small hole in the screw and tap the extractor into the hole. Back the screw out with a wrench on the extractor. See **Figure 40**.

CHAPTER ONE

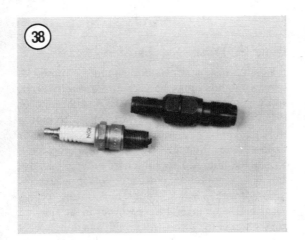

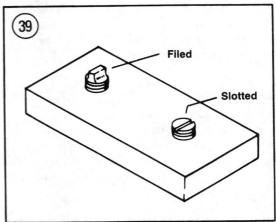

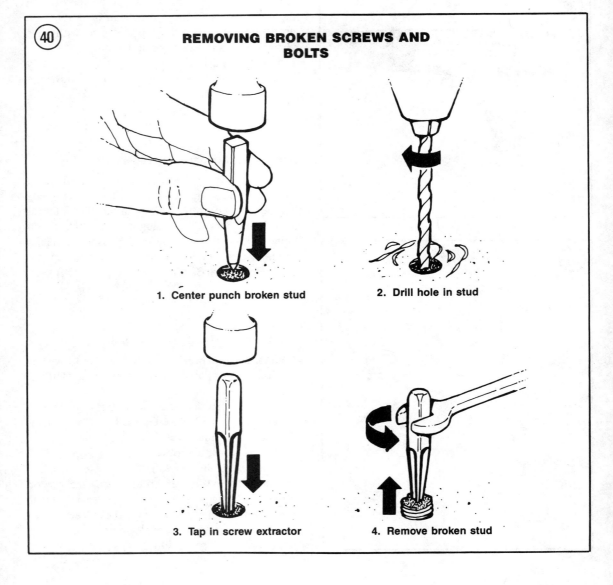

GENERAL INFORMATION

Table 1 ENGINE SERIAL NUMBERS

Model number and year	Engine serial No. start to end
1983 KDX200-A1	DX200AE000001-003000
1984 KDX200-A2	DX200AE003001-007400
1985 KDX200-A3	DX200AE008401-on
1986 KDX200-C1	DX200CE000001-005500
1987 KDX200-C2	DX200CE005501-010500
1988 KDX200-C3	DX200CE010501-on

Table 2 DECIMAL AND METRIC EQUIVALENTS

Fractions	Decimal in.	Metric mm	Fractions	Decimal in.	Metric mm
1/64	0.015625	0.39688	33/64	0.515625	13.09687
1/32	0.03125	0.79375	17/32	0.53125	13.49375
3/64	0.046875	1.19062	35/64	0.546875	13.89062
1/16	0.0625	1.58750	9/16	0.5625	14.28750
5/64	0.078125	1.98437	37/64	0.578125	14.68437
3/32	0.09375	2.38125	19/32	0.59375	15.08125
7/64	0.109375	2.77812	39/64	0.609375	15.47812
1/8	0.125	3.1750	5/8	0.625	15.87500
9/64	0.140625	3.57187	41/64	0.640625	16.27187
5/32	0.15625	3.96875	21/32	0.65625	16.66875
11/64	0.171875	4.36562	43/64	0.671875	17.06562
3/16	0.1875	4.76250	11/16	0.6875	17.46250
13/64	0.203125	5.15937	45/64	0.703125	17.85937
7/32	0.21875	5.55625	23/32	0.71875	18.25625
15/64	0.234375	5.95312	47/64	0.734375	18.65312
1/4	0.250	6.35000	3/4	0.750	19.05000
17/64	0.265625	6.74687	49/64	0.765625	19.44687
9/32	0.28125	7.14375	25/32	0.78125	19.84375
19/64	0.296875	7.54062	51/64	0.796875	20.24062
5/16	0.3125	7.93750	13/16	0.8125	20.63750
21/64	0.328125	8.33437	53/64	0.828125	21.03437
11/32	0.34375	8.73125	27/32	0.84375	21.43125
23/64	0.359375	9.12812	55/64	0.859375	21.82812
3/8	0.375	9.52500	7/8	0.875	22.22500
25/64	0.390625	9.92187	57/64	0.890625	22.62187
13/32	0.40625	10.31875	29/32	0.90625	23.01875
27/64	0.421875	10.71562	59/64	0.921875	23.41562
7/16	0.4375	11.11250	15/16	0.9375	23.81250
29/64	0.453125	11.50937	61/64	0.953125	24.20937
15/32	0.46875	11.90625	31/32	0.96875	24.60625
31/64	0.484375	12.30312	63/64	0.984375	25.00312
1/2	0.500	12.70000	1	1.00	25.40000

Table 3 GENERAL TORQUE SPECIFICATIONS

Thread diameter	N·m	ft.-lb.
5 mm	3.4-4.9	30-43 in.-lb.
6 mm	5.9-7.8	52-69 in.-lb.
8 mm	14-19	10.0-13.5
10 mm	25-39	19-25
12 mm	44-61	33-45
14 mm	73-98	54-72
16 mm	115-155	83-115
18 mm	165-225	125-165
20 mm	225-325	165-240

CHAPTER TWO

TROUBLESHOOTING

Diagnosing mechanical problems is relatively simple if you use orderly procedures and keep a few basic principles in mind.

The troubleshooting procedures in this chapter analyze typical symptoms and show logical methods of isolating causes. These are not the only methods. There may be several ways to solve a problem, but only a systematic approach can guarantee success.

Never assume anything. Do not overlook the obvious. If you are riding along and the bike suddenly quits, check the easiest, most accessible problem spots first. Is there gasoline in the tank? Is the fuel shutoff valve in the ON position? Has the spark plug wire fallen off?

If nothing obvious turns up in a quick check, look a little further. Learning to recognize and describe symptoms will make repairs easier for you or a mechanic at the shop. Describe problems accurately and fully. Saying that "it won't start" isn't the same thing as saying "it quit while climbing a hill and won't start," or that "it sat in my garage for 3 months and then wouldn't start."

Gather as many symptoms as possible to aid in diagnosis. Note whether the engine lost power gradually or all at once, what color smoke came from the exhaust and so on. Remember that the more complicated a machine is, the easier it is to troubleshoot because symptoms point to specific problems.

After the symptoms are defined, areas which could cause problems are tested and analyzed. Guessing at the cause of a problem may provide the solution, but it can easily lead to frustration, wasted time and a series of expensive, unnecessary parts replacements.

You do not need fancy equipment or complicated test gear to determine whether repairs can be attempted at home. A few simple checks could save a large repair bill and lost time while the bike sits in a dealer's service department. On the other hand, be realistic and do not attempt repairs beyond your abilities. Service departments tend to charge heavily for putting together a disassembled engine that may have been abused. Some won't even take on such a job—so use common sense, don't get in over your head.

OPERATING REQUIREMENTS

An engine needs 3 basics to run properly: correct fuel/air mixture, compression and a spark at the right time. If one basic requirement is missing, the engine will not run. Two-stroke engine operating principles are described in Chapter Four under *Engine Principles*. The ignition system is the weakest link of the 3 basics. More problems result from ignition breakdowns than from any other source. Keep that in mind before you begin tampering with carburetor adjustments and the like.

If a bike has been sitting for any length of time and refuses to start, check and clean the spark plug and then look to the gasoline delivery system. This includes the tank, fuel shutoff valve and fuel line to the carburetor. Gasoline tends to lose its firepower after standing for long periods. Condensation may contaminate it with water. Drain the gas from the fuel tank and carburetor and try starting with a fresh tankful.

TROUBLESHOOTING INSTRUMENTS

Chapter One lists the instruments needed and detailed instruction on their use.

STARTING THE ENGINE

When your engine refuses to start, frustration can cause you to forget basic starting principles and procedures. The following outline will guide you through basic starting procedures.

Starting a Cold Engine

1. Shift the transmission into NEUTRAL.
2. Apply the front brake and rock the bike back and forth. This will help to mix the fuel in the tank.
3. Turn the fuel valve to ON.
4. Pull the choke knob up (**Figure 1**) or push the choke lever down (**Figure 2**).
5. With the throttle completely *closed*, kick the engine over.
6. When the engine starts, work the throttle slightly to keep it running.
7. Let the engine idle approximately a minute or until the throttle responds cleanly and the choke can be closed.

Starting a Warm or Hot Engine

1. Shift the transmission into NEUTRAL.
2. Turn the fuel valve to ON.

TROUBLESHOOTING

3. The choke knob should be pushed down (**Figure 1**) or the choke lever should be pulled up (**Figure 2**).

4. Open the throttle slightly and kick the engine over.

Starting a Flooded Engine

If the engine is flooded, open the throttle all the way and kick the engine over until it starts.

NOTE
*If the engine refuses to start, check the carburetor overflow hose attached to the fitting at the bottom of the float bowl (**Figure 3**). If fuel is running out of the hose, the floats may be stuck open.*

STARTING DIFFICULTIES

When the bike is difficult to start, or won't start at all, it does not help to kick away at the kick starter. Check for obvious problems even before getting out your tools. Go down the following list step-by-step. Do each one. If the bike still will not start, refer to the appropriate troubleshooting procedures which follow in this chapter.

1. Is there fuel in the tank? Remove the filler cap and rock the bike from side to side. Listen for fuel sloshing around.

WARNING
Do not use an open flame to check in the tank. A serious explosion is certain to result. When checking for fuel flow, place the disconnected fuel hose end into an approved gasoline container.

2. If there is fuel in the tank, pull off the fuel line at the carburetor. Turn the fuel valve to RES (**Figure 4**) and see if fuel flows freely. If none comes out and there is a fuel filter installed in the fuel line, remove the filter and turn the fuel valve to RES again. If fuel flows, the filter is clogged and should be replaced. If no fuel comes out, the fuel valve may be shut off, blocked by foreign matter, or the fuel cap vent may be plugged. If the carburetor is getting usable fuel, turn to the electrical system next.

3. Make sure the kill button is not stuck or working improperly or that the wire is broken and shorting out. See **Figure 5**.

4. Is the spark plug wire on tight (**Figure 6**)? Push it on and slightly rotate it to clean the electrical connection between the plug and the connector.

5. Is the choke knob or lever in the right position? Refer to *Starting the Engine* in this chapter.

ENGINE STARTING TROUBLES

An engine that refuses to start or is difficult to start is very frustrating. More often than not, the problem is very minor and can be found with a simple and logical troubleshooting approach.

The following items show a beginning point from which to isolate engine starting problems.

Engine Fails to Start

Perform the following spark test to determine if the ignition system is operating properly.

CAUTION
Before removing the spark plug in Step 1, clean all dirt and debris from the

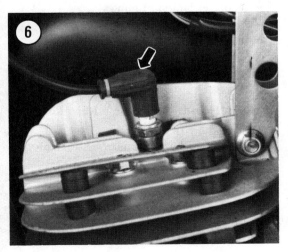

plug base. *Dirt that falls into the cylinder will cause rapid piston, piston ring and cylinder wear.*

NOTE
If you are checking the spark plug while on the trail, be careful that dirt does not fall into the cylinder.

1. Remove the spark plug (**Figure 6**).
2. Connect the spark plug wire and connector to the spark plug and touch the spark plug base to the cylinder head to ground it (**Figure 7**). Position the spark plug so you can see the electrode.

WARNING
In Step 3, do not hold the spark plug, wire or connector or a serious electrical shock may result.

3. Crank the engine over with the kickstarter. A fat blue spark should be evident across the spark plug electrode.
4. If the spark is good, check for one or more of the following possible malfunctions:
   a. Obstructed fuel line or fuel filter.
   b. Leaking head or cylinder base gasket.
5. If spark is not good, check for one or more of the following:
   a. Loose electrical connections.
   b. Dirty electrical connections.
   c. Loose or broken ignition coil ground wire.
   d. Weak ignition coil.
   e. Weak CDI unit.

Engine is Difficult to Start

Check for one or more of the following possible malfunctions:
   a. Fouled spark plug.
   b. Improperly operating choke.
   c. Contaminated fuel system.
   d. Improperly adjusted carburetor.
   e. Loose electrical connections.
   f. Dirty electrical connections.
   g. Weak CDI unit.
   h. Weak ignition coil.
   i. Poor compression.

Engine Will Not Crank

If the engine will not crank because of a mechanical problem, check for one or more of the following possible malfunctions.

   a. Defective kickstarter and/or gear.
   b. Seized piston.
   c. Seized crankshaft bearings.
   d. Broken connecting rod.

ENGINE PERFORMANCE

In the following check list, it is assumed that the engine runs, but is not operating at peak performance. This will serve as a starting point from which to isolate a performance malfunction.

The possible causes for each malfunction are listed in a logical sequence and in order of probability.

Engine Will Not Idle

   a. Carburetor incorrectly adjusted.
   b. Pilot jet clogged.
   c. Fouled spark plug.
   d. Head gasket leaking.

Engine Misses at High Speed

   a. Fouled or improperly gapped spark plug.
   b. Improper carburetor main jet selection.
   c. Carburetor main jet and/or needle jet clogged.
   d. Obstructed fuel line or fuel shutoff valve.
   e. Ignition timing incorrect.

Engine Overheating

   a. Incorrect carburetor jetting or fuel/oil ratio mixture.
   b. Incorrect ignition timing.
   c. Improper spark plug heat range.
   d. Intake system or crankcase air leak.
   e. Damaged or blocked cooling fins.
   f. Dragging brake(s).

Smoke in Exhaust and Engine Runs Roughly

   a. Clogged air filter element.
   b. Carburetor adjustment incorrect—mixture too rich.
   c. Carburetor floats damaged or incorrectly adjusted.
   d. Choke not operating correctly.
   e. Water or other contaminants in fuel.
   f. Excessive piston-to-cylinder clearance.

TROUBLESHOOTING

Engine Loses Power

a. Carburetor incorrectly adjusted.
b. Engine overheating.
c. Ignition timing incorrect due to improper timing or defective ignition component(s).
d. Incorrectly gapped spark plug.
e. Obstructed silencer.
f. Dragging brake(s).

Engine Lacks Acceleration

a. Carburetor adjustment incorrect.
b. Clogged fuel line.
c. Ignition timing incorrect due to improper timing or faulty ignition component(s).
d. Dragging brake(s).

ENGINE NOISES

1. *Knocking or pinging during acceleration*—May be caused by using a lower octane fuel than recommended. It may also be caused by poor quality fuel. Pinging can also be caused by a spark plug of the wrong heat range and incorrect carburetor jetting. Refer to *Correct Spark Plug Heat Range* in Chapter Three.

2. *Slapping or rattling noises at low speed or during acceleration*—May be caused by piston slap, i.e., excessive piston-cylinder wall clearance.

3. *Knocking or rapping while decelerating*—Usually caused by excessive rod bearing clearance.

4. *Persistent knocking and vibration*—Usually caused by worn main bearings.

5. *Rapid on-off squeal*—Compression leak around cylinder head gasket or spark plug.

EXCESSIVE VIBRATION

This can be difficult to find without disassembling the engine. Usually this is caused by loose or broken engine mounting bolts.

TWO-STROKE PRESSURE TESTING

Many owners of 2-stroke bikes are plagued by hard starting and generally poor running, for which there seems to be no cause. Carburetion and ignition may be good, and compression tests may show that all is well in the engine's upper end.

What a compression test does not show is lack of primary compression. The crankcase in a 2-stroke engine is alternately under pressure and vacuum. After the piston closes the intake port, further downward movement of the piston causes the entrapped mixture to be pressurized so that it can rush quickly into the cylinder when the transfer ports are opened. Upward piston movement creates a slight vacuum in the crankcase, enabling the fuel/air mixture to be drawn in from the carburetor.

NOTE
The operational sequence of a two-stroke engine is illustrated in Chapter Four under **Engine Principles**.

If crankcase seals or cylinder gaskets leak, the crankcase cannot hold pressure or vacuum, and proper engine operation becomes impossible. Any other source of leakage such as a defective cylinder base gasket or porous or cracked crankcase castings will result in the same conditions. See **Figure 8**.

It is possible, however, to test for and isolate engine pressure leaks. The test is simple but requires special equipment. A typical two-stroke pressure test kit is shown in **Figure 9**. Briefly, what is done is to seal off all natural engine openings, then apply air pressure. If the engine does not hold air, a leak or leaks is indicated. Then it is only necessary to locate and repair all leaks.

The following procedure describes a typical pressure test.

1. Remove the carburetor.

⑧

TWO-STROKE CRANKCASE PRESSURE TESTING

Excessive exhaust smoke, oil fouled spark plug or transmission & clutch oil loss ───

Check:
- Leaking right-hand side crankshaft seal.
- Leaking crankcase mating seal.
- Porous crankcase casting.

White spark plug reading, pinging or pre-ignition, power surging, piston seizure or holed piston ───

Check:
- Leaking spark plug seal.
- Leaking left-hand side crankshaft seal.
- Leaking intake manifold.
- Leaking crankcase mating seal.
- Porous crankcase casting.
- Porous cylinder head casting.

Difficult starting, white spark plug reading or low compression ───

Check:
- Leaking spark plug seal.
- Leaking head gasket.
- Porous cylinder head casting.

TROUBLESHOOTING

> *NOTE*
> *Do not remove the intake manifold. The manifold should remain on the engine during this test as it may be causing the leak.*

2. Take a rubber plug and insert it tightly in the intake manifold.

3. Remove the exhaust pipe and block off the exhaust port, using suitable adapters and fittings.

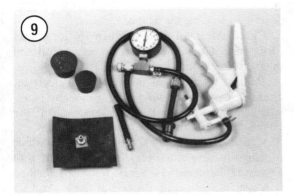

4. Remove the spark plug and install the pressure gauge adapter into the spark plug hole. Connect the pressurizing lever and gauge to the pressure fitting installed where the spark plug was, then continue to squeeze the lever until the gauge indicates approximately 5 psi.

> *CAUTION*
> *Do not apply more than 8 psi or the crankcase seals may be damaged.*

5. Observe the pressure gauge. If the engine is in good condition, the pressure should hold for 3-5 minutes. If the pressure starts to drop immediately, there is a leak. Before condemning the engine, first be sure that there are no leaks in the test equipment or sealing plugs. If the equipment shows no signs of leakage, go over the entire engine carefully. Large leaks can be heard; smaller ones can be found by going over every possible leakage source with a small brush and soap suds. Possible leakage points are listed below:
   a. Crankshaft seals. See **Figure 10** (left-hand seal) or **Figure 11** (right-hand seal).
   b. Spark plug (**Figure 6**).
   c. Cylinder head joint.
   d. Cylinder base joint.
   e. Reed valve manifold.
   f. Crankcase joint.
   g. Porous crankcase, cylinder or cylinder head casting.

> *NOTE*
> *To check the left-hand and right-hand crankcase seals, the clutch and magneto assemblies must be removed. Refer to Chapter Five and Chapter Seven for details.*

CLUTCH

The three basic clutch troubles are:
   a. Improper clutch disengagement.
   b. Clutch slipping.
   c. Clutch noise.

All clutch troubles, except adjustments, require partial engine disassembly to identify and cure the problem. Refer to Chapter Six for procedures.

The troubleshooting procedures outlined in **Figure 12** will help you solve the majority of clutch troubles in a systematic manner.

TRANSMISSION

The basic transmission troubles are:
a. Difficult shifting.
b. Gears pop out of mesh.
c. Incorrect shift lever operation.
d. Excessive gear noise.

Transmission symptoms are sometimes hard to distinguish from clutch symptoms. Be sure that the clutch is not causing the trouble before working on the transmission.

The troubleshooting procedures outlined in **Figure 13** will help you solve the majority of transmission troubles.

IGNITION SYSTEM

All KDX200 models are equipped with a capacitor discharge ignition (CDI) system. This solid state system uses no contact breaker pointd or other moving parts. Because of the solid state design, problems with the capacitor discharge system are relatively few. However, when problems arise they can create one of the following conditions:
a. Weak spark.
b. No spark.

It is possible to check CDI systems that:
a. Do not spark.
b. Have a weak spark.

It is difficult to check CDI systems that malfunction due to:
a. Vibration problems.
b. Components that malfunction only when the engine is hot or under a load.

The troubleshooting procedures in **Figure 14** will help you isolate the ignition problem fast. When troubleshooting the ignition system, consider the following:

1. Disconnect the kill switch (**Figure 5**) and see if the problem still exists.
2. Remove the magneto rotor, then make sure that the stator plate screws (**Figure 15**) are tight. If the screws are loose, recheck the ignition timing as described in Chapter Three.
3. Check the stator plate (**Figure 15**) for cracks or damage that would cause the pulser coil and magneto to be out of alignment.
4. Remove the fuel tank and untape all electrical connectors. Make sure the connectors are connected properly. If necessary, clean the connectors with electrical contact cleaner.
5. Check the left- and right-hand crankshaft bearings for excessive play. See **Figure 10** and **Figure 11**. Remove the magneto rotor as described in Chapter Nine. Grab the end of the crankshaft and try to move it up and down. Any noticeable play indicates worn crankshaft bearings. Refer to Chapter Five.

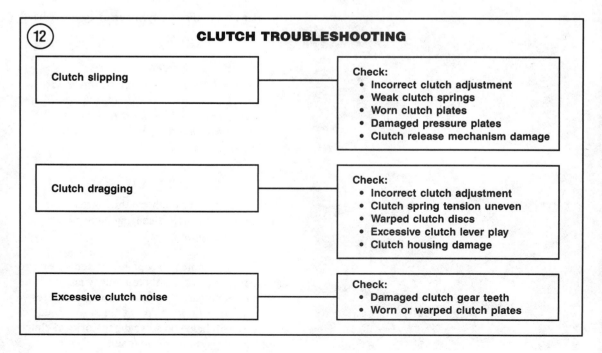

TROUBLESHOOTING

⑬

TRANSMISSION TROUBLESHOOTING

Excessive gear noise

Check:
- Worn bearings
- Worn or damaged gears
- Excessive gear backlash

Difficult shifting

Check:
- Damaged gears
- Damaged shift forks
- Damaged shift drum
- Samaged shift lever assembly
- Incorrect main shaft and countershaft engagement
- Incorrect clutch disengagement

Gears pop out of mesh

Check:
- Worn gear or transmission shaft splines
- Shift forks worn or bent
- Worn dog holes in gears
- Insufficient shift lever spring tension
- Damages shift lever linkage

Incorrect shift lever operation

Check:
- Bent shift lever
- Bent or damaged shift lever shaft
- Damaged shift lever linkage or gears

Incorrect shifting after engine reassembly

Check:
- Missing transmission shaft shims
- Incorrectly installed parts
- Shift forks bent during reasembly
- Incorrectly assembled transmission
- Incorrect clutch adjustment
- Incorrectly assembled shift linkage assembly

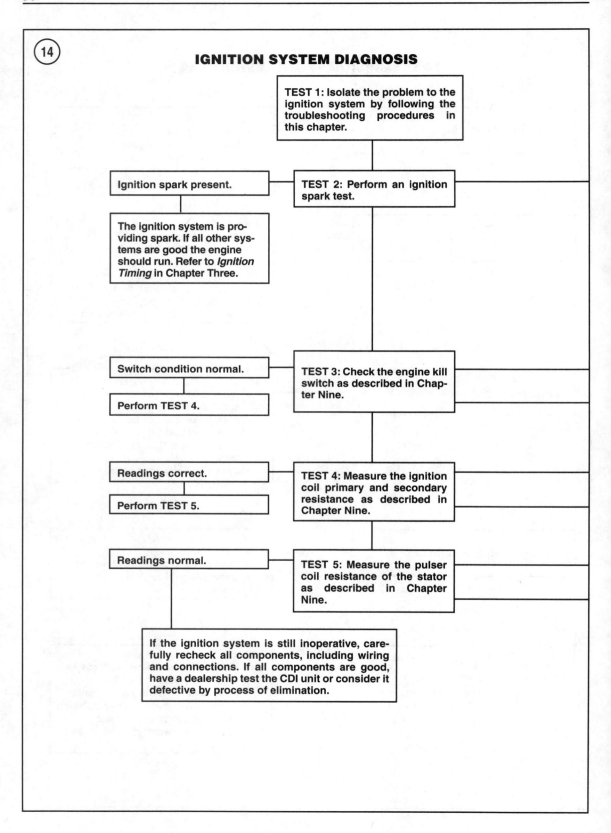

TROUBLESHOOTING

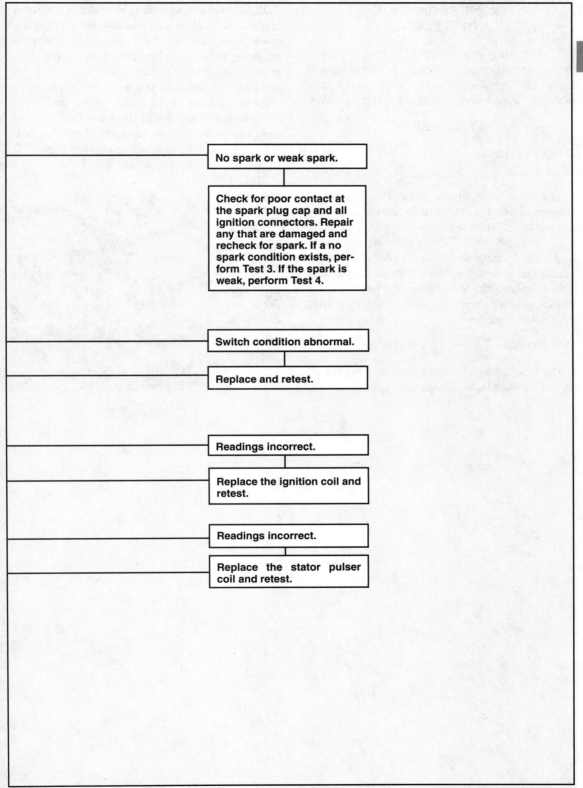

FRONT SUSPENSION AND STEERING

Poor handling may be caused by improper front or rear tire pressure, a damaged or bent frame or front steering components, worn swing arm bushings, worn wheel bearings or dragging brakes.

BRAKES

Front Disc Brake (1986-on)

The front disc brake should be inspected frequently and any problems located and repaired immediately. When replacing or refilling the brake fluid, use only DOT 3 brake fluid from a closed and sealed container. See Chapter Twelve for additional information on brake fluid and disc brake service. The troubleshooting procedures in **Figure 16** will help you isolate the majority of front disc brake troubles.

Drum Brakes

The front (1983-1985) and rear drum brakes are relatively simple in design and operation. The KDX200 brakes have always been one of the better brake units installed on a production dirt bike. Yet, many riders do not get full stopping power because the shoes and drum are covered with residue. This residue buildup is due mainly to lack of maintenance. To work properly, the drum brakes must be cleaned and serviced before each ride. Periodic maintenance will also allow inspection of parts so that they can be replaced before they fail.

Refer to the troubleshooting chart in **Figure 17** for drum brake problems and checks.

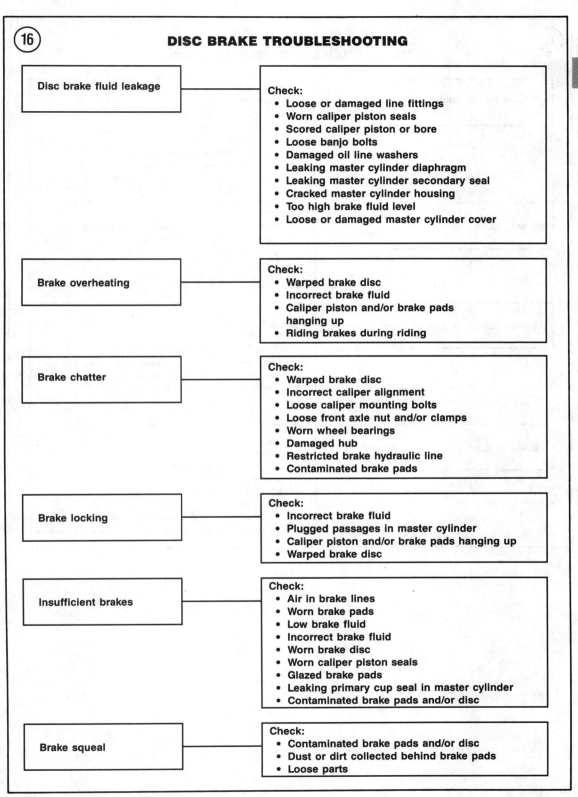

34 CHAPTER TWO

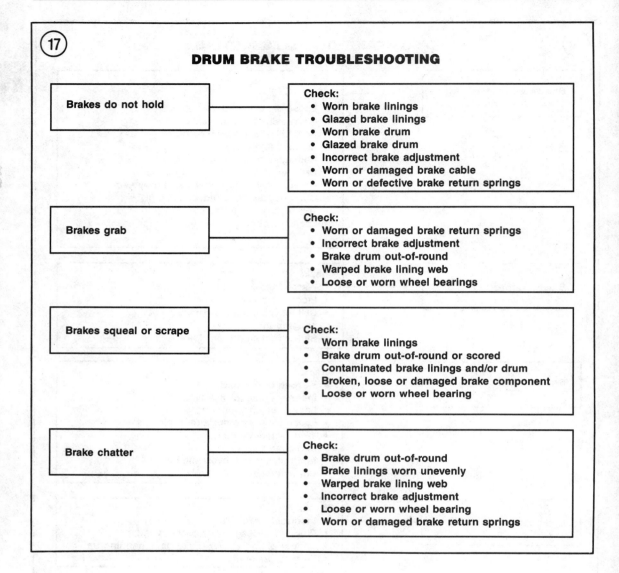

CHAPTER THREE

LUBRICATION, MAINTENANCE AND TUNE-UP

This chapter covers all of the regular maintenance required to keep your KDX200 in top shape. Regular maintenance is something you can't afford to ignore whether you are racing competitively or just trail riding on weekends. Because off-road motorcycles are subjected to tremendous heat, stress and vibration, they must be inspected and serviced at regular intervals.

When neglected, any bike becomes unreliable and actually dangerous to ride. By maintaining a routine service schedule as described in this chapter, costly mechanical problems and unexpected breakdowns can be prevented.

This chapter explains lubrications, maintenance and tune-up procedures required for 1983 and later Kawasaki KDX200 models. **Table 1** and **Table 2** are suggested maintenance schedules. **Tables 1-17** are at the end of the chapter.

PRE-CHECKS

The following checks should be performed prior to each race or before the first ride of the day.
1. Inspect the fuel line and fittings for wetness.
2. Make sure the fuel tank is full and has the correct fuel/oil mixture. Refer to *Engine Lubrication* in this chapter.
3. Make sure the air cleaner is clean and that the cover is securely in place.
4. Check the clutch/transmission oil level.
5. Check the operation of the clutch and adjust if necessary.
6. Check that the clutch and brake levers operate properly with no binding.
7. Inspect the condition of the front and rear suspension. Make sure it has a good solid feel with no looseness.
8. Check the drive chain for wear and correct tension.

9. Check tire pressure (**Table 3**).

NOTE
*While checking tire pressure, also check the position of the valve stem. If the valve stem is cocked sideways like that shown in **Figure 1**, your riding time could end quickly because of a flat tire. Refer to **Tires and Wheels** in this chapter.*

10. Check the exhaust system for damage.
11. Check the tightness of all fasteners, especially engine mounting hardware.
12. Check the rear sprocket and bolts as follows:
    a. Check the sprocket holes for signs of egg-shaping. If the sprocket is found in this condition, the sprocket bolts have loosened during operation. Replace the sprocket before the hub is destroyed.
    b. Check the sprocket bolts for tightness. If Allen head bolts (**Figure 2**) are used on your model, always tighten the nut rather than the bolt. Also, check the surface between the countersunk bolt head and the machined countersunk area in the hub. The bolt should sit flush in the countersunk area.
    c. Replace nuts that have started to round at their corners.

TIRES AND WHEELS

Tire Pressure

Tire pressure should be checked and adjusted to maintain good traction and handling. An accurate gauge should be carried in your tool box. The approximate tire inflation pressure specification for all models is listed in **Table 3**. When racing, track conditions usually dictate tire air pressure. Lower air pressures can be used for soft, smooth or muddy track conditions. If the track is rougher with a number of big jumps or rocks, you may need a higher air pressure.

Tire Inspection

The tires take a lot of punishment due to the variety of terrain they are subject to. Inspect them periodically for excessive wear, cuts, abrasions, etc. Sidewall tears are the most common cause of tire failure. This type of damage is usually caused by sharp rocks or other trail conditions. Often, sidewall tears cannot be seen from the outside. If necessary, remove the tire from the rim as described in Chapter Ten. Run your hand around the inside of the tire casing to feel for tears or sharp objects embedded in the casing. The outside of the tire can be inspected visually.

NOTE
If a regular standard inner tube is used, replace it every 10 events. A stronger heavy-duty tube will last longer and is not as easy to puncture. The stronger tube weighs more but it's a small sacrifice for the additional durability.

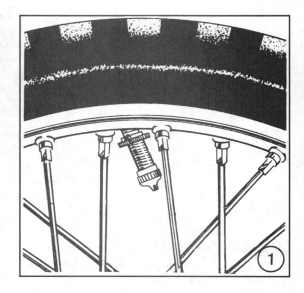

LUBRICATION, MAINTENANCE AND TUNE-UP

While checking the tires, also check the position of the valve stem. If the valve stem is cocked sideways like that shown in **Figure 1**, your riding day could end because of a flat tire. Refer to *Valve Stem Alignment* in this chapter.

Wheel Spoke Tension

Tap each spoke with a wrench. The higher the pitch of sound it makes, the tighter the spoke. The lower the sound frequency, the looser the spoke. A "ping" is good, a "clunk" says the spoke is too loose.

If one or more spokes are loose, tighten them as described under *Front Wheel* in Chapter Ten.

NOTE
*Most spokes loosen as a group rather than individually. Extra-loose spokes should be tightened carefully. Overtightening just a few spokes will put improper pressure across the wheel, which will result in excessive wobble. Refer to **Front Wheel** in Chapter Ten.*

Rim Inspection

Frequently inspect the condition of the wheel rims. If a rim has been damaged it may be enough to cause excessive side-to-side play. Refer to *Front Wheel* in Chapter Ten.

Tube Alignment

Before each riding day, check each tube's valve stem alignment. **Figure 1** shows a valve stem that has slipped. If the tube is not repositioned, the valve stem will eventually pull away from the tube, causing a flat. However, don't get your tire irons out yet. The tube can be aligned without removing the tire.

1. Wash the tire if it is very dirty or caked with mud.

2. Remove the valve stem core and release all air pressure from the tube.

3. Loosen the rim locknut (**Figure 3**).

4. With an assistant steadying the bike, squeeze the tire and break the tire-to-wheel seal all the way around the wheel. If the tire seal is very tight, it may be necessary to lay the bike on its side and break the tire seal with your foot or a rubber mallet. Use care, though; have an assistant steady the bike so that it doesn't rock and damage the handlebars or a control lever.

5. After the tire seal is broken, put the bike on a stand so that the wheel clears the ground.

6. Apply a mixture of soap and water from a spray container (like that used when changing a tire) along the tire bead on both sides of the tire.

7. Have an assistant apply the brake "hard." If necessary, tighten the front or rear brake adjuster.

8. Using both of your hands, grab hold of the tire and turn it and the tube until the valve stem is straight up (90°). See **Figure 4**.

9. When the valve stem is straight up, install the valve stem core and inflate the tire. If the soap and

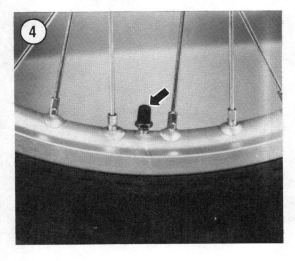

water solution has dried, reapply it to help the tire seat on the rim. Check the tire to make sure it seats all the way around the rim.

WARNING
Do not overinflate the tire and tube. If the tire will not seat properly, remove the valve stem core and re-lubricate the tire.

10. Tighten the rim lock (**Figure 3**) securely.
11. Adjust the tire pressure (**Table 3**). When installing the valve stem nut, do not tighten it against the rim. If the tire and tube slip again, the valve stem will pull away from the tube and cause a flat. Instead, tighten the nut against the valve cap as shown in **Figure 4**. This will allow the valve stem to slip without damage until you can reposition the tire and tube.

LUBRICANTS

Clutch/Transmission Oil

Oil is graded according to its viscosity, which is an indication of how thick it is. The Society of Automotive Engineers (SAE) system distinguishes oil viscosity by numbers, called "weights." Thick (heavy) oils have higher viscosity numbers than thin (light) oils. For example, a 5 weight (SAE 5) oil is a light oil while a 90 weight (SAE 90) oil is relatively heavy.

Grease

A good quality grease—preferably waterproof—should be used for many of the parts on your KDX200. Water does not wash grease off parts as easily as it washes oil off. In addition, grease maintains its lubricating qualities better than oil on long and strenuous events.

CLEANING SOLVENT

A number of solvents can be used to remove old dirt, grease and oil. Kerosene is readily available and comparatively inexpensive. Another inexpensive solvent similar to kerosene is ordinary diesel fuel. Both of these solvents have a very high temperature flash point and can be used safely in any adequately ventilated area away from open flames.

WARNING
Never use gasoline for cleaning parts. Gasoline is extremely volatile and contains tremendously destructive potential energy. The slightest spark from metal parts accidentally hitting, or a tool slipping, could cause a fatal explosion.

ENGINE LUBRICATION

WARNING
Serious fire hazards always exist around gasoline. Do not allow any smoking in areas where fuel is being mixed or while refueling your machine. Always have a fire extinguisher, rated for gasoline and electrical fires, within reach just to play it safe.

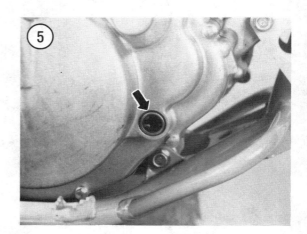

LUBRICATION, MAINTENANCE AND TUNE-UP

The engines in all KDX200 models are lubricated by oil mixed with gasoline. Refer to **Table 4** for recommended oils and fuel. Mix the oil and gasoline thoroughly in a separate clean, sealable container larger than the quantity being mixed to allow room for agitation. Always measure the quantities exactly. **Table 5** lists fuel/oil mixture ratios for all models. Fuel capacity for the various models is given in **Table 6**. Use a good grade of premium fuel rated at 90+ octane.

Use a discarded baby bottle with graduations in cubic centimeters (cc) or fluid ounces (oz.) on the side. Pour the required amount of oil into the mixing container and add approximately half the required amount of gasoline. Agitate the mixture thoroughly, then add the remaining fuel and agitate again until all is mixed well.

NOTE
Always mix a fresh amount of fuel the morning of the race or ride; do not mix more than you will use that day. Do not keep any fuel overnight. Dispose of any excess properly.

To avoid any contaminants entering into the fuel system, use a funnel with a filter when pouring the fuel into the bike's tank.

CAUTION
Do not mix castor bean oils with petroleum lubricants. A gum will form and may cause serious engine damage.

PERIODIC LUBRICATION

Transmission Oil
Checking and Changing

The transmission oil lubricates both the transmission and the clutch. Proper operation and long service for the clutch and transmission require clean oil. Oil should be changed at the intervals indicated in **Table 1** or **Table 2**. Check the oil level frequently and add as necessary to maintain the correct level. Refer to **Table 7** for oil capacities for the various models.

Try to use the same brand of oil. Do not mix 2 brand types at the same time as they all vary slightly in their composition. Use of oil additives is not recommended as it may cause clutch slippage.

Checking

1. Start the engine and let it warm up approximately 2-3 minutes. Shut it off.
2. Place the bike in an upright position.
3. Check the oil level through the inspection window (**Figure 5**) located at the front of the clutch cover. The oil level should be in the middle of the window.
4. If necessary, turn the oil fill cap (**Figure 6**) counterclockwise and remove it.
5. Add the recommended weight of oil (**Table 4**) through the oil fill opening to correct the level.

NOTE
If the oil level is too high, siphon some of the oil out through the oil fill opening with a fork oil level gauge or some other type of syringe.

Changing

To drain the oil you will need the following:
a. Drain pan.
b. Funnel.
c. Can opener or pour spout.
d. 1 quart of oil.

NOTE
Never dispose of motor oil in the trash or pour it on the ground, or down a storm drain. Many service stations accept used motor oil. Many waste haulers provide curbside used motor oil collection. Do not combine other fluids with motor oil to be recycled. To find a recycling location contact the American Petroleum Institute (API) at www.recycle.org.

1. Start the engine and let it reach operating temperature.
2. Shut it off and place a drain pan under the engine.
3. Wipe all dirt and debris from around the drain plug. Then remove the engine drain plug. Remove the oil fill cap (**Figure 6**) to help speed up the flow of oil.
4. Let the oil completely drain.
5. Inspect the sealing washer on the drain plug. Replace if necessary.
6. Install the drain plug and tighten it to the torque specification in **Table 8**.
7. Fill the transmission with the correct weight and quantity oil. Refer to **Table 4** and **Table 7**.

8. Screw in the oil fill cap and start the engine. Let it idle for 2-3 minutes. Check for leaks.
9. Turn the engine off and check for correct oil level. Adjust as necessary.

Front Fork Oil Change

The fork oil should be changed at the interval described in **Table 1** or **Table 2**. If it becomes contaminated with dirt or water, change it immediately.

1. Support the motorcycle with a stand or blocks so that the front wheel clears the ground.
2. Remove the fork tube air valve cap (**Figure 7**). Use a small screwdriver or punch and release all air pressure in the fork (A, **Figure 8**).

CAUTION
Release the air pressure gradually. If released too fast, oil may spurt out with the air. Protect your eyes accordingly.

3. Place a drain pan underneath the drain screw (**Figure 9**). Remove the drain screw and allow the oil to drain. Never reuse the oil.

CAUTION
Do not allow the fork oil to contact any of the brake components or to run onto the front tire.

4. Remove the stand or blocks from underneath the bike. With both of the bike's wheels on the ground, grab the front brake lever and push down on the handlebar. Repeat this action until all the oil is released from the fork tube.
5. Check the drain screw seal. Replace it if worn or damaged.

LUBRICATION, MAINTENANCE AND TUNE-UP

6. Apply Loctite 242 (blue) onto the screw threads and reinstall the drain screw. Tighten it securely.

7. Repeat Steps 1-6 for the opposite fork.

8. Place the motorcycle on a stand or blocks so that the front wheel clears the ground.

9. Loosen the top fork pinch bolts (B, **Figure 8**).

10. Using a speeder bar and socket (**Figure 10**), loosen and remove the fork cap. See **Figure 11**.

11. Remove the spacer (**Figure 12**).

12. Remove the spring seat (**Figure 13**).

13. Remove the fork spring (**Figure 14**).

14. Fill each fork with the specified weight and quantity of fork oil. See **Table 4** and **Table 9**.

15. Repeat Steps 9-13 for the opposite fork.

16. With an assistant's help, roll the bike off of the stand so that the forks are placed in a vertical position.

17. Allow the oil to settle for a few minutes. Then with an assistant's help, push the front wheel up and down to remove all air bubbles from the fork oil.

NOTE
*A tape measure or ruler (**Figure 15**) can be used to perform Step 18. However, to assure a precise oil level, you may want to invest in a fork oil level gauge offered by Kawasaki or one of the numerous companies dealing in motocross accessories.*

18. Using a fork oil level gauge (**Figure 16**), measure the distance from the top of the fork tube to the top of the oil (**Figure 17**). Refer to **Table**

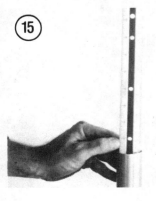

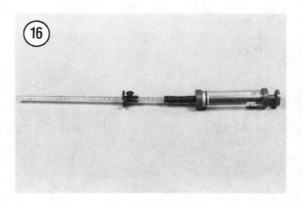

for the correct specifications. Repeat for the opposite fork. **Figure 18** shows a fork oil level gauge being used with the forks removed. If the oil level is too high, use the gauge to siphon some of the oil out of the fork tube. If the oil level is too low, pour some fork oil into the fork tube. Measure the fork oil level.

19. Place the bike onto the stand so that the front wheel clears the ground. Push down on the front wheel so that the forks are completely extended.
20. Check the O-ring in the fork cap (**Figure 19**). Replace it if worn or damaged.
21. Install the fork spring (**Figure 14**), spring seat (**Figure 13**) and spacer (**Figure 12**).
22. Place the fork cap on the spring seat and push it down with a speeder bar and sprocket. Install the fork cap by carefully threading it into the fork. Don't cross thread it. Tighten the fork cap securely.
23. Tighten the fork tube pinch bolts (B, **Figure 8**) to the torque specification in **Table 8**.
24. Inflate each fork tube to the correct amount of air pressure as described in this chapter.

Drive Chain

The drive chain should be cleaned after each race or weekend trail ride. The chain should be lubricated before each ride and during the day as required. A properly maintained chain will provide maximum service life and reliability.

1. Disconnect the master link (**Figure 20**) and remove the chain from the motorcycle.

> *CAUTION*
> *If an O-ring drive chain has been installed (**Figure 21**), use only kerosene or diesel fuel for cleaning to prevent O-ring damage. Do not use gasoline or other solvents that will cause the O-rings to swell or deteriorate.*

2. Immerse the chain in a pan of cleaning solvent and allow it to soak for about a half hour. Move it around and flex it during this period so that the dirt between the pins and rollers may work its way out.
3. Scrub the rollers and side plates with a stiff brush and rinse away loosened dirt. Rinse it a couple of times to make sure all dirt and grit are washed out. Hang up the chain and allow it to thoroughly dry.

4. Lubricate the chain with a good grade of chain lubricant, carefully following the manufacturer's instructions.

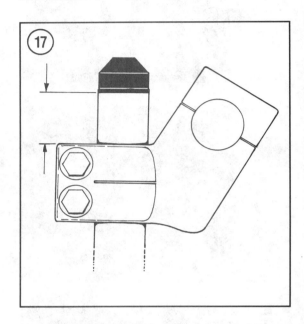

LUBRICATION, MAINTENANCE AND TUNE-UP

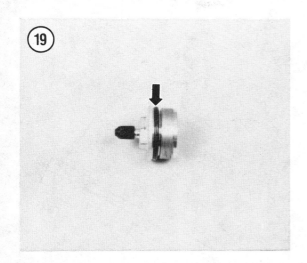

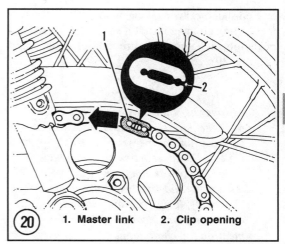

1. Master link   2. Clip opening

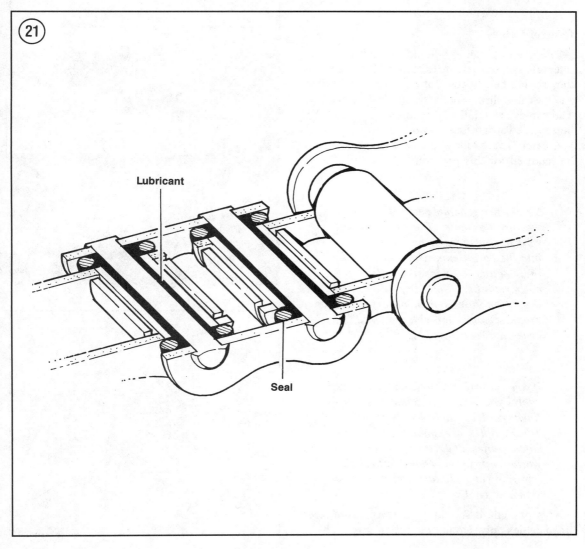

Lubricant

Seal

5. Reinstall the chain on the motorcycle. Use a new master link clip and install it so that the closed end of the clip is facing the direction of chain travel (**Figure 20**).

> *WARNING*
> *Always check the master link clip after the bike has been rolled backwards such as unloading from a truck or trailer. The master link clip may have snagged on the chain guide or tensioner and become disengaged. Obviously, losing a chain while riding can cause a serious spill, not to mention the chain damage which may occur.*

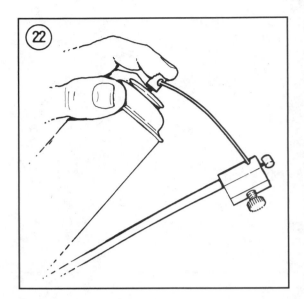

Control Cables

The control cables should be lubricated at intervals as described in **Table 1** or **Table 2**. Also they should be inspected at this time for fraying, and the cable sheath should be checked for chafing. The cables are relatively inexpensive and should be replaced when found to be faulty.

A can of cable lube and a cable lubricator will be required for this procedure.

> *CAUTION*
> *Never use a graphite cable lubricate on the throttle cable. The graphite will work its way through the cable and exit into the carburetor. The graphite can then cause excessive slide-to-carburetor bore wear. Replacement of the carburetor is then necessary. A graphite lubricant can be used on brake and clutch cables.*

> *NOTE*
> *If you are having trouble with the stock cables you may want to install Teflon-lined cables, such as Terrycables. These cables are smoother than the stock cables and can be washed in warm soapy water. They don't require any oiling and will last longer than the standard cables.*

This procedure should be performed on steel lined cables only. Do not oil Teflon-lined cables.

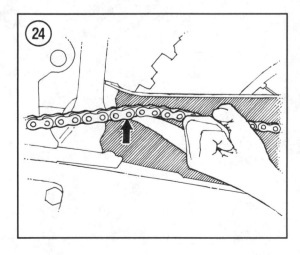

LUBRICATION, MAINTENANCE AND TUNE-UP

1. Disconnect the cables from the clutch lever and the throttle grip assembly and from where they attach to the carburetor and clutch mechanism.
2. Attach a cable lubricator following the manufacturer's instructions (**Figure 22**).
3. Insert the nozzle of the lubricant can in the lubricator, press the button on the can and hold down until the lubricant begins to flow out of the other end of the cable.

NOTE
Place a shop cloth at the end of the cable to catch the oil as it runs out the end or place the end in an empty container. Discard the excess oil properly.

4. Remove the lubricator, reconnect the cable(s) and adjust the cable(s) as described in this chapter.

Miscellaneous Lubrication Points

Lubricate the clutch lever, front brake lever, rear brake pedal pivot point and the sidestand pivot point.

PERIODIC MAINTENANCE

Drive Chain Free Play Inspection

The drive chain (**Figure 23**) must have adequate play so that the chain is not strung tight when the swing arm is horizontal. On the other hand, too much play may cause the chain to jump off the sprockets with potentially disastrous results. Set free play within the specifications listed in **Table 11**.

When riding in mud and sand, dirt buildup will make the chain tighter. Recheck chain play and readjust as required. See **Table 11**.

1. Place the bike on a stand so that the rear wheel clears the ground. Spin the wheel and check the chain for tightness at several spots. Check and adjust the chain at its tightest point.
2. Lower the bike so that both wheels are on the ground and the bike is in a vertical position. There should not be a rider on the bike when performing this adjustment.
3A. *1983-1985:* Push the middle of the upper chain run up away from the swing arm. The play should be within the specifications in **Table 11** when measured between the chain and the swing arm at the rear of the swing arm protector (**Figure 24**).
3B. *1986-on:* Push the middle of the upper chain run up away from the swing arm. The play should be within the specifications in **Table 11** when measured between the chain and the swing arm (**Figure 24**).

Drive Chain Adjustment

When adjusting the drive chain, you must also maintain rear wheel alignment. A misaligned rear wheel can cause poor handling and pulling to one side, as well as increased sprocket and chain wear.

On all KDX200 models, cam type chain adjusters (**Figure 25**) are used. Slots (A) are cut into the outside of the adjuster that align with a series of numbers. The slots engage a hardened pin (B) installed in each side of the swing arm. When both adjusters are set at the same mark the rear wheel should be aligned correctly.

1. Loosen the axle nut (**Figure 26**).
2. Turn both adjuster cams so that the narrower end of the cam contacts the pin and kick the rear wheel forward until the chain is loose.
3. Turn each adjuster cam back an equal amount until the chain play is within specification. The pin

in front of the adjusters should be positioned at the same adjuster alignment mark on each side of the wheel.

4. When the chain play is correct, check wheel alignment. Sight along the top of the drive chain from the rear sprocket to see that it is correctly aligned. It should leave the top of the rear sprocket in a straight line (A, **Figure 27**). If it is cocked to one side or the other (B and C, **Figure 27**) the wheel is incorrectly aligned and must be corrected.

NOTE
If the chain alignment is incorrect, check the cam adjusters (A, Figure 25) for damage. If the adjusters are okay, *check the hardened pin (B, Figure 25) installed in each side of the swing arm.*

NOTE
*To prevent a spongy-feeling brake, **partially** tighten the axle nut, spin the wheel, stop it forcefully with the brake pedal, then tighten the axle nut. This centers the brake backing plate in the brake drum.*

5. Tighten the axle nut (**Figure 26**) to the torque specification in **Table 8**.
6. Recheck chain play.
7. Adjust the rear brake if required. *See Rear Brake Adjustment* in this chapter.

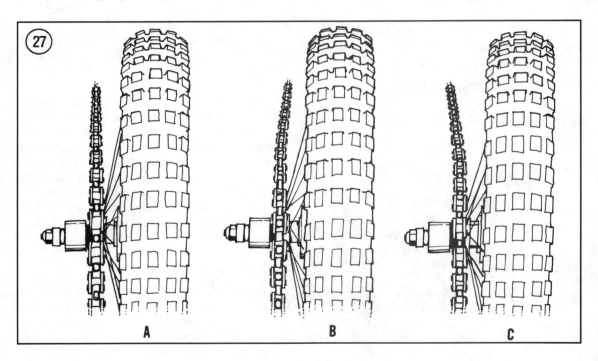

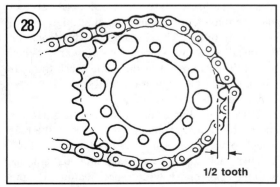

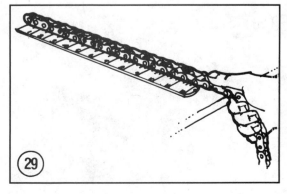

LUBRICATION, MAINTENANCE AND TUNE-UP

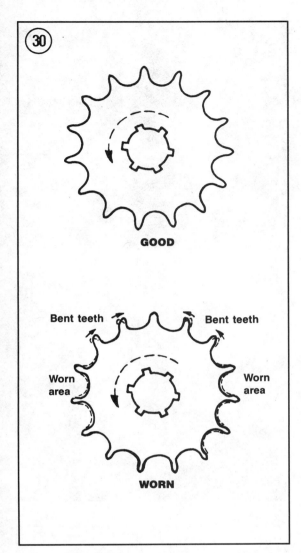

Drive Chain Inspection

Kawasaki recommends replacing the drive chain when it has worn longer than 2% of its original length.

A quick check will give you an indication of when to actually measure chain wear. At the rear sprocket, pull one of the links away from the sprocket. If the link pulls away more than half the height of a sprocket tooth, the chain has probably worn out (**Figure 28**).

To measure chain wear, perform the following:
1. Remove the drive chain and stretch it tight on the workbench, or loosen the axle nut and tighten the chain adjusters to move the wheel rearward until the chain is taut.
2. Lay a scale along the top chain run (**Figure 29**), and measure the length of any 20 links in the chain, from the center of the first pin you select to the 21st pin. If the link length is more than the limit given in **Table 12**, install a new drive chain.
3. If the drive chain is worn, inspect the rear wheel sprocket and engine drive sprocket for undercutting or sharp teeth (**Figure 30**). If wear is evident, replace the sprockets too, or you'll soon wear out a new drive chain.

NOTE
*Check the inner faces of the inner plates (**Figure 31**). They should be lightly polished on both sides. If they show considerable wear on both sides, the sprockets are not aligned. Adjust alignment as described under **Drive Chain Adjustment** in this chapter.*

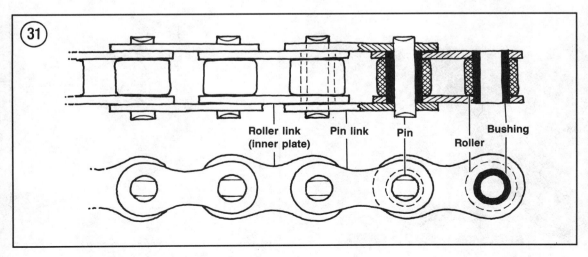

Drive Chain Guard and Rollers Replacement

The drive chain rollers (**Figure 32**) and guides (**Figure 33** and **Figure 34**) should be inspected and replaced as necessary. It is a good idea to inspect them prior to each race. A worn or damaged chain roller or guard can allow the drive chain to damage the swing arm.

Front Brake Lever Adjustment (Drum Brakes)

The front brake lever should be adjusted to suit your own personal preference, but should maintain a minimum cable slack of 4-5 mm (5/32-3/16 in.). Refer to **Figure 35**. The brake lever should travel this amount before the brake shoes come in contact with the drum, but it must not be adjusted so closely that the brake shoes contact the drum with the lever released. The primary adjustment should be made at the hand lever.

1. Slide back the rubber boot.
2. Loosen the locknut (A, **Figure 36**) and turn the adjusting barrel (B, **Figure 36**) in or out to achieve the correct amount of free play. Tighten the locknut.
3. Because of normal brake wear, this adjustment will eventually be "used up." It is then necessary to loosen the locknut (A, **Figure 36**) and screw the adjusting barrel (B, **Figure 36**) all the way in toward the hand grip. Tighten the locknut.
4. At the adjuster on the brake panel, loosen the locknut (**Figure 37**) and turn the adjuster nut (**Figure 38**) until the brake lever can be used once again for the fine adjustment. Be sure to tighten the locknut.

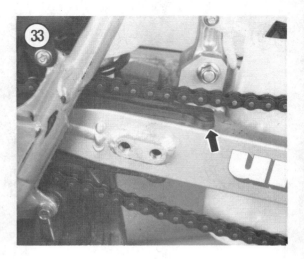

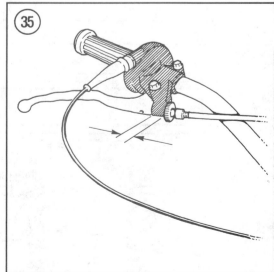

LUBRICATION, MAINTENANCE AND TUNE-UP

36

37

38

39

5. If proper adjustment cannot be achieved by the use of these adjustment points the cable has stretched and must be replaced.

Front Brake Lever Adjustment (Disc Brake)

The front brake lever free play must be maintained properly to prevent excessive brake drag which could cause premature brake pad wear. Set the brake lever free play to best suit your riding conditions. To adjust, turn the screw at the brake lever in or out so that there is some free play before the screw contacts the master cylinder piston assembly (**Figure 39**).

Rear Brake Pedal Adjustment

Rear brake adjustment is largely a matter of personal preference.

To adjust the rear brake, turn the brake adjusting nut on the brake arm at the rear wheel (**Figure 40**). Normal pedal travel is approximately 20-30 mm (25/32-1 3/16 in.).

The brake pedal height (**Figure 41**) can be changed to suit individual riding preferences.

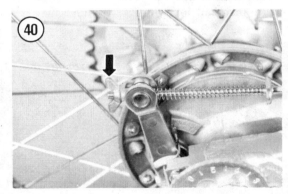

Loosen the adjuster bolt locknut and turn the bolt as required to reposition the brake pedal. Tighten the locknut. See **Figure 42** (1983-1985) or **Figure 43** (1986-on).

Rotate the rear wheel and check for brake drag. Also operate the pedal several times to make sure it returns to the at-rest position immediately after release.

NOTE
Brake drag can sometimes be difficult to check because of the drag induced by the drive chain. If you are having brake problems and you want to be sure you have removed all brake drag, remove the master link and slip the drive chain off of the rear sprocket. Spin the rear wheel and check the rear brake. Adjust the rear brake as required and reconnect the drive chain.

Front Brake Fluid Level Check (1986-on)

The front brake reservoir should always be kept more than half full with DOT 3 brake fluid.

NOTE
If the brake fluid level lowers rapidly, check the disc brake line and fittings. If the brake fluid level is very low, check the front brake pads for wear.

1. Place the bike on level ground and position the handlebar so the master cylinder reservoir is level.
2. Clean any dirt from the top cover prior to removing the cover.
3. Remove the 2 top cover screws and remove the cover (A, **Figure 44**) and diaphragm.
4. Add fresh DOT 3 brake fluid from a sealed container.

WARNING
Use brake fluid clearly marked DOT 3 and specified for disc brakes. Others may vaporize and cause brake failure. Do not intermix different brands or types of brake fluid as they may not be compatible. Do not intermix a silicone

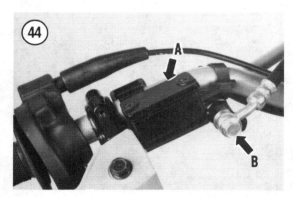

LUBRICATION, MAINTENANCE AND TUNE-UP

based (DOT 5) brake fluid as it can cause brake component damage leading to brake system failure.

CAUTION
Be careful when handling brake fluid. Do not spill it on painted or plastic surfaces as it will destroy the surface. If spilled, wash the area immediately with soap and water and thoroughly rinse it off.

5. Reinstall the diaphragm and top cover. Install the screws and tighten securely.

Disc Brake Lines

Check the brake line between the master cylinder and the brake caliper. If there is any leakage, tighten the connections and bleed the brake as described in Chapter Twelve. See B, **Figure 44** and **Figure 45**. If this does not stop the leak or if a brake line is obviously damaged, cracked or chafed, replace the brake line and bleed the system.

Disc Brake Pad Wear

Inspect brake pads for excessive or uneven wear, scoring and oil or grease on the friction surface. Refer to Chapter Twelve.

Disc Brake Fluid Change

Every time the reservoir cap is removed, a small amount of dirt and moisture enters the brake fluid. The same thing happens if a leak occurs or any part of the hydraulic system is loosened or disconnected. Dirt can clog the system and cause unnecessary wear. Water in the brake fluid vaporizes at high temperature, impairing the hydraulic action and reducing the brake's stopping ability.

To maintain peak performance, change the brake fluid once a year. To change brake fluid, follow the *Bleeding the Brake System* procedure in Chapter Twelve.

WARNING
Use brake fluid clearly marked DOT 3 only. Others may vaporize and cause brake failure.

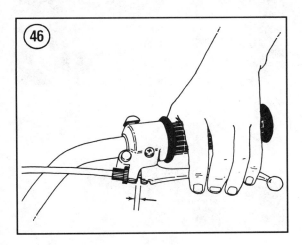

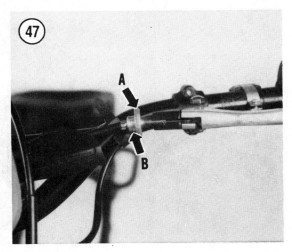

Clutch Adjustment

It is normal for the clutch cable to stretch over a period of time. For the clutch to operate correctly, the clutch cable free play (**Figure 46**) must be maintained at 2-3 mm (3/32-1/8 in.). If there is no clutch cable free play, the clutch cannot disengage completely. This would cause clutch slippage and rapid clutch plate wear.

1. Pull the clutch lever toward the handlebar. When cable resistance is felt, hold the lever and measure the gap shown in **Figure 46** with a ruler; this is clutch cable free play. If resistance was felt as soon as you pulled the clutch lever, there is no cable free play.
2. See **Figure 47**. At the hand lever loosen the locknut (A) and turn the adjusting barrel (B) in or out to obtain the correct amount of free play. Tighten the locknut.

3. If the proper amount of free play cannot be achieved at the handlebar adjuster, perform the following:
   a. Loosen the locknut (A, **Figure 47**) and turn the adjuster (B, **Figure 47**) all the way in toward the clutch lever.
   b. Loosen the clutch cable's midline adjuster locknut and turn the adjusting barrel in or out to take up clutch cable slack. See **Figure 48** (1983-1985) or **Figure 49** (1986-on). Tighten the locknut.
   c. Working at the hand lever again, loosen the locknut (A, **Figure 47**) and turn the adjusting barrel (B, **Figure 47**) in or out to obtain the correct amount of free play. Tighten the locknut.

4. If the clutch cable free play cannot be achieved using these adjustment points, the clutch cable has stretched excessively and must be replaced.

Throttle Cable Adjustment and Operation

For correct operation, the throttle cable should have 2-3 mm (3/32-1/8 in.) free play. In time, the throttle cable free play can become excessive from cable stretch. This will delay throttle response and affect low speed operation. On the other hand, if there is no throttle cable free play, an excessively high idle can result.

1. Start the engine and allow it to idle.

2. With the engine at idle, twist the throttle (A, **Figure 50**) to raise engine speed.

3. Determine the amount of movement (free play) at the throttle grip required to raise the engine speed from idle. If the free play is incorrect, perform the following.

4. Slide the upper adjuster cover (**Figure 51**) down the throttle cable.

5. See **Figure 52**. Loosen the adjuster locknut and turn the adjuster in or out to achieve proper free play. Tighten the locknut securely.

6. If there is not enough adjustment at the throttle grip, perform the following:
   a. Slide the lower adjuster cover (A, **Figure 53**) up the throttle cable at the carburetor cap.
   b. Loosen the adjuster locknut (B, **Figure 53**) and turn the adjuster in or out to achieve proper free play. Tighten the locknut freely.

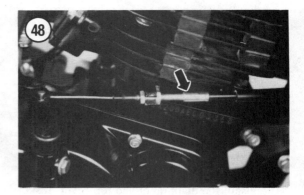

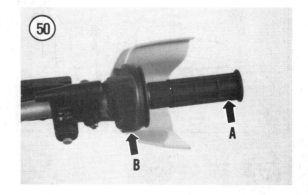

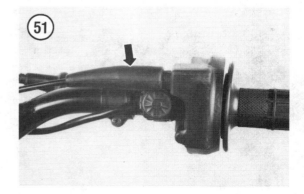

LUBRICATION, MAINTENANCE AND TUNE-UP

7. Slide the throttle cable adjuster covers back into place.
8. Make sure the throttle grip rotates freely from a fully closed to fully open position.
9. Start the engine and allow it to idle. Turn the handlebar from side to side. If the idle increases, the throttle cable is routed incorrectly or there is not enough cable free play.

> **WARNING**
> *Correct the problem immediately. Do not ride the bike in this unsafe condition.*

Throttle Grip

After each race, the throttle grip and throttle housing should be cleaned and serviced.
1. Remove the Phillips screws securing the throttle housing (B, **Figure 50**).
2. Separate the throttle housings.

3. Disconnect the throttle cable at the twist grip.
4. Clean the inner twist grip bore with electrical contact cleaner.
5. Clean the throttle housings thoroughly.
6. Check the end of the handlebar for burrs or other damage that would cause the twist grip to stick or operate sluggishly. If necessary, smooth the end of the handlebar with a file.
7. Install by reversing these steps. Make sure the throttle grip rotates freely from a fully closed to fully open position.

Air Filter

The air filter element should be removed, cleaned, and re-oiled at intervals indicated in **Table 1** or **Table 2**.

The air filter removes dust and abrasive particles from the air before it enters the carburetor and engine. Very fine particles that may enter into the engine will cause rapid wear to the piston rings, cylinder and bearings and may clog small passages in the carburetor. Never run your KDX200 without the air filter element installed.

Proper air filter servicing can do more to insure long service from your engine than any other single item.

> **NOTE**
> *The Kawasaki KDX200 cylinders are aluminum with a molybdenum coated bore called Electro-Fusion. These cylinders **cannot** be bored oversize. Boring the cylinder would remove the cylinder coating and the engine would quickly seize. For this reason, it is critical to properly and routinely service the air filter element. If dirt enters the engine, more than likely the cylinder will have to be replaced. In any case, replacement parts will be expensive.*

All models are equipped with a foam air filter element. To work properly, the filter element must be properly, cleaned and oiled with a foam air filter oil.
1. Remove the left-hand side cover.

2. Remove the screws securing the air filter side cover and remove the cover. See **Figure 54** (1983-1985) or **Figure 55** (1986-on).
3. Remove the wing nuts securing the air filter into the air box and remove the element. See **Figure 56** (1983-1985) or **Figure 57** (1986-on).
4. Pull the plastic support out of the filter (**Figure 58**).
5. Stuff a clean shop rag into the carburetor opening.
6. Examine the inside of the air box. There should be no signs of dust or dirt on the inside of the air box cover or sides. If dirt is noticeable, the air filter may be damaged or it was improperly serviced.
7. Clean the inside of the air box with a clean shop rag soaked in solvent or soap and water.
8. After the air box has dried, coat the inside of the air box with a layer of wheel bearing grease. Apply the grease with your hands so that it covers all inside surfaces of the air box. The grease works like an additional filter and will help to catch passed dirt.

CAUTION
Do not clean the air filter element with gasoline. Besides being a fire hazard, gasoline will break down your filter's seam glue and corrode the seam stitching.

9. Fill a clean pan with liquid cleaner and warm water. If you are using an accessory air filter, the manufacturer may sell a special air filter cleaner.
10. Submerge the filter into the cleaning solution and gently work the cleaner into the filter pores. Soak and squeeze (gently) the filter to clean it. See **Figure 59**.

CAUTION
Do not wring or twist the filter when cleaning it. This harsh action could damage a filter pore or tear the filter at a seam. This would allow unfiltered air to enter the engine and cause severe and rapid wear.

11. Rinse the filter under warm water while soaking and gently squeezing it.
12. Repeat Step 10 and Step 11 two or three times or until there are no signs of dirt being rinsed from the filter.

LUBRICATION, MAINTENANCE AND TUNE-UP

13. After cleaning the filter, inspect it. If it is torn or broken in any area it should be replaced. Do not run the engine with a damaged filter as it may allow dirt to enter the engine and cause severe engine wear.

14. Set the filter aside and allow it to dry thoroughly.

CAUTION
A water damp filter will not trap fine dust. Make sure the filter is completely dry before oiling it.

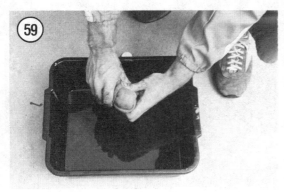

15. Properly oiling an air filter element is a messy job. You may want to wear a pair of disposable rubber gloves when performing this procedure. Oil the filter as follows:
   a. Purchase a box of gallon size resealable storage bags. The bags can also be used when cleaning the filter as well as for storing engine and carburetor parts during disassembly.
   b. Place the cleaned filter into a storage bag.
   c. Pour foam air filter oil onto the filter to soak it.
   d. Gently squeeze and release the outside of the bag to soak filter oil into the filter's pores. Repeat until all of the filter's pores are discolored with the oil.
   e. Remove the filter from the bag and check the pores for uneven oiling. This is indicated by light or dark areas. If necessary, soak the filter and squeeze it again.
   f. When the filter oiling is even, squeeze the filter a final time.

16. Remove the filter from the bag. Install the plastic filter support inside the filter, if so equipped.

17. Apply a coat of thick wheel bearing grease to the filter's sealing surface (**Figure 58**).

18. Align the air filter with the housing and install the filter. Secure the filter with the 2 wingnuts. See **Figure 56** (1983-1985) or **Figure 57** (1986-on).

19. Install the outer filter cover and secure it with the attaching screws.

20. Install the left-hand side cover.

21. Pour the left-over filter oil from the bag back into the bottle for reuse.

22. Dispose of the plastic bag.

Fuel Line Inspection

Inspect the fuel line from the fuel tank to the carburetor (**Figure 60**). If it is cracked or starting to deteriorate it must be replaced. Make sure the small hose clamps are in place and holding securely. Also make sure that the overflow and vent tubes are in place.

WARNING
A damaged or deteriorated fuel line presents a very dangerous fire hazard to both the rider and the machine if fuel should spill onto a hot engine or exhaust pipe.

NOTE
If you have been experiencing fuel contamination that is plugging up carburetor jets (especially the pilot jet), install a fuel filter in the fuel line between the gas tank and the carburetor. Use the stock Kawasaki fasteners to hold the line to the filter.

Wheel Bearings

The non-sealed wheel bearings should be cleaned and repacked once a year or more often if the vehicle is operated often in water (especially salt water). The correct service procedures are covered in Chapter Ten (front) and Chapter Eleven (rear).

Steering Head Adjustment Check

Tapered roller bearings are installed in the upper and lower bearing mounting areas. Because the KDX200 models are often ridden in rough terrain, bearing play should be checked and adjusted frequently. A loose bearing adjustment will hamper steering and cause premature bearing and race wear. In severe conditions, a loose bearing adjustment can cause loss of control.

1. Place the bike on a stand so that the front wheel clears the ground.

2. Center the front wheel. Push lightly against the left handlebar grip to start the wheel turning to the right, then let go. The wheel should continue turning under its own momentum until the forks hit their stop. Try the same in the other direction.

3. If, with a light push in either direction, the front wheel will turn all the way to the top, the steering adjustment is loose enough.

4. Center the front wheel and kneel in front of it. Grasp the bottoms of the fork legs. Try to pull the forks toward you, and then try to push them toward the engine. If no play is felt, the steering adjustment is tight enough.

5. If the steering adjustment is too tight or too loose, readjust it as described under *Steering Adjustment* in Chapter Ten.

Handlebars

Inspect the handlebars weekly for any signs of damage. A bent or damaged handlebar should be replaced. The knurled section of your bars should be very rough for maximum grip. Keep the clamps clean with a wire brush. Any time that the bars slip in the clamps (like when you land flat and they move forward slightly) they should be removed and wire brushed clean to prevent small balls of aluminum from gathering in the clamps and reducing gripping abilities.

Nuts, Bolts and Other Fasteners

Constant vibration can loosen many of the fasteners on the motorcycle. Check the tightness of all fasteners, especially those on:
  a. Engine mounting hardware.
  b. Engine crankcase covers.

LUBRICATION, MAINTENANCE AND TUNE-UP

c. Handlebar and front forks.
d. Gearshift lever.
e. Kickstarter lever.
f. Brake pedal and lever.
g. Exhaust system.

ENGINE TUNE-UP

The number of definitions of the term "tune-up" is probably equal to the number of people defining it. For the purposes of this book, a tune-up is general adjustment and maintenance to insure peak engine performance.

The following paragraphs discuss each facet of a proper tune-up which should be performed in the order given. Unless otherwise specified, the engine should be thoroughly cool before starting any tune-up procedure.

Have the new parts on hand before you begin.

To perform a tune-up on your KDX200, you will need the following tools and equipment:
a. 14 mm spark plug wrench.
b. Socket wrench and assorted sockets.
c. Phillips head screwdriver.
d. Spark plug wire feeler gauge and gapper tool.
e. Flywheel puller.
f. Compression gauge.

Cylinder and Cylinder Head Nuts

The engine must be at room temperature for this procedure.

1. Place support blocks under the frame to hold the bike securely.

2. Remove the seat.

3. Remove the fuel tank as described in Chapter Eight.

4. Remove the exhaust system as described in Chapter Eight.

5. Tighten each cylinder nut (**Figure 61**) in a crisscross pattern to the tightening torque in **Table 8**.

6. Tighten each cylinder head nut (**Figure 62**) equally in a crisscross pattern to the tightening torque in **Table 8**.

7. Leave the seat and fuel tank off for the following steps.

Cylinder Compression

A cylinder cranking compression check is one of the quickest ways to check the internal condition of the engine: rings, head gasket, etc. It's a good idea to check compression at each tune-up, write it down, and compare it with the reading you get at the next tune-up. This will help you spot any developing problems.

1. Warm the engine to normal operating temperature.
2. Remove the spark plug.
3. Insert the tip of a compression gauge into the hole. Make sure the gauge is seated properly.

NOTE
You may have to remove the fuel tank to provide clearance for the gauge. See Chapter Eight.

NOTE
Press the kill switch while performing Step 4.

4. Hold the throttle wide open and crank the engine several revolutions until the gauge gives its highest reading. Record the figure. Refer to **Table 13** for compression readings. If the compression is very low, it's likely that a ring is broken or there is a hole in the piston.

Correct Spark Plug Heat Range

The proper spark plug is very important in obtaining maximum performance and reliability. The condition of a used spark plug can tell a trained mechanic a lot about engine condition and carburetion.

Select plugs of the heat range designed for the loads and conditions under which the bike will be run. Use of incorrect heat ranges can cause a seized piston, scored cylinder wall, or damaged piston crown.

In general, use a hot plug for low speeds and low temperatures. Use a cold plug for high speeds, high engine loads and high temperatures. The plug should operate hot enough to burn off unwanted deposits, but not so hot that it burns itself or causes preignition. A spark plug of the correct heat range will show a light tan color on the portion of the insulator within the cylinder after the plug has been in service. See **Figure 63**.

CHAPTER THREE

SPARK PLUG CONDITIONS

NORMAL USE

OIL FOULED

CARBON FOULED

OVERHEATED

GAP BRIDGED

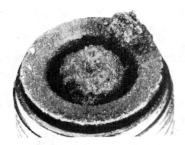

SUSTAINED PREIGNITION

WORN OUT

LUBRICATION, MAINTENANCE AND TUNE-UP

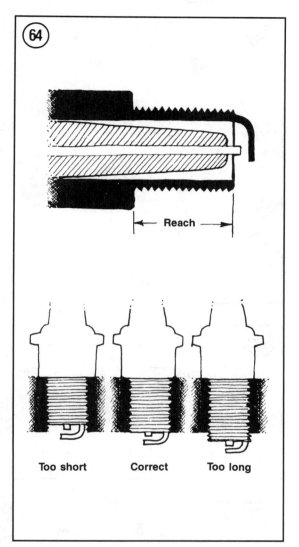

The reach (length) of a plug is also important. A longer than normal plug could interfere with the piston, causing permanent and severe damage. Refer to **Figure 64**.

The standard heat range spark plug for the various models is listed in **Table 14**.

Spark Plug Removal/Cleaning

1. Grasp the spark plug lead (**Figure 65**) as near the plug as possible and pull it off the plug. If it is stuck to the plug, twist it slightly to break it loose.

2. Blow away any dirt that has accumulated next to the spark plug base.

> *CAUTION*
> *The dirt could fall into the cylinder when the plug is removed, causing serious engine damage.*

3. Remove the spark plug with a 14 mm spark plug wrench.

> *NOTE*
> *If the plug is difficult to remove, apply penetrating oil, like WD-40 or Liquid Wrench, around the base of the plug and let it soak in about 10-20 minutes.*

4. Inspect the plug carefully. Look for a broken center porcelain, excessively eroded electrodes, and excessive carbon or oil fouling. See **Figure 63**.

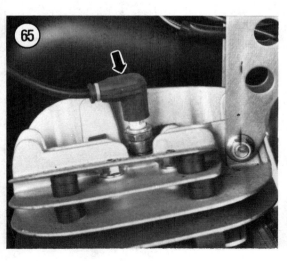

Gapping and Installing the Plug

A new spark plug should be carefully gapped to ensure a reliable, consistent spark. You must use a special spark plug gapping tool and a wire feeler gauge.

1. Remove the new spark plug from the box. Make sure the terminal nut is installed (**Figure 66**).

2. Insert a wire feeler gauge between the center and side electrode (**Figure 67**). The correct gap is listed in **Table 14**. If the gap is correct, you will feel a slight drag as you pull the wire through. If there is no drag, or the gauge won't pass through, bend the side electrode with a gapping tool (**Figure 68**) to set the proper gap.

3. Apply anti-seize compound to the plug threads before installing the spark plug.

> *NOTE*
> *Anti-seize compound can be purchased at most automotive parts stores.*

4. Screw the spark plug in by hand until it seats. Very little effort is required. If forced is necessary, you have the plug cross-threaded. Unscrew it and try again.

5. Use a spark plug wrench and tighten the plug an additional 1/4 to 1/2 turn after the gasket has made contact with the head or tighten it to the torque specification in **Table 8**. If you are installing an old, regapped plug and reusing the old gasket, tighten only an additional 1/4 turn.

> *CAUTION*
> *Do not overtighten. This will only squash the gasket and destroy its sealing ability.*

6. Install the spark plug wire. Make sure it is on tight.

> *CAUTION*
> *Make sure the spark plug wire is pulled away from the exhaust pipe.*

7. Reinstall the seat, fuel tank and exhaust system.

Reading Spark Plugs

Much information about engine and spark plug performance can be determined by careful examination of the spark plug. This information is more valid after performing the following steps.

1. Ride the bike a short distance at full throttle in any gear.

2. Push on the kill switch before closing the throttle and simultaneously pull in the clutch or shift to neutral; coast and brake to a stop.

3. Remove the spark plug and examine it. Compare it to **Figure 63**.

If the insulator is white or burned, the plug is too hot and should be replaced with a colder one.

A too-cold plug will have sooty or oil deposits.

If the plug has a light tan or gray colored deposit and no abnormal gap wear or electrode erosion is evident, the plug and the engine are running properly.

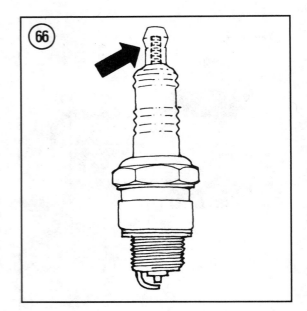

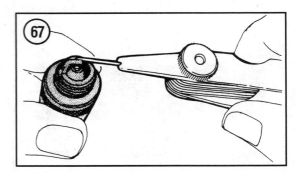

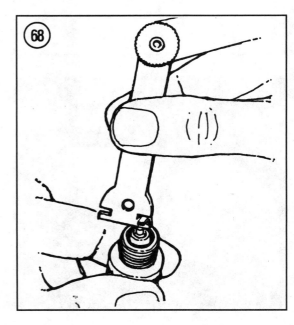

LUBRICATION, MAINTENANCE AND TUNE-UP

If the plug exhibits a black insulator tip, damp oily film over the firing end, and a carbon layer over the entire nose, it is oil fouled. An oil fouled plug can be cleaned, but it is better to replace it.

Ignition Timing

These models are equipped with a capacitor discharge ignition (CDI). This system uses no breaker points, which greatly simplifies ignition timing and makes the ignition system much less susceptible to failures caused by dirt, moisture and wear.

Since there are no components to wear, adjusting the ignition timing is necessary only after the engine has been disassembled or if the base plate screws have worked loose.

1. Place the bike on the sidestand.
2. Remove the ignition cover (**Figure 69**).
3. Remove the rotor as described in Chapter Nine.
4. Remove the Phillips screw indicated in **Figure 70**.
5. Check that the timing mark on the stator plate aligns with the mark on the crankcase (**Figure 71**).
6. If the timing marks align, the ignition timing is correct. Install and tighten the Phillips screw.
7. If the timing marks do not align, loosen the other Phillips screw and reposition the stator plate to align the timing marks.
8. Tighten the stator plate screws securely.
9. Install the rotor as described in Chapter Nine.

Carburetor Idle Speed Adjustment

Proper idle speed is a balance between a low enough idle to give adequate compression braking and a high enough idle to prevent engine stalling (if desired). The idle air/fuel mixture affects transition from idle to part throttle openings.

1983-1987

1. Make sure that the throttle cable free play is correct.
2. Start the engine and allow it to warm up for 2-3 minutes.
3. Turn the idle speed adjustment screw (**Figure 72**) to set the idle speed.

1988

A pilot air screw has been added to the carburetor installed on these models.

1. Make sure that the throttle cable free play is correct.
2. Turn the pilot air screw (A, **Figure 73**) in until it seats lightly, then back it out 1 1/2 turns.

> **CAUTION**
> Never turn the pilot air screw in tight. You'll damage the screw or the soft aluminum seat in the carburetor.

3. Warm up the engine completely. Then turn the idle speed screw (B, **Figure 73**) to set the idle as low as possible without stalling the engine.
4. Turn the pilot air screw (A, **Figure 73**) until the engine speed drops off quickly, then turn it back until the idle shoots up. The midpoint between high and low engine idle is the correct pilot air screw adjustment.

> **NOTE**
> The pilot air screw should not be opened more than 3 turns or it may vibrate out. If you cannot get the bike to idle properly, check that the air filter is clean. If air filter is okay and other engine systems are operating correctly, the pilot jet size may be incorrect. Refer to Chapter Eight.

5. Reset the idle speed (B, **Figure 73**) as desired.

> **NOTE**
> After this adjustment is completed, test ride the bike. Throttle response from idle should be rapid and without any hesitation. If there is any hesitation, turn the pilot air screw in or out in 1/4 turn increments until this problem is solved.

> **WARNING**
> With the engine idling, move the handlebar from side to side. If idle speed increases during this movement, the throttle cable needs adjusting or it may be incorrectly routed through the frame. Correct this problem immediately. Do not ride the bike in this unsafe condition.

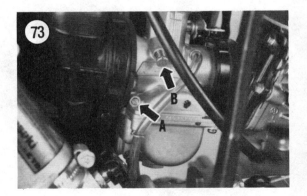

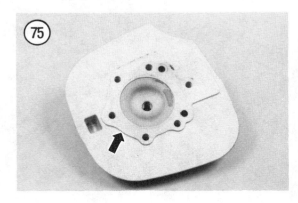

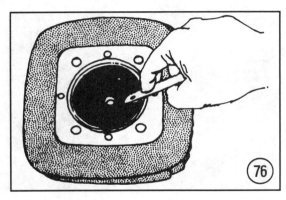

LUBRICATION, MAINTENANCE AND TUNE-UP

Decarbonizing

The carbon deposits should be removed from the piston, cylinder head, exhaust port and muffler as indicated in **Table 1** or **Table 2**. If it is not cleaned off it will cause reduced performance, preignition (ping) or overheating.

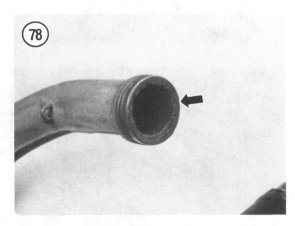

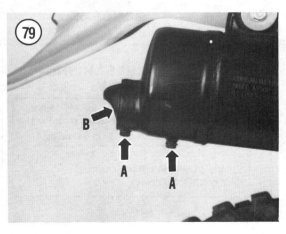

Engine Decarbonizing

1. Remove the cylinder head and cylinder as described under *Cylinder Removal/Installation* in Chapter Four.
2. Stuff a shop cloth into the opening in the crankcase to keep any residue from entering into it. Gently scrape off carbon deposits from the top of the piston (**Figure 74**) and cylinder head (**Figure 75**) with a dull screwdriver or end of a hacksaw blade (**Figure 76**). Do not scratch the surface.
3. Wipe the surfaces clean with a cloth dipped in cleaning solvent.
4. Scrape off the carbon in the exhaust port (**Figure 77**) with a dull screwdriver or end of a hacksaw blade. Do not scratch the surface.
5. Install the cylinder and cylinder head as described in Chapter Four.

Exhaust System Decarbonizing

1. Remove the exhaust pipe assembly as described under *Exhaust System Removal/Installation* in Chapter Eight.
2. Gently scrape off carbon deposits from the interior of the head pipe (**Figure 78**) where it attaches to the cylinder.
3. Remove the baffle bolts (A, **Figure 79**) and remove the baffle (B, **Figure 79**) from the silencer assembly. Clean the baffle of all carbon and oil deposits.

> **WARNING**
> *If a length of cable is used in an electric drill to clean the inside of the exhaust pipe, do not start the drill **until** the cable is inserted into the exhaust pipe. Operating the drill with the cable out of the pipe could cause serious injury if the cable should whip against your face or body.*

4. Clean out the rest of the interior of the expansion chamber by running a piece of used motorcycle drive chain around in it. Another way is to chuck a length of wire cable, with one end frayed, in an electric drill. Run it around in the front portion a couple of times. Shake out all loose carbon. Also tap on the outer shell of the exhaust pipe assembly with a plastic mallet to break any additional carbon loose.

5. Blow out the expansion chamber with compressed air.
6. Clean out the interior of the silencer.
7. Reinstall the baffle into the silencer. Install the attaching bolts and tighten securely. See **Figure 79**.
8. Visually inspect the entire exhaust pipe assembly, especially in the welded areas for cracks or other damage. Replace if necessary, or repair as described in Chapter Eight.
7. Install the exhaust pipe assembly. See Chapter Eight.

SUSPENSION ADJUSTMENT

Air Pressure Adjustment

Air pressure will increase or decrease through the entire fork travel range. Because air pressure makes the fork action harsh, many riders do not pressurize their forks. Instead, they use the air valves on the fork caps to bleed off air that builds up inside the forks after each ride. When bleeding off air pressure, prop the front wheel up so that it clears the ground. Then depress the air valve (**Figure 80**) and bleed off all air pressure. Raising the front wheel off the ground prevents a vacuum from building in the fork tubes.

If your front forks seem soft and are bottoming harshly, you may want to add a small amount of air pressure. Consider the following when adjusting fork air pressure:
   a. Decreasing air pressure will soften fork travel.
   b. Increasing air pressure will stiffen fork travel.

CAUTION
*Do not exceed the air pressure specifications in **Table 15**.*

1. Place the bike on a stand so that the forks are fully extended and the front wheel clears the ground.
2. Remove the air valve caps.

WARNING
*Use only compressed air or nitrogen— do **not** use any other type of compressed gas as an explosion may result. Never heat the front forks with*

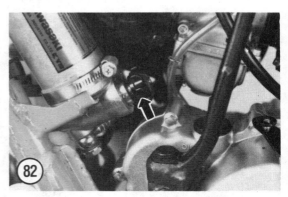

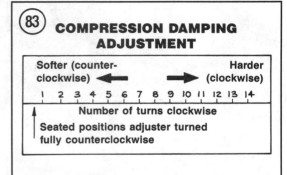

LUBRICATION, MAINTENANCE AND TUNE-UP

a torch or place them near an open flame or extreme heat.

3. Use a small manual air pump. Attach it to the air fitting (**Figure 80**) and inflate the fork to the desired setting.
4. Repeat for the opposite side.

NOTE
The air pressure difference between the 2 fork tubes should be 0.1 kg/cm² (1.4 psi) or less.

5. Reinstall the air caps.
6. Test ride the bike.

Rear Shock Absorber Damping Adjustment

1983-1985

The shock on these models has a 4-way damping adjuster at the top of the shock absorber (**Figure 81**). To adjust, remove the right-hand side cover. Then turn the adjuster with a screwdriver to the desired position. The damping range runs from soft (No. 1 postion) to hard (No. 4 position). Install the side cover after adjusting the damping.

1986-on

The shock on these models has both compression and rebound damping adjustments:

1. *Compression damping adjustment:* Perform the following:
   a. The compression damping adjuster (**Figure 82**) is mounted on the shock absorber reservoir.
   b. Referring to **Figure 83**, turn the adjuster as required. Count each click when turning the adjuster.
   c. If you want to start at the softest position, turn the compression damping adjuster (**Figure 82**) counterclockwise until it stops. Then turn the adjuster clockwise and count the clicks until you reach the desired adjustment position.
2. *Rebound damping adjustment:* Perform the following:
   a. Remove the right-hand side cover.
   b. The rebound compression damping adjuster (**Figure 84**) is mounted at the top of the shock absorber.

NOTE
Figure 84 shows the shock absorber removed for clarity. It is not necessary to remove the shock absorber when adjusting the rebound damping adjuster.

   c. Referring to **Figure 85**, turn the adjuster as required. Count each click when turning the adjuster.
   d. If you want to start at the softest position, turn the rebound damping adjuster (**Figure 84**) counterclockwise until it stops. Then turn the adjuster clockwise and count the clicks until you reach the desired adjustment position.
   e. Install the right-hand side cover.

Rear Shock Absorber Spring Preload Adjustment

1. Remove the shock absorber as described in Chapter Eleven.
2. Referring to **Figure 86**, measure the distance from the center of the lower shock bolt hole to the edge of the spring adjuster. This measurement is the spring adjustment length. Refer to **Table 16** for spring adjustment length specifications.

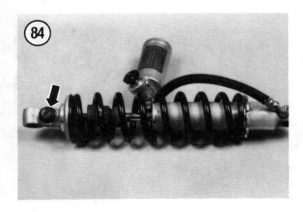

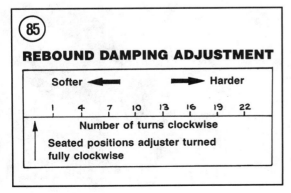

3. To change spring preload, mount the shock housing in a vise with soft jaws. Using the Kawasaki hook wrenches (part No. 57001-1101) or equivalent, loosen the locknut (**Figure 86**). Then turn the spring adjuster (**Figure 86**) as required to change preload. Make sure to stay within the adjustment range listed in **Table 16**.

NOTE
The standard spring preload is 530 N (119 lb.) on 1983-1985 models; turning the spring adjuster 1 turn changes the preload 53 N (12 lb.). The standard spring preload on 1986 and later models is 430 N (97 lb.); turning the spring adjuster 1 turn changes the preload 86 N (19.4 lb.).

4. After adjusting the spring preload, tighten the spring locknut.

5. Reinstall the shock absorber as described in Chapter Eleven.

Uni-Trak Nitrogen Pressure Adjustment

All Uni-Trak shock absorbers have a nitrogen gas valve at the reservoir (**Figure 87**). See **Table 17** for the standard pressure and range of adjustment. A higher nitrogen pressure has an effect similar to higher spring preload.

WARNING
Use only nitrogen gas to pressurize the shock absorber. Air or other gases may cause corrosion or explosion. Do not exceed the maximum recommended pressure in Table 17.

Have the nitrogen adjustment performed by a Kawasaki dealer or qualified suspension specialist.

STORAGE

Several months of inactivity can cause serious problems and a general deterioration of your KDX200. This is especially true in areas of weather extremes. During the winter months it is advisable to specially prepare the bike for lay-up.

Selecting a Storage Area

Most riders store their bikes in their home garages. If you do not have a home garage, facilities suitable for long-term motorcycle storage are readily available for rent or lease in most areas. In selecting a building, consider the following points.

1. The storage area must be dry, free from dampness and excessive humidity. Heating is not necessary, but the building should be well insulated to minimize extreme temperature variations.

2. Buildings with large window areas should be avoided, or such windows should be masked (also a good security measure) if direct sunlight can fall on the bike.

3. Buildings in industrial areas, where factories are likely to emit corrosive fumes, are not desirable, nor are facilities near bodies of salt water.

4. The area should be selected to minimize the possibility of loss from fire, theft or vandalism. The area should be fully insured, perhaps with a package covering fire, theft, vandalism, weather and liability. Talk this over with your insurance agent and get approval on these matters. The building should be fireproof and items such as the security of doors and windows, alarm facility and proximity of police should be considered.

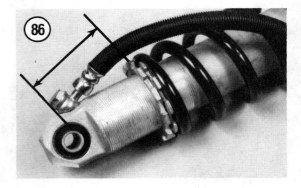

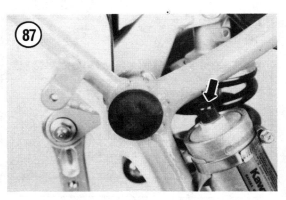

LUBRICATION, MAINTENANCE AND TUNE-UP

Preparing Bike for Storage

Careful preparation will minimize deterioration and make it easier to restore the bike to service later. Use the following procedure.
1. Wash the bike completely. Make certain to remove all dirt in all the hard to reach parts like the cooling fins on the head and cylinder. Completely dry all parts of the bike to removal all moisture. Wax all painted and polished surfaces, including any chromed areas.
2. Run the bike for about 20-30 minutes to warm up the oil in the clutch and transmission. Drain the oil, regardless of the time since the last oil change. Refill with the normal quantity and type of oil.
3. Drain all gasoline from the fuel tank, interconnecting hose and the carburetor. Leave the fuel shutoff valve in the ON position. As an alternative, a fuel preservative may be added to the fuel. This preservative is available from many motorcycle shops and marine equipment suppliers.
4. Lubricate the drive chain and control cables; refer to specific procedures in this chapter.
5. Remove the spark plug and add about one teaspoon of two-stroke engine oil into the cylinder. Reinstall the spark plug and turn the engine over to distribute the oil to the cylinder walls and piston. Depress the engine kill switch while doing this to prevent it from starting.
6. Tape or tie a plastic bag over the end of the silencer to prevent the entry of moisture.
7. Check the tire pressure, inflate to the correct pressure and move the bikes to the storage area. Place it securely on a sturdy crate or wood blocks with both wheels off the ground.
8. Remove the batteries from the timer unit. See Chapter Nine.
9. Cover the bike with a heavy blanket or blankets. Do not use any plastic material, as it may trap moisture causing condensation.

Inspection During Storage

Try to inspect the bike weekly while in storage. Any deterioration should be corrected as soon as possible. For example, if corrosion of bright metal parts is observed, cover them with a light coat of grease or silicone spray after a thorough polishing.

Turn the engine over a couple of times. Don't start it; use the kickstarter and hold the kill switch on. Pump the front forks to keep the seals lubricated.

Restoring Bike to Service

A bike that has been properly prepared and stored in a suitable area requires only light maintenance to restore to service. It is advisable, however, to perform a spring tune-up.
1. Before removing the bike from the storage area, reinflate the tires to the correct pressure. Air loss during storage may have nearly flattened the tires, and moving the bike can cause damage to tires, tubes and rims.
2. When the bike is brought to the work area, turn the fuel shutoff valve to the OFF position, and refill the fuel tank with the correct fuel/oil mixture. Remove the main jet cover on the base of the carburetor, turn the fuel shutoff valve to the ON position, and allow several cups of fuel to pass through the fuel system. Turn the fuel shutoff valve to the OFF position and install the main jet cover.

WARNING
Place a metal container under the carburetor to catch all expelled fuel–this presents a real fire danger if allowed to drain onto the bike and the floor. Dispose of the fuel properly.

3. Remove the spark plug and squirt a small amount of fuel into the cylinder to help remove the oil coating.
4. Install a fresh spark plug and start up the engine.
5. Perform the standard tune-up as described earlier in this chapter.
6. Check the operation of the engine kill switch. Oxidation of the switch contacts during storage may make it inoperative.
7. Install fresh batteries into the timer unit (Chapter Nine).
8. Clean and test ride the motorcycle.

WARNING
If any type of preservative (Armor All or equivalent) has been applied to the tire treads be sure the tires are well "scrubbed-in" prior to any fast riding or cornering on a hard surface. If not they will slip right out from under you.

Table 1 PERIODIC MAINTENANCE* (1983-1985)

Before each ride	Lubricate drive chain
	Check drive chain free play and adjust if necessary
Initial 60 miles (100 km); thereafter every 200 miles (300 km)	Check Uni-trak bearing and sleeve wear
	Lubricate the Uni-trak bearings
Initial 60 miles (100 km); thereafter every 300 miles (500 km)	Check clutch adjustment
	Check throttle cable adjustment
	Check carburetor adjustment
	Clean the air filter element **
	Check brake adjustment
	Check spoke tightness
	Check rim runout
	Check front fork operation
	Clean and flush fuel system
	Check steering stem play
Initial 60 miles (100 km); thereafter every 600 miles (1,000 km)	Change transmission oil
	Check all external suspension and engine fasteners
Every 300 miles (500 km)	Check brake pad wear
	Replace the drive chain
	Check sprocket wear; replace if necessary
	Lubricate the swing arm bearings
	Check the frame and swing arm for cracks or other damage
Every 600 miles (1,000 km)	Decarbonize engine top end
	Check piston condition
	Check cylinder condition
	Check piston to cylinder clearance
	Check piston ring wear
	Check small end bearing
	Check main bearings
	Check crankshaft big end bearing
	Replace shock oil
Every 1,200 miles (2,000 km)	Change front fork oil
	Grease brake camshafts
	Grease wheel bearings

* The service intervals should be performed more frequently if the bike is ridden in wet or dusty conditions or if the bike is used in competition.
** Replace the air filter element after every 5 cleanings.

LUBRICATION, MAINTENANCE AND TUNE-UP

Table 2 PERIODIC MAINTENANCE* (1986-ON)

Before each ride	Lubricate drive chain
	Check drive chain free play and adjust if necessary
Initial 60 miles (100 km); thereafter every 300 miles (500 km)	Check clutch adjustment
	Check throttle cable adjustment
	Clean and regap spark plug
	Check carburetor adjustment
	Check brake adjustment
	Check spoke tightness
	Check rim runout
	Check front fork operation
	Clean and flush fuel system
	Check steering stem play
Initial 60 miles (100 km); thereafter every 600 miles (1,000 km)	Check all external suspension and engine fasteners
Every 300 miles (500 km)	Clean the air filter element
	Check brake pad wear
	Check the brake fluid level
	Check drive chain wear
	Check sprocket wear
	Check the swing arm pivot shaft
	Check the Uni-trak linkage pivot shafts
	Lubricate the swing arm bearings
	Lubricate the Uni-trak linkage bearings
Every 600 miles (1,000 km)	Replace transmission oil
	Decarbonize engine top end
	Check piston condition
	Check cylinder condition
	Check piston to cylinder clearance
	Check piston ring wear
	Check small end bearing
	Check main bearings
	Check crankshaft big end bearing
	Check the exhaust advancer system
	Replace the exhaust pipe O-ring
Every 1,200 miles (2,000 km)	Change front fork oil
	Grease brake camshafts
	Grease wheel bearings
	Grease steering stem
Every 2,500 miles (4,000 km)	Clean the spark arrester
Every year	Replace rear shock oil
Every 2 years	Change brake fluid
	Replace the master cylinder cups and seals
	Replace the brake caliper cups and seals
Every 4 years	Replace the brake hydraulic hose
	Replace the fuel hoses

* The service intervals should be performed more frequently if the bike is ridden in wet or dusty conditions or if the bike is used in competition.
** Replace the air filter element after every 5 cleanings.

Table 3 TIRE INFLATION PRESSURE

Front	1.0 kg/cm² (14 psi)
Rear	1.0 kg/cm² (14 psi)

Table 4 RECOMMENDED LUBRICANTS AND FUEL

Engine oil	Kawasaki 2-stroke racing oil
Transmission oil	SAE 10W/30 or 10W/40 automotive engine oil
Front fork oil	10 wt fork oil
Air filter	Foam air filter oil
Drive chain	Chain lube
Control cables	Cable lube
Control lever pivots	10W/30 motor oil
Swing arm assembly	Lithium grease base grease
Steering head, wheel bearings	Wheel bearing, waterproof type
Fuel	Premium grade—Research octane 90 or higher
Brake fluid (1986-on)	DOT 3

Table 5 FUEL/OIL PREMIX RATIO

Model	Premix ratio with Kawasaki Racing Oil
1983	20:1
1984	30:1
1985-on	32:1

RATIO 20:1

Gasoline U.S. gal.	Oil Oz.	cc
1	6.4	190
2	12.8	380
3	19.2	570
4	25.6	760
5	32	945

RATIO 30:1

Gasoline U.S. gal.	Oil Oz.	cc
1	4.3	127
2	8.5	251
3	12.8	379
4	17.1	506
5	21.3	630

RATIO 32:1

Gasoline U.S. gal.	Oil Oz.	cc
1	4	118
2	8	237
3	12	355
4	16	473
5	20	591

LUBRICATION, MAINTENANCE AND TUNE-UP

Table 6 FUEL TANK CAPACITY

Model	U.S. Gal.	Liters
1983	3.3	12.5
1984-1985	3.2	12.0
1986-on	3.3	12.5

Table 7 CLUTCH/TRANSMISSION OIL CAPACITY

Model	cc	qts.
1983-1985	600	0.63
1986-on	700	0.74

Table 8 MAINTENANCE TORQUE SPECIFICATIONS

Item	N·m	ft.-lb.
Cylinder head nuts	25	18
Cylinder nuts		
1983-1985	34	25
1986-on	25	18
Transmission drain plug	20	14.5
Spark plug	27	20
Front axle nut		
1983-1985	64	47
1986-on	78	58
Fork tube pinch bolts	20	14.5
Handlebar clamp bolts		
1983-1985	14	10
1986-on	21	15
Swing arm pivot shaft nut	78	58
Rear axle nut	98	72

Table 9 FRONT FORK OIL CAPACITY

Model	cc	oz.
1983-1985	441-449	14.91-15.18
1986	631-639	21.3-21.6
1987-on	626-634	21.2-21.4

Table 10 FRONT FORK OIL LEVEL

Model	Standard range mm	Standard range in.	Adjustable range mm	Adjustable range in.
1983-1985	163-167	6.42-6.57	—	—
1986	148-152	5.8-6.0	120-152	4.7-6.0
1987-on	133-137	5.2-5.4	105-160	4.1-6.3

Table 11 DRIVE CHAIN SLACK

Model	mm	in.
Normal or dry conditions	50-60	1.96-2.36
Muddy conditions	55-65	2.2-2.6

Table 12 DRIVE CHAIN LENGTH MEASUREMENT

Model	Standard mm (in.)	Wear limit mm (in.)
1983-on	317.5 (12.50)	323 (12.7)

Table 13 ENGINE COMPRESSION

Model	Standard kg/cm^2 (psi)	Range kg/cm^2 (psi)
1983-on	11.0-13.0 (156-185)	8.4-13 (119-185)

Table 14 SPARK PLUG TYPE AND GAP

Model	Type	Gap mm (in.)
U.S.	B9ES	0.7-0.8 (0.028-0.032)
All other	BR9ES	0.7-0.8 (0.028-0.032)

Table 15 FRONT FORK AIR PRESSURE

Model	kg/cm^2	psi
1983-1985		
Maximum	2.5	36
Operating range	0-2.5	0-36
1986-on		
Maximum	2.5	36
Operating pressure	0.4	6

Table 16 REAR SHOCK SPRING LENGTH

Model	Acceptable range mm	in.	Standard mm	in.
1983-1985	75-95	2.95-3.74	85	3.35
1986-on	67-87	2.6-3.4	77	3.0

Table 17 REAR SHOCK NITROGEN PRESSURE ADJUSTMENT*

Model	Acceptable range kg/cm^2	psi	Standard setting kg/cm^2	psi
1983-on	10-15	142-213	10	142

* Nitrogen pressure adjustment should only be performed by a Kawasaki dealer or suspension specialist.

CHAPTER FOUR

ENGINE TOP END

This chapter covers service to the cylinder head, cylinder, piston, piston rings and reed valve. Engine lower end service (crankshaft, transmission removal, shift drum and shift forks) is covered in Chapter Five. Clutch and kickstarter service is covered in Chapter Six. Transmission disassembly is covered in Chapter Seven.

Prior to removing and disassembling the engine top end, clean the entire engine and frame with a good grade commercial degreaser, like Gunk or Bel-Ray engine degreaser or equivalent. It is easier to work on a clean engine and you will do a better job.

Make certain that you have all the necessary tools available and purchase replacement parts (gaskets, oil seals, etc.) prior to disassembly. Some parts must be purchased after disassembly and inspection since it is difficult to know the condition of internal engine parts until the engine is disassembled. Also make sure you have a clean place to work.

It is a good idea to identify and mark parts as they are removed so that errors will be avoided during assembly and installation. Clean all parts thoroughly upon removal, then place them in trays or boxes with their associated mounting hardware. Do not rely on memory alone as it may be days or weeks before you complete the job. In the text there is frequent mention of the left-hand and right-hand sides of the engine. This refers to the engine as it sits in the bike's frame, not as it sits on your workbench.

Engine specifications are listed in **Table 1** and **Table 2**. Tightening torques are listed in **Table 3**. **Tables 1-3** are found at the end of the chapter.

ENGINE PRINCIPLES

Figure 1 explains how a typical 2-stroke engine works. This will be helpful when troubleshooting or repairing the engine.

ENGINE LUBRICATION

Engine lubrication is provided by the fuel/oil mixture used to power the engine. Refer to Chapter Three for oil and ratio recommendations.

ENGINE COOLING

Cooling is provided by air passing over the cooling fins on the engine cylinder head and cylinder. To prevent engine damage from overheating, it is important to keep these fins free from a buildup of dirt, oil, grease, and other

CHAPTER FOUR

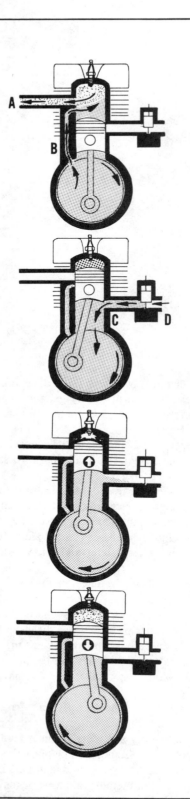

2-STROKE OPERATING PRINCIPLES

The crankshaft in this discussion is rotating in a clockwise direction.

As the piston travels downward, it uncovers the exhaust port (A) allowing the exhaust gases, which are under pressure, to leave the cylinder. A fresh fuel/air charge, which as been compressed slightly, travels from the crankcase into the cylinder through the transfer port (B). Since this charge enters under pressure, it also helps to push out the exhaust gases.

While the crankshaft continues to rotate, the piston moves upward, covering the transfer port (B) and exhaust port (A). The piston is now compressing the new fuel/air mixture and creating a low pressure area in the crankcase at the same time. As the piston continues to travel, it uncovers the intake port (C). A fresh fuel/air charge, from the carburetor (D), is drawn into the crankcase through the intake port, because of the low pressure within it.

Now, as the piston almost reaches the top of its travel, the spark plug fires, thus igniting the compressed fuel/air mixture. The piston continues to top dead center (TDC) and is pushed downward by the expanding gases.

As the piston travels down, the exhaust gases leave the cylinder and the complete cycle starts all over again.

ENGINE TOP END

foreign matter. Brush out the fins with a whisk broom or small stiff paint brush.

> *CAUTION*
> *Remember, cooling fins are thin and may be damaged if struck too hard.*

CLEANLINESS

Repairs go much faster and easier if your engine is clean before you begin work. This is especially important when servicing your engine's top end. If the top end is being serviced while the engine is installed in the frame, note that dirt trapped underneath the fuel tank or upper frame tube can fall into the cylinder or crankcase opening. There are special cleaners for washing the engine and related parts. Just spray or brush on the cleaning solution, let it stand, then rinse it away with a garden hose. See Chapter One. If you are servicing the bike at a race track, you may not have access to soap and water to clean the bike. Instead, wrap a large clean cloth around the gas tank and upper frame tube. This will prevent dirt from falling into the engine with the top end removed.

SERVICING ENGINE IN FRAME

Some of the components can be serviced while the engine is mounted in the frame (the bike's frame is a great holding fixture—especially for breaking loose stubborn bolts and nuts):
 a. Cylinder head.
 b. Cylinder.
 c. Piston.
 d. Carburetor.
 e. Magneto.
 f. Clutch.
 g. External shift mechanism.

CYLINDER HEAD

The cylinder head is bolted to the top of the cylinder with 4 nuts or bolts. A gasket separates the cylinder head and cylinder.

Removal/Installation

> *CAUTION*
> *To prevent warpage and damage to any component, remove the cylinder head only when the engine is at room temperature.*

1. Remove the seat, side covers and fuel tank.
2. Remove the exhaust system as described under *Exhaust System Removal/Installation* in Chapter Eight.
3. Disconnect the spark plug wire at the plug (**Figure 2**).

> *NOTE*
> *If you think that it may be necessary to remove the spark plug later, loosen it now while the cylinder head is bolted down.*

4. Remove the nuts and bolts for the cylinder head-to-frame brace, then remove the brace. See **Figure 3** (1983-1985) or **Figure 4** (1986-on).
5. Remove the cylinder head nuts and washers in a crisscross pattern.

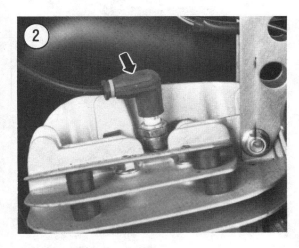

6. Loosen the head by tapping around the perimeter with a rubber or plastic mallet.

CAUTION
Remember, the cooling fins are fragile and may be damaged if tapped or pried too hard. Never use a metal hammer.

NOTE
Do not pry the head if it is stuck. Sometimes it is possible to loosen the head with engine compression. Rotate the engine with the kickstarter (with the spark plug installed). As the piston reaches top dead center (TDC) on the compression stroke, it will pop the head loose.

7. Remove the cylinder head (**Figure 5**) by pulling straight up and off the cylinder studs. Store the cylinder head with the gasket surface placed on a thick piece of cardboard.
8. Remove the cylinder head gasket and discard it.

NOTE
It is not necessary to remove the exhaust valve assembly on 1986 and later models when removing the cylinder head. If you do remove the exhaust valve assembly, it must be installed in a specific manner to assure proper operation. Refer to Cylinder in this chapter.

9. Bring the piston to top dead center (TDC). Lay a rag over the cylinder to prevent dirt from falling into the cylinder.
10. Inspect the cylinder head as described in this chapter.
11. Install the cylinder head by reversing these steps. Note the following:
  a. Always install a new cylinder head gasket. On 1986 and later models, the gasket must align with the exhaust valve assembly as shown in **Figure 6**.
  b. Install the cylinder head and screw on the nuts finger-tight.
  c. Tighten the nuts (**Figure 7**) in a crisscross pattern to the torque specification in **Table 3**. To avoid cylinder head damage, tighten the nuts in 2 or 3 stages, a little at a time.
  d. Install the engine brace and tighten the bolts and nuts securely.

ENGINE TOP END

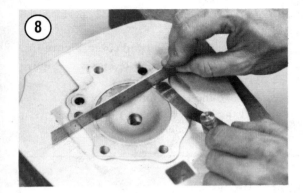

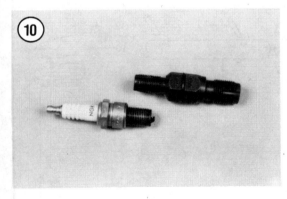

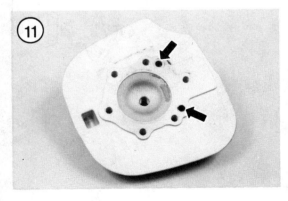

Inspection
(All Models)

1. Clean the cylinder head as described under *Engine Decarbonizing* in Chapter Three.

2. Use a straightedge and feeler gauge and measure the flatness of the cylinder head (**Figure 8**). If the cylinder head warpage exceeds 0.03 mm (0.0012 in.), resurface the cylinder head as follows:

   a. Tape a piece of 400-600 grit wet emery sandpaper onto a piece of thick plate glass or surface plate.

   b. Slowly resurface the head by moving it in figure-eight patterns on the sandpaper.

   c. Rotate the head several times to avoid removing too much material from one side. Check progress often with the straightedge and feeler gauge.

   d. If the cylinder head warpage still exceeds the service limit, it will be necessary to have the head resurfaced by a machine shop. Removing excessive amounts of material from the cylinder head mating surface will change the compression ratio and could also result in contact between the piston top and cylinder head. If the cylinder head is resurfaced on a lathe, the squish band of the combustion chamber must be restored to its original depth and width. Consult with the machinist on this critical measurement.

> *CAUTION*
> *Always use an aluminum thread fluid or kerosene on the tap and threads when performing Step 3.*

3. With the spark plug removed, check the spark plug threads in the cylinder head (**Figure 9**) for any signs of carbon buildup or cracking. The carbon can be removed with a 14 mm spark plug tap (**Figure 10**).

4. Check the flatness of the cylinder head nut or bolt surfaces. Remove any burrs with a file or sandpaper.

5. *1986-on:* Check the exhaust valve shaft holes in the cylinder head (**Figure 11**) for cracks or other damage.

6. Wash the cylinder head in hot soapy water and rinse thoroughly before installation.

CHAPTER FOUR

CYLINDER

Removal

1. Remove the cylinder head as described under *Cylinder Head Removal/Installation* in this chapter.
2. Remove the carburetor as described under *Carburetor Removal/Installation* in Chapter Eight.
3. *1986-on:* Referring to **Figure 12**, perform the following:

    a. Remove the left-hand port cover (**Figure 13**).
    b. Remove the right-hand lever cover (**Figure 14**).
    c. Remove the lever bolt (**Figure 15**).
    d. Lift the lever (**Figure 16**) up and remove it from the cylinder.

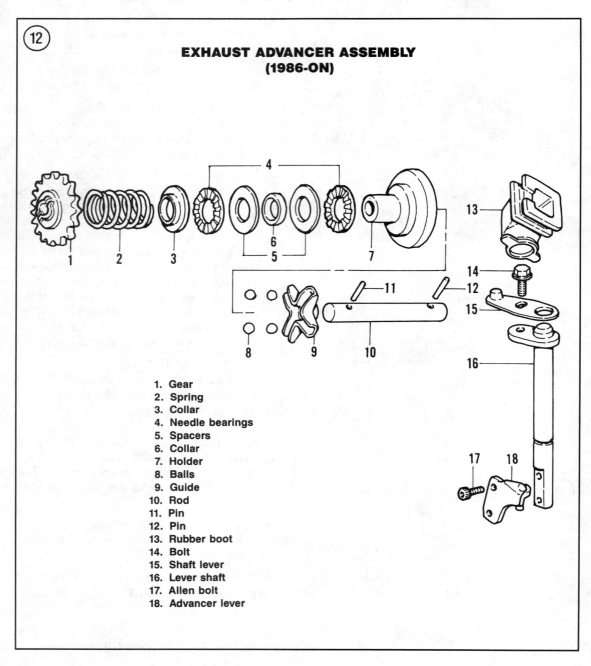

EXHAUST ADVANCER ASSEMBLY (1986-ON)

1. Gear
2. Spring
3. Collar
4. Needle bearings
5. Spacers
6. Collar
7. Holder
8. Balls
9. Guide
10. Rod
11. Pin
12. Pin
13. Rubber boot
14. Bolt
15. Shaft lever
16. Lever shaft
17. Allen bolt
18. Advancer lever

ENGINE TOP END

4. Loosen the cylinder base nuts in a crisscross pattern (**Figure 17**). Then remove the nuts.

5. Loosen the cylinder by tapping around the perimeter with a rubber or plastic mallet.

CAUTION
Do not twist the cylinder during removal. The piston rings could snap into a port and it could damage the piston rings and piston. If this should happen, remove the reed valve assembly and push the rings back into position.

6. Rotate the engine so the piston is at the bottom of its stroke. Pull the cylinder (**Figure 18**) straight up and off the crankcase studs and piston.

CAUTION
Remember, the cooling fins are fragile and may be damaged if tapped or pried too hard. Do not use a metal hammer.

7. Remove the cylinder base gasket and discard it.

8. Place a clean shop cloth into the crankcase opening to prevent the entry of foreign material. See **Figure 19**.

Exhaust Power Valve (1986-on) Removal/Inspection/Installation

Refer to **Figure 12** for this procedure.
1. Remove the small circlip and slide the rod collar (**Figure 20**) off of the valve operating rod.
2. Remove the Phillips screw (**Figure 21**) and remove the exhaust valve holder (**Figure 22**).
3. Pull the valve operating rod (**Figure 23**) out. Then remove the valve guides (**Figure 24**) and exhaust valves (**Figure 25**).
4. Completely remove the valve operating rod.
5. Clean and inspect the exhaust power valve assembly as follows:
   a. Using a small wire brush, clean the 2 port holes (**Figure 26**) thoroughly of all oil and carbon debris.
   b. Clean all exhaust valve parts in solvent to remove all traces of oil and carbon buildup.
   c. Check the valve guides (A, **Figure 27**) for scoring or other damage.

ENGINE TOP END

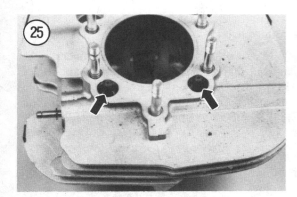

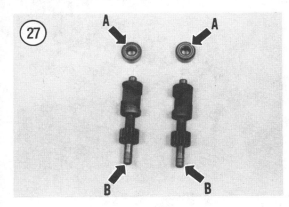

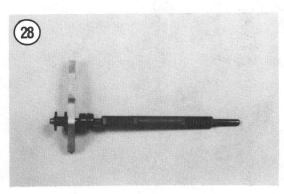

d. Check the exhaust valves (B, **Figure 27**) for scoring or gear damage.
e. Check the valve operating rod (**Figure 28**) for bending or gear damage.
f. Replace all worn or damaged parts.

6. Apply molybdenum disulfide grease to the valve operating rod teeth and the exhaust valve teeth.

7. Before installing the exhaust valves (**Figure 29**), note the following:

   a. The exhaust valves (**Figure 29**) can be identified by the number of grooves cut into the top of each valve shaft. The valve with one groove (A) is installed on the left-hand side. The valve with two grooves (B) is installed on the right-hand side.
   b. The top of each exhaust valve has a punch mark (**Figure 30**) to help with alignment when installing the valve.

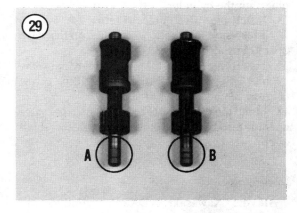

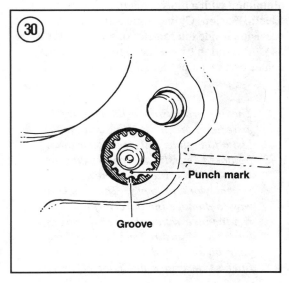

8. Referring to **Figure 31**, install the left-hand exhaust valve (A) and right-hand exhaust valve (B) into its correct port.
9. Turn each exhaust valve so that the punch mark (**Figure 30**) aligns with the cylinder mark.
10. See **Figure 32**. Lift the exhaust valves slightly and install the valve operating rod (A). The teeth on the valve operating rod should point to the back of the cylinder.
11. After inserting the valve operating rod all the way into the cylinder, check that the punch mark on each exhaust valve is still aligned with the cylinder mark (**Figure 30**). If a punch mark is not aligned correctly, remove the valve operating rod and repeat Step 10.
12. **Figure 32** shows the plug and its O-ring (B). Make sure the plug is installed on the valve operating rod as shown in **Figure 32**. After the valve operating rod is properly installed, push the plug into the cylinder.
13. Install the valve guides (**Figure 24**).
14. Make sure the circlip is installed on the valve operating rod (**Figure 33**).
15. Install the exhaust valve holder onto the cylinder (**Figure 22**). Install the Phillips screw (**Figure 21**) and tighten it securely.
16. Install the rod collar (**Figure 20**) onto the valve operating rod. Secure the collar with the small circlip.

Inspection

All the Kawasaki KDX200 cylinders are aluminum with a molybdenum coated bore called Electro-Fusion. Cylinder measurement requires a precision inside micrometer or equivalent (**Figure 34**). If you don't have the right tools, have your dealer or a machine shop take the measurements.

NOTE
The Electro-Fusion cylinder bore is extremely hard and durable and should last a long time. This cylinder cannot be bored oversize to compensate for wear, so it is critical that the air filter system work properly. The quickest way to damage the bore surface is to run the bike with a dirty or damaged air filter. To insure long service from your bike's cylinder, service the air filter as described in Chapter Three.

1. Remove and inspect the reed valve as described in this chapter.
2. Measure the cylinder bore with a cylinder gauge or inside micrometer, at the point shown in **Figure 35**. Measure in 2 axes—in line with the wrist pin and at 90° to the pin. If bore exceeds the wear limit in **Table 2**, the cylinder must be replaced.

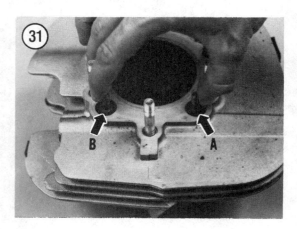

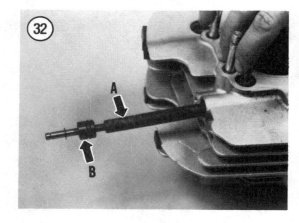

ENGINE TOP END

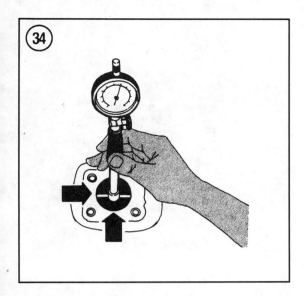

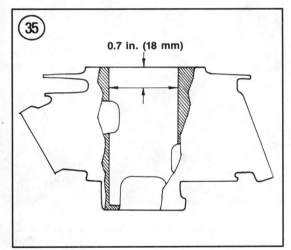

3. When installing a new cylinder, give the bike the same break-in procedure you would use on a new machine.

CAUTION
Electro-Fusion cylinders cannot be bored oversize since the cylinder coating is very thin for maximum heat transfer.

4. Check the cylinder studs (**Figure 36**) for thread damage or looseness. If thread damage is minor, they may be cleaned up with an M8 × 1.25 metric die. If the studs are damaged or loose, replace them as follows:

a. Thread two nuts onto the damaged cylinder stud as shown in **Figure 37**. Then tighten the 2 nuts against each other so that they are locked.
b. Turn the bottom nut counterclockwise (**Figure 38**) and unscrew the stud.

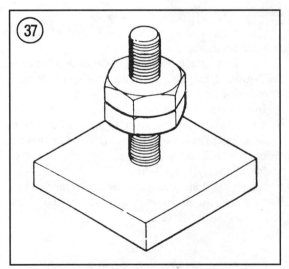

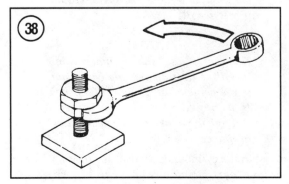

c. Clean the threads in the cylinder with solvent or electrical contact cleaner and allow to thoroughly dry.
d. Install 2 nuts on the top half of the new stud as in sub-step a. Make sure they are locked securely.
e. Coat the bottom half of a new stud with Loctite 271 (red).
f. Turn the top nut clockwise and thread the new stud into the cylinder. Tighten to 15 N·m (11 ft.-lb.).
g. Remove the nuts and repeat for each stud as required.
h. Follow Loctite's directions on cure time before installing the cylinder head and cylinder head nuts.

5. Before installing the cylinder, wash the bore in hot soapy water. Then after drying the cylinder, lubricate the bore with Kawasaki 2-stroke oil.

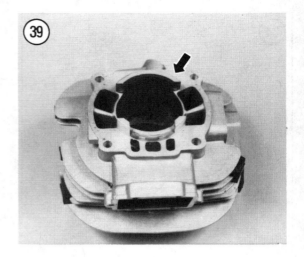

Installation

1. Clean the cylinder bore as described under *Inspection* in this chapter.
2. Check that the top surface of the crankcase and the bottom surface of the cylinder (**Figure 39**) are clean prior to installation.
3. Install a new base gasket.
4. Make sure the end gaps of the piston rings are lined up with the locating pins in the ring grooves (**Figure 40**). Lightly oil the piston rings and the inside of the cylinder bore.
5. Install a piston holding fixture under the piston. Then rotate the crankshaft until the piston skirt seats against the fixture.

NOTE
*A piston holding fixture can be easily made out of wood to the specifications in **Figure 41**.*

CAUTION
Do not rotate the cylinder while installing it. A piston ring could snag in the cylinder intake port and break. If a ring does snag, try to reach through the intake port to push it back in place.

6. Start the cylinder down over the piston *with the exhaust port facing forward*. See **Figure 42**.

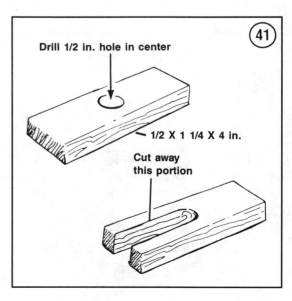

ENGINE TOP END

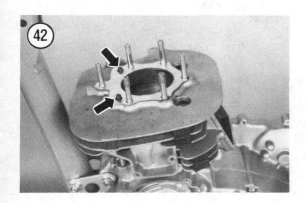

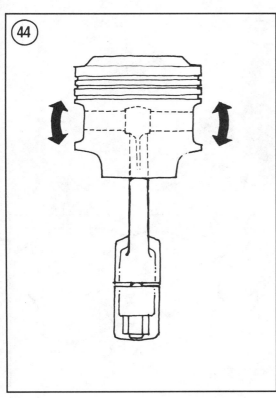

7. Compress each ring, with your fingers, as the cylinder starts to slide over it.

NOTE
Make sure the rings are still properly aligned with the locating pins in the piston.

8. Slide the cylinder down until it bottoms on the piston holding fixture.
9. Remove the piston holding fixture and slide the cylinder into place on the crankcase.
10. Hold the cylinder in place with one hand and push the kickstarter lever down with the other hand. If the piston catches or stops in the cylinder, the piston rings were not lined up properly. The piston should move up and down smoothly.
11. Install the cylinder base nuts and tighten them securely in a crisscross pattern (**Figure 43**) to the torque specification in **Table 3**.
12. Install the cylinder head as described under *Cylinder Head Removal/Installation* in this chapter.
13. Install the carburetor as described under *Carburetor Removal/Installation* in Chapter Eight.
14. Follow the *Break-in Procedure* in this chapter if the cylinder was replaced.

PISTON, WRIST PIN AND PISTON RINGS

The piston is made of an aluminum alloy. The wrist pin is a precision fit and is held in place by a clip at each end. A caged needle bearing is used on the small end of the connecting rod.

Piston and Piston Ring Removal

1. Remove the cylinder head and cylinder as described in this chapter.
2. Before removing the piston, hold the rod tightly and rock the piston as shown in **Figure 44**. Any rocking motion (do not confuse with the normal sliding motion) indicates wear on the wrist pin, needle bearing, wrist pin bore or more likely a combination of all three.

NOTE
Wrap a clean shop cloth under the piston so that the clips will not fall into the crankcase.

WARNING
Safety glasses should be worn when performing Step 3.

3. Remove the clips from each side of the wrist pin bore (**Figure 45**) with a small screwdriver or scribe. Hold your thumb over one edge of the clip when removing it to prevent it from springing out.
4. Use a proper size wooden dowel or socket extension and push out the wrist pin.

CAUTION
If the piston seized, the wrist pin will probably be very difficult to remove. However, do not drive the wrist pin out of the piston. This will damage the piston, needle bearing and connecting rod. If the wrist pin will not push out by hand, remove it as described in Step 5.

5. If the wrist pin is tight, fabricate the tool shown in **Figure 46**. Assemble the tool onto the piston and pull the wrist pin out of the piston. Make sure to install a pad between the piston and piece of pipe to prevent from scoring the side of the piston.
6. Lift the piston off the connecting rod.
7. Remove the needle bearing from the connecting rod (**Figure 47**).
8. If the piston is going to be left off for some time, place a piece of foam insulation tube, or shop cloth, over the end of the rod to protect it.

NOTE
Always remove the top piston ring first.

9. First remove the top ring by spreading the ends with your thumbs just enough to slide it up over the piston (**Figure 48**). Repeat for the other ring.

Wrist Pin and Needle Bearing Inspection

1. Clean the needle bearing in solvent and dry it thoroughly. Use a magnifying glass and inspect the bearing cage for cracks at the corners of the needle slots (A, **Figure 49**) and inspect the needles themselves for cracking. If any cracks are found, the bearing must be replaced.
2. Check the wrist pin (B, **Figure 49**) for severe wear, scoring or chrome flaking. Also check the wrist pin for cracks along the top and side. Replace the wrist pin if necessary.

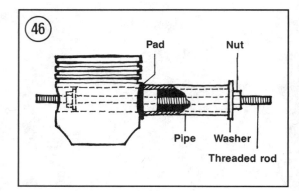

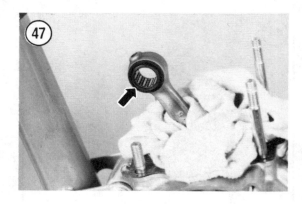

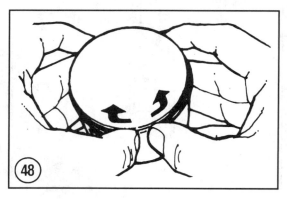

ENGINE TOP END

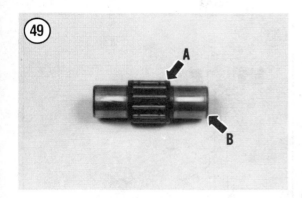

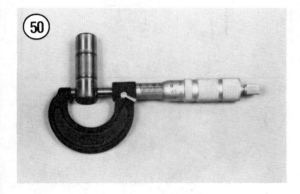

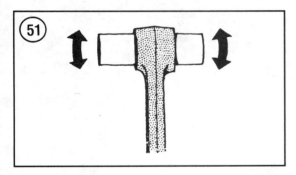

3. Measure the wrist pin outside diameter in the bearing area with a micrometer (**Figure 50**) and compare to the wear limit in **Table 2**. If the wrist pin outside diameter is too small, replace it.

4. Oil the needle bearing and pin and install it in the connecting rod. Slowly rotate the pin and check for radial play (**Figure 51**). If any play exists, the pin and bearing should be replaced, providing the rod bore is in good condition. If the condition of the rod bore is in question, the old pin and bearing can be checked with a new connecting rod.

CAUTION
If there are signs of piston seizure or overheating (blue), replace the wrist pin and bearing. These parts may have been weakened from excessive heat and could fail unexpectedly.

Connecting Rod Inspection

1. Wipe the wrist pin bore in the connecting rod with a clean rag and check it for galling, scratches or any other signs of wear or damage. If any of these conditions exist, replace the connecting rod as described in Chapter Five.

2. Measure the inside diameter of the small end of the connecting rod with a snap gauge and a micrometer (**Figure 52**). If the inside diameter is larger than the limit given in **Table 2**, install a new connecting rod.

3. Check the connecting rod big end bearing play. You can make a quick check by simply rocking the

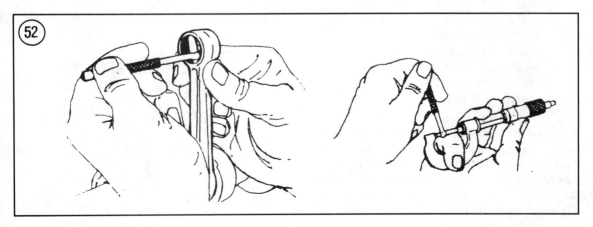

connecting rod back and forth (**Figure 53**). If there is more than a very slight rocking motion (some side to side clearance is normal), you should remove the crankshaft assembly and measure big-end bearing play. See Chapter Five.

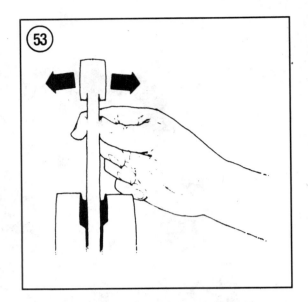

Piston Inspection

1. Carefully check the piston for cracks at the top edge of the transfer cutaways (**Figure 54**) and replace if found. Check the piston skirt (A, **Figure 55**) for brown varnish buildup. More than a slight amount is an indication of worn or sticking rings which should be replaced.
2. Check the piston skirt for galling and abrasion which may have resulted from piston seizure. If light galling is present, smooth the affected area with No. 400 emery paper and oil or a fine oilstone. However if galling is severe or if the piston is deeply scored, replace it.
3. Check the piston ring locating pin(s) in the piston (B, **Figure 55**). The pins should be tight and the piston should show no signs of cracking around the pin. If any locating pin is loose, replace the piston. A loose pin will eventually fall out and cause severe engine damage.

> *NOTE*
> *Maintaining proper piston ring end gap helps to ensure peak engine performance. Always check piston ring end gap at the intervals specified in Chapter Three. Excessive ring end gap reduces engine performance and can cause overheating. Insufficient ring end gap will cause the ring ends to butt together and cause the ring to break. This would cause severe engine damage. To avoid waiting for parts, always order extra cylinder head and base gaskets to have on hand for routine top end inspection and maintenance.*

4. Measure piston ring end gap. Place a ring into the cylinder and push it in about 20 mm (3/4 in.) with the crown of the piston (**Figure 56**). This ensures that the ring is square in the cylinder bore. Measure the gap with a flat feeler gauge (**Figure 57**) and compare to the wear limit in **Table 2**. If

ENGINE TOP END

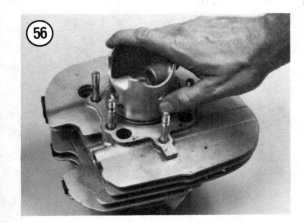

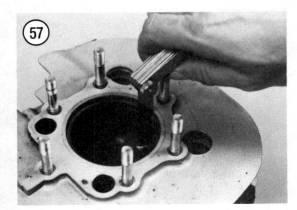

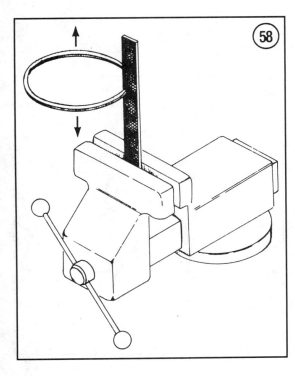

the gap is greater than specified, the rings should be replaced.

NOTE
*When installing new rings, measure their end gap in the same manner as for old ones. If the gap is less than specified, you may have the wrong size rings. If you have the correct rings and the gap is too small, carefully file the ends with a fine cut file until the gap is correct (**Figure 58**).*

5. Carefully remove all carbon buildup from the ring grooves with a broken ring (**Figure 59**). Inspect the grooves carefully for burrs, nicks, or broken and cracked lands. Recondition or replace the piston if necessary.

6. Measure the side clearance of each ring in its groove with a flat feeler gauge (**Figure 60**) and

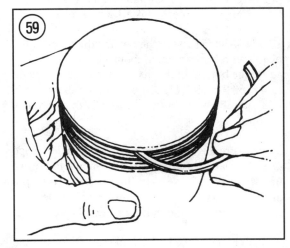

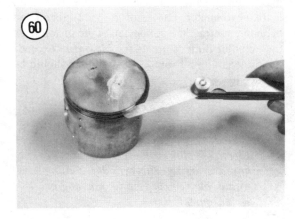

compare to the wear limit in in **Table 2**. If the clearance is greater than specified, the rings must be replaced, and if the clearance is still excessive with the new rings, the piston must also be replaced.

7. If the piston appears okay, measure the piston outside diameter as described under *Piston/Cylinder Clearance* in this chapter.

Piston/Cylinder Clearance

The following procedure requires the use of highly specialized and expensive measuring tools. If such equipment is not readily available, have the measurements performed by a dealer or machine shop.

1A. *1983:* Measure the outside diameter of the piston with a micrometer about 12 mm (0.47) below the piston crown, at a 90° angle to the piston pin (**Figure 61**). If the diameter is less than the wear limit in **Table 2**, install a new piston.

1B. *1984-on:* Measure the outside diameter of the piston with a micrometer about 18.5 mm (0.73 in.) above the bottom of the piston skirt, at a 90° angle to the piston pin (**Figure 62**). If the diameter is less than the wear limit in **Table 2**, install a new piston.

2. Measure the cylinder bore with a cylinder gauge or inside micrometer, at the point shown in **Figure 63**. Measure in 2 axes—in line with the wrist pin and at 90° to the pin. If the bore exceeds the wear limit in **Table 2**, the cylinder must be replaced.

3. Piston clearance is the difference between the maximum piston diameter and the minimum cylinder diameter. For a run-in (used) piston and cylinder, subtract the dimension of the piston from the cylinder dimension. If the clearance exceeds the dimension in **Table 2**, the cylinder should be replaced.

> *NOTE*
> *All Kawasaki KDX200 cylinders use a coated bore called Electro-Fusion. Electro-Fusion cylinders cannot be bored oversize. The cylinder coating would be removed, and the engine would quickly seize.*

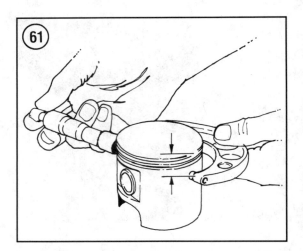

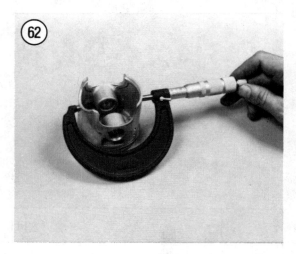

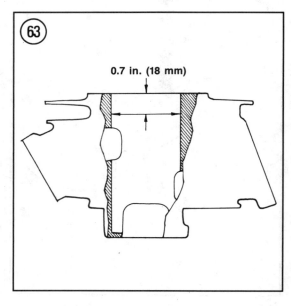

ENGINE TOP END

Piston Installation

1. Apply assembly oil to the needle bearing and install it in the connecting rod (**Figure 64**).
2. Oil the wrist pin and install it in the piston until the end of it extends slightly beyond the inside of the boss.
3. Place the piston over the connecting rod with the arrow on the piston crown pointing forward. Line up the pin with the bearing and push the pin into the piston until it is even with the wrist pin clip grooves.

> *CAUTION*
> *If the wrist pin will not slide in the piston smoothly, use the homemade tool described during **Piston Removal** to install the wrist pin (**Figure 46**). When using the homemade tool, the pipe and pad are not required. Instead, run the threaded rod through the wrist pin. Secure the end of the wrist pin next to the piston with the small washer and nut. Slide the large washer onto the threaded rod so that it is next to the wrist pin. Install the nut next to the large washer and tighten the nut to push the wrist pin into the piston.*

4. Install new wrist pin clips (**Figure 65**) in the ends of the pin boss. Make sure they are seated in the grooves.
5. Check the installation by rocking the piston back and forth around the pin axis and from side to side along the axis. It should rotate freely back and forth but not from side to side.
6. Install the piston rings—first the bottom one, then the top—by carefully spreading the ends of the ring with your thumbs and slipping the ring over the top of the piston. Make sure that the marks on the piston rings are toward the top of the piston.
7. Make sure the rings are seated completely in the grooves, all the way around the circumference, and that the ends are aligned with the locating pins.
8. Follow the *Break-in Procedure* in this chapter if new piston or ring(s) were installed.

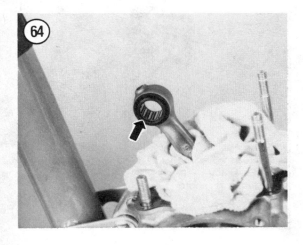

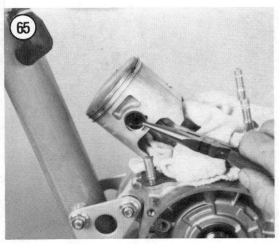

BREAK-IN PROCEDURE

If the rings were replaced, a new piston installed or the cylinder replaced, the engine must be run in at moderate speeds and loads for no less than 2 hours. Don't exceed 75% of normal allowable rpm during break-in. After the first half hour, remove the spark plug and check its condition. The electrode should be dry and clean and the color of the insulation should be light to medium tan. If the insulation is white (indicating a too lean fuel/air mixture) or if it is dark and oily (indicating a too rich fuel/air mixture ratio), correct the condition with a main jet change; both incorrect conditions produce excessive engine heat and can lead to damage to the rings, piston, and cylinder before they have had a chance to seat in.

Refer to Chapter Three for further information on how to read a spark plug and to Chapter Eight for carburetor jet change.

REED VALVE ASSEMBLY

All models are equipped with a reed valve assembly (**Figure 66**) installed in the intact tract between the carburetor and crankcase. The reed is a thin, flexible one-way valve made of stainless steel or fiber material. The reed valve regulates the air/fuel mixture drawn from the carburetor into the crankcase.

Particular care must be taken when handling and repairing the reed valve assembly.

Removal/Installation

The reed valve can be removed with the cylinder removed or installed on the bike.

1. If the reed valve is going to be removed with the cylinder installed on the bike, note the following:
    a. Wash the bike thoroughly before disassembly.
    b. Remove the carburetor.
2. Remove the bolts securing the intake manifold (**Figure 67**) to the cylinder.
3. Pull the reed cage assembly (**Figure 68**) out of the cylinder intake tract.

NOTE
Some mechanics choose to seal the reed cage against the cylinder with a chemical sealer. This is not necessary (unless mating surfaces are damaged) and it can make removal of the reed cage difficult. If the reed cage on your model is secured with a sealer, do not pry the cage off. Undoubtedly this will damage the mating surfaces and cause an air leak. Instead, tap the side (non-gasket area) of the cage with a rubber or plastic mallet until the cage breaks free of the sealer. Do not use a drift or screwdriver to tap the reed cage off; this will flare the edge of the reed cage surface and cause an air leak. If you are working on a bike in which a sealer was used, check the reed cage carefully for pry marks or other damage.

4. Remove and discard the reed cage gasket. If a sealer was used, carefully scrape all gasket residue from the cylinder mating surface.

5. Inspect the reed valve assembly as described in this chapter.
6. Install a new gasket and insert the reed valve assembly into the cylinder.

CAUTION
Overtightening the reed valve mounting bolts will create an air leak.

7. Install the intake manifold (**Figure 67**) and tighten the mounting bolts evenly in a crisscross pattern.

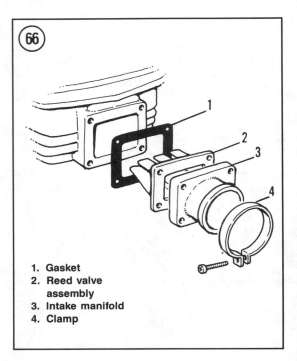

1. Gasket
2. Reed valve assembly
3. Intake manifold
4. Clamp

ENGINE TOP END

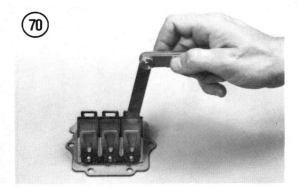

Inspection

1. Carefully examine the reed valve assembly (**Figure 69**) for visible signs of wear, distortion or damage.
2. Use a flat feeler gauge and check the clearance between the reed plate and the gasket (**Figure 70**). Refer to the service limit in **Table 2**. If the clearance exceeds this dimension the reed plate(s) must be replaced.
3. Remove the screws securing the reed stop to the reed body. Be careful that the screwdriver does not slip off and damage the reed plate.
4. Carefully examine the reed plate, reed stop and gasket. Check for signs of cracks, metal fatigue, distortion or foreign matter damage. Pay particular attention to the rubber gasket seal. The reed stops and reed plates are available as replacement parts, but if the rubber gasket seal is damaged the entire assembly should be replaced.
5. Check the threaded holes in the reed cage. If the threads are stripped, do not repair the threads. Instead, it will be safer to replace the reed cage. Loose screws can fall into the engine and cause expensive damage.
6. Reassemble the unit. Apply Loctite 242 (blue) to the threads prior to installation and tighten securely.

NOTE
Make sure that all parts are clean and free of any small dirt particles or lint from a shop cloth as they may cause a small amount of distortion in the reed plate.

7. Reinstall the reed valve assembly as previously described.

Tables are on the following pages.

Table 1 GENERAL ENGINE SPECIFICATIONS

Bore × stroke	66.0 × 58.0 mm (2.60 × 2.28 in.)
Displacement	198 cc (12.08 cu. in.)
Compression ratio	
1983-1987	7.7:1
1988	7.5:1
Port timing	
1983-1985	
Intake	
Open	—
Close	—
Transfer	
Open	62° BBDC
Close	62° ABDC
Exhaust	
Open	93° BBDC
Close	93° ABDC
1986-on	
Intake	
Open	—
Close	—
Transfer	
Open	60° BBDC
Close	60° ABDC
Exhaust	
Open	89° BBDC
Close	89° ABDC
Lubrication	Fuel/oil premix

Table 2 ENGINE TOP END SERVICE SPECIFICATIONS

	Standard mm (in.)	Wear limit mm (in.)
Cylinder bore		
1983	66.006-66.021 (2.5987-2.5993)	66.1 (2.60)
1984-on	66.016-66.031 (2.5991-2.5996)	66.1 (2.60)
Piston diameter		
1983	65.833-65.848 (2.5919-2.5925)	65.70 (2.587)
1984-1985	65.954-65.969 (2.5966-2.5972)	65.80 (2.591)
1986-on	65.939-65.954 (2.5960-2.5966)	65.80 (2.591)
Piston-to-cylinder clearance		
1983	0.049-0.059 (0.0019-0.0023)	—
1984-1985	0.057-0.077 (0.0022-0.0030)	—
1986-on	0.067-0.087 (0.0026-0.0034)	—
Piston ring end gap	0.15-0.35 (0.006-0.014)	0.7 (0.028)
Piston ring groove clearance		
1983-1987	0.04-0.08 (0.0016-0.0032)	0.18 (0.0071)
1988	*	

(continued)

ENGINE TOP END

Table 2 ENGINE TOP END SERVICE SPECIFICATIONS (continued)

	Standard mm (in.)	Wear limit mm (in.)
Piston ring groove thickness		
1983-1987	1.23-1.25 (0.0484-0.0492)	1.33 (0.0524)
1988	*	
Piston ring thickness		
1983-1987	1.170-1.190 (0.0461-0.0469)	1.10 (0.043)
1988	*	
Wrist pin outside diameter	15.995-16.000 (0.6297-0.6299)	15.96 (0.628)
Wrist pin hole ID	16.000-16.005 (0.6299-0.6301)	16.07 (0.633)
Connecting rod small end ID	21.003-21.014 (0.8269-0.8273)	21.05 (0.829)
Reed valve-to-plate clearance		0.7 (0.028)

* Not specified by Kawasaki for this model.

Table 3 ENGINE TOP END TIGHTENING TORQUES

	N·m	ft.-lb.
Cylinder head nuts	25	18
Cylinder base nuts		
1983-1985	34	25
1986-on	25	18
Exhaust advancer lever bolt		
1986	10	87 in.-lb.
1987-on	9	78 in.-lb.
Exhaust advancer lever		
shaft bolts	4	35 in.-lb.
Spark plug	27	20

CHAPTER FIVE

ENGINE LOWER END

This chapter describes service procedures for the following lower end components:
a. Crankcases.
b. Crankshaft.
c. Connecting rod.
d. Transmission (removal and installation).
e. Internal shift mechanism (removal and installation).

Transmission and internal shift mechanism overhaul procedures are described in Chapter Seven.

Prior to removing and disassembling the crankcase, clean the entire engine and frame with a good grade commercial degreaser, like Gunk or Bel-Ray engine degreaser. It is easier to work on a clean engine and you will do a better job.

Make certain that you have all the necessary tools available, especially any special tool(s), and purchase replacement parts prior to disassembly. Also make sure you have a clean place to work.

It is a good idea to identify and mark parts as they are removed so that errors will be avoided during assembly and installation. Clean all parts thoroughly upon removal, then place them in trays or boxes with their associated mounting hardware. Do not rely on memory alone as it may be days or weeks before you complete the job. In the text there is frequent mention of the left-hand and right-hand sides of the engine. This refers to the engine as it sits in the bike's frame, not as it sits on your workbench.

Crankshaft specifications are listed in **Table 1**. Tightening torques are listed in **Table 2**. **Table 1** and **Table 2** are found at the end of the chapter.

SERVICING ENGINE IN FRAME

Some of the components can be serviced while the engine is mounted in the frame (the bike's frame is a great holding fixture—especially for breaking loose stubborn bolts and nuts):
a. Cylinder head.
b. Cylinder.
c. Piston.
d. Carburetor.
e. Magneto.
f. Clutch.
g. External shift mechanism.

ENGINE

Removal/Installation

The engines covered in this manual are very compact and can be easily removed by one adult. If the engine is going to be removed for non-engine

ENGINE LOWER END

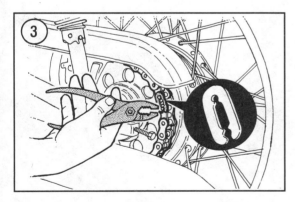

related service, engine disassembly is not required. Instead, remove the engine as a unit. If service requires crankcase disassembly, use the frame as a holding tool and remove all of the engine sub-assemblies while the engine is mounted in the frame. After the sub-assemblies are removed, the crankcase can be removed as a unit and then serviced as required.

1. Place a milk crate or wood block(s) under the frame to support the bike securely.
2. Remove the seat and both side covers.
3. Remove the fuel tank as described in under *Fuel Tank Removal/Installation* in Chapter Eight.
4. Remove the exhaust system as described under *Exhaust System Removal/Installation* in Chapter Eight.
5. Remove the carburetor as described under *Carburetor Removal/Installation* in Chapter Eight.
6. Remove the shift lever pinch bolt and slide the lever (**Figure 1**) off of the shift shaft. If the lever is tight, pry the lever slot open with a screwdriver and pull the lever off.
7. Remove the sprocket cover bolts and remove the cover (**Figure 2**).
8. If necessary, remove the master link on the drive chain (**Figure 3**). Then disconnect the drive chain and remove it.
9. Remove the circlip and remove the countershaft sprocket (**Figure 4**).
10. See **Figure 5**. At the handlebar, loosen the clutch cable adjuster locknut (A) and turn the adjuster (B) toward the clutch lever to loosen the clutch cable. Then disconnect the clutch cable at the engine. See **Figure 6** (1983-1985) or **Figure 7** (1986-on).

11. If you plan on disassembling the crankcases, remove the following engine sub-assemblies:
   a. Cylinder head (Chapter Four).
   b. Cylinder (Chapter Four).
   c. Piston (Chapter Four).
   d. Magneto (Chapter Nine).
   e. Clutch (Chapter Six).
   f. Kickstarter (Chapter Six).

12. Disconnect the magneto electrical connector. See **Figure 8** (1983-1985) or **Figure 9** (1986-on).

13. Remove the cylinder head mounting brace. See **Figure 10** (1983-1985) or **Figure 11** (1986-on).

14. Remove the engine assembly (**Figure 12**) as follows:

   a. Remove the front engine mounting bolts and brackets (**Figure 13**).
   b. Loosen the swing arm pivot shaft nut (**Figure 14**).
   c. Remove the lower engine mount nut and bolt (**Figure 15**).
   d. Remove the engine-to-swing arm pivot shaft nut (**Figure 14**) and withdraw the pivot shaft (**Figure 16**).
   e. Lift the engine (**Figure 15**) out of the frame.
   f. The swing arm is now loose from its mounting on the frame. If it is necessary to move the bike, align the swing arm with the frame and install the pivot shaft and nut (**Figure 16**).

15. While the engine is removed, check the engine frame mounts for cracks or other damage. See **Figure 17** and **Figure 18**.

16. Install by reversing these removal steps.

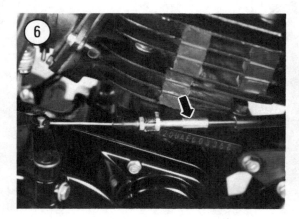

ENGINE LOWER END

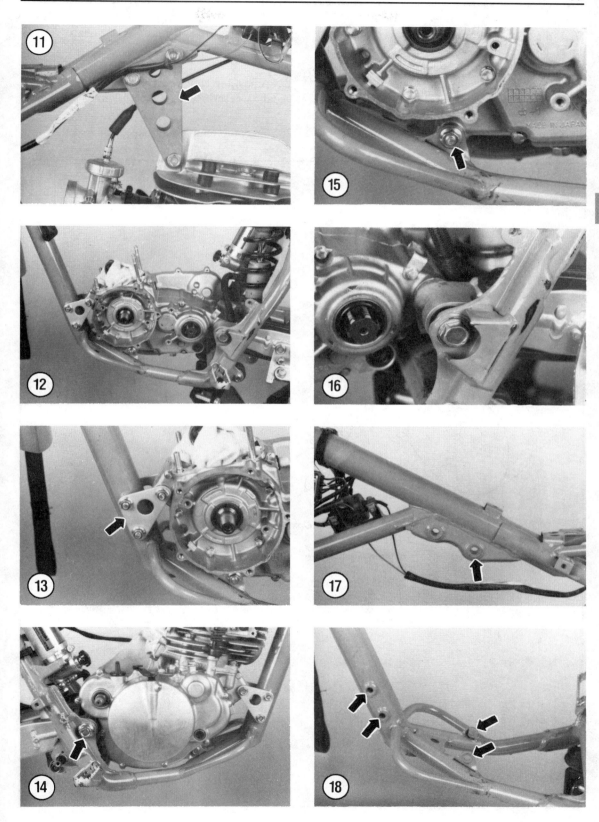

17. If the clutch/transmission oil was drained, fill the clutch/transmission with the correct type and quantity oil as described under *Transmission Oil* in Chapter Three.

18. Reinstall the drive chain. Connect the master link so that the closed end of the Chain faces the direction of chain travel (**Figure 3**).

19. Adjust the clutch, drive chain and rear brake pedal as described in Chapter Three.

20. Start the engine and check for leaks.

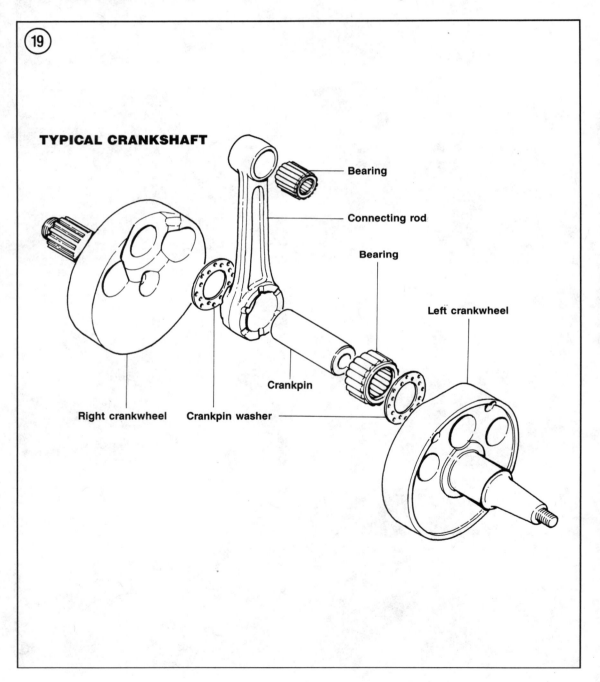

ENGINE LOWER END

ENGINE SPROCKET

The engine sprocket is mounted on the left end of the transmission countershaft, with a sleeve and O-ring inside of it. The sprocket is secured with a circlip.

Removal/Installation

1. Remove the engine sprocket cover (**Figure 2**).
2. Remove the circlip with circlip pliers.
3. Remove the engine sprocket (**Figure 4**), spacer and O-ring.
4. Installation is the reverse of these steps.

CRANKCASE AND CRANKSHAFT

Disassembly of the crankcase—splitting the cases—and removal of the crankshaft assembly require that the engine be removed from the frame. However, the cylinder head, cylinder and all other attached assemblies should be removed with the engine in the frame.

The crankcase is made in 2 halves of precision diecast aluminum alloy and is of the "thin-walled" type. To avoid damage to them do not hammer or pry on any of the interior or exterior projected walls. These areas are easily damaged if stressed beyond what they are designed for. They are assembled without a gasket; only gasket sealer is used while dowel pins align the crankcase halves when they are bolted together.

The crankshaft assembly is made up of 2 full-circle flywheels pressed together on a hollow crankpin. The connecting rod's big end rotates on a needle bearing (**Figure 19**). The crankshaft assembly is supported by a ball bearing in each crankcase half.

The procedure which follows is presented as a complete, step-by-step major lower end rebuild that should be followed if an engine is to be completely reconditioned.

Remember that the right- and left-hand sides of the engine relate to the engine as it sits in the bike's frame, not as it sits on your workbench.

Special Tools

When splitting the crankcase assembly, a few special tools will be required. These tools allow easy disassembly and reassembly of the engine without prying or hammering. Remember, the crankcase halves can be easily damaged by improper disassembly or reassembly techniques.

   a. Kawasaki crankcase separating tool (Part No. 57001-1098) (**Figure 20**). This tool threads into the crankcase and is used to separate the crankcase halves and to press the crankshaft out of the crankcase. The tool is very simple in design and a similar type of tool, such as a steering wheel puller can be substituted.

   b. Some type of press will be required to assemble the crankcase assembly. While a floor-model hydraulic press is the preferred tool, a special hand press tool can be used.

Crankcase Disassembly

This procedure describes disassembly of the crankcase halves and removal of the crankshaft, transmission and internal shift mechanism.

1. Remove all exterior engine assemblies as described in this chapter and other related chapters.

> *NOTE*
> *Drain the clutch/transmission oil as described in Chapter Three. To avoid misplacing the drain bolt, reinstall it after the oil is completely drained.*

2. Remove the O-ring (**Figure 21**) from its groove in the countershaft.

> *NOTE*
> *Make sure to remove the entire external shift mechanism assembly as described in Chapter Six for your model.*

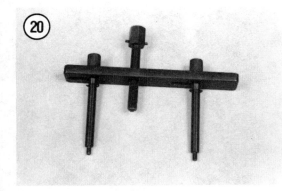

3. Place the engine assembly on a couple of wood blocks with the left-hand side facing up (**Figure 22**).
4. Loosen all screws securing the crankcase halves together one-quarter turn. To prevent warpage, loosen them in a crisscross pattern.
5. Remove all screws loosened in Step 4. Be sure to remove all of them.

NOTE
To prevent loss and to ensure proper location during assembly, draw the crankcase outline on cardboard, then punch holes to correspond with screw locations. Insert the screws in their appropriate locations. Also record the position of any clips that hold electrical wires or drain tubes.

CAUTION
*Perform this operation over and close down to the work bench as the crankcase halves may easily separate. **Do not** hammer on the crankcase halves as they will be damaged.*

CAUTION
On models in which the shift drum segment is permanently mounted onto the end of the shift drum, make sure to align the segment with the slots in the case to prevent damaging the case.

6. Install the crankcase separating tool (**Figure 23**) into the threaded holes on the right-hand crankcase. Center the pressure bolt on the end of the crankshaft. Tighten the securing bolts into the crankcase, making sure the tool body is parallel with the crankcase. If necessary, back out one of the separating tool bolts.
7. Screw the puller *clockwise* until both cases begin to separate.

CAUTION
*While tightening the puller make sure the body is kept parallel to the crankcase surface during this operation (**Figure 24**). Otherwise it will put an uneven stress on the case halves and may damage them.*

8. Use a plastic or rubber mallet and tap the crankcase half and transmission shaft to help during separation.

CAUTION
*Crankcase separation requires only hand pressure on the puller screw. If extreme pressure seems to be needed, or if both halves will not remain parallel, **stop immediately**. Check for crankcase screws not removed, or any*

ENGINE LOWER END

part that is still attached, or transmission shafts hung up in a bearing. Relieve puller pressure immediately.

CAUTION
Never pry between case halves. Doing so will result in oil leaks, requiring replacement of the case halves.

9. Remove the 2 dowel pins (**Figure 25**) after removing the left-hand crankcase half.
10. Unscrew the crankcase separator tool.
11. The transmission assemblies and the crankshaft assemblies will usually stay in the right-hand case half (**Figure 25**).

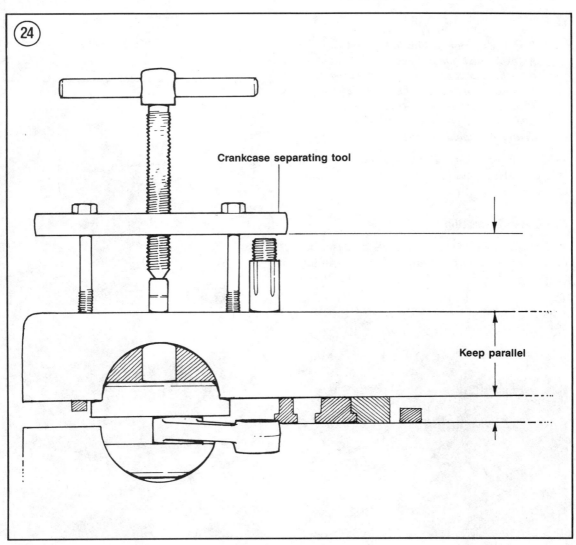

12A. *1983-1985:* Remove the transmission assembly as follows:
   a. Remove the shift fork shafts (**Figure 26**).
   b. Remove the 3 shift forks.
   c. See **Figure 27**. Remove the screws securing the shift drum holder and remove the shift drum.
   d. Remove the transmission shafts (**Figure 28**).

12B. *1986-on:* Remove the transmission assembly as follows:
   a. Remove the shift fork shafts (**Figure 26**).
   b. Swing the shift forks away from the shift drum grooves, then lift the shift drum (**Figure 29**) out of the crankcase.
   c. Remove the 3 shift forks (**Figure 30**).
   d. Remove the transmission shafts (**Figure 28**).

NOTE
*Step 13 describes crankshaft removal. As explained under **Special Tools** in this chapter, a press will be required to remove and install the crankshaft. If you do not have a press or access to one, have the crankshaft removed by a dealer or machine shop.*

13. If it is necessary to remove the crankshaft (**Figure 31**), press it out of the right-hand crankcase.

Crankcase Inspection

1. Remove the crankcase oil seals as described under *Bearing and Oil Seal Replacement* in this chapter.

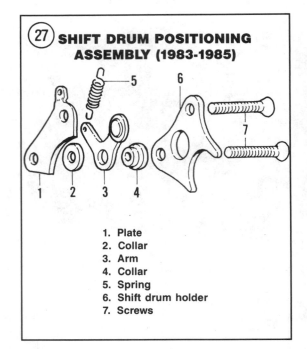

1. Plate
2. Collar
3. Arm
4. Collar
5. Spring
6. Shift drum holder
7. Screws

ENGINE LOWER END

2. Clean both crankcase halves inside and out with cleaning solvent. Thoroughly dry with compressed air and wipe off with a clean shop cloth. Be sure to remove all traces of old gasket sealer from all mating surfaces.

3. Oil the crankshaft main bearings (**Figure 32**) with clean two-stroke engine oil before checking the bearings in Steps 4 and 5.

4. Check the crankshaft main bearings (**Figure 32**) for roughness, pitting, galling, and play by rotating them slowly by hand. If any cracks roughness or play can be felt in the bearing it must be replaced.

NOTE
Always replace both crankcase main bearings as a set.

5. Inspect the other bearings as described in the previous step. See **Figure 33** and **Figure 34**.
6. Replace any worn or damaged bearings as described under *Bearing and Oil Seal Replacement* in this chapter.
7. Carefully inspect the cases (**Figure 35**) for cracks and fractures, especially in the lower areas

where they are vulnerable to rock damage. Also check the areas around the stiffening ribs, around bearing bosses and threaded holes. If any are found, have them repaired by a shop specializing in the repair of precision aluminum castings or replace them.

8. Check the kickstarter stop (**Figure 36**) for damage. Also check the stop bolts for tightness.
9. Check the shift shaft pin (**Figure 37**) for looseness. Tighten the pin if necessary.

Bearing and Oil Seal Replacement

1. Pry out the oil seals with a screwdriver (**Figure 38**). Place a rag or wood block underneath the screwdriver to prevent damaging the crankcase. If the seals are old and difficult to remove, heat the cases as described later and use an awl and punch a small hole in the steel backing of the seal. Install a small sheet metal screw into the seal and pull the seal out with a pair of pliers.

CAUTION
Do not install the screw too deep or it may contact and damage the bearing behind it.

2. Some bearings are held in position by a retainer plate (**Figure 39**) or with bolts and washers (**Figure 40**). Remove the retainers before removing the bearings. If it is not necessary to remove the bearings, check the retainer plate bolts for tightness.

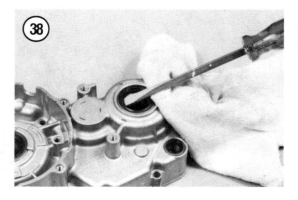

NOTE
*It will be necessary to remove the left-hand crankshaft main bearing (**Figure 32**) before removing the left-hand crankshaft oil seal (**Figure 41**).*

CAUTION
Before heating the crankcases in this procedure to remove the bearings, wash the cases thoroughly with detergent and water. Rinse and rewash the cases as required to remove all traces of oil and debris.

3. The bearings are installed with a slight interference fit. The crankcase must be heated to a temperature of about 212° F (100° C)

ENGINE LOWER END

in an oven or on a hot plate. An easy way to check to see that it is at the proper temperature is to drop tiny drops of water on the case; if they sizzle and evaporate immediately, the temperature is correct. Heat only one case at a time.

CAUTION
Do not heat the cases with a torch (propane or acetylene)—never bring a flame into contact with the bearing or case. The direct heat will destroy the case hardening of the bearing and will likely warp the case half.

4. Remove the case from the oven or hot plate and hold onto the 2 crankcase studs with a kitchen pot holder, heavy gloves, or heavy shop cloths—it is *hot*.

5. Remove the oil seals if not already removed.

NOTE
A suitable size socket and extension work well for removing and installing bearings.

6. Hold the crankcase with the bearing side down and tap the bearing out. Repeat for all bearings in that case half.

7. While heating up the crankcase halves, place the new bearings in a freezer if possible. Chilling them will slightly reduce their overall diameter while the hot crankcase is slightly larger due to heat expansion. This will make installation much easier.

NOTE
Be sure to apply lithium based grease to the lips of new grease seals.

8. While the crankcase is still hot, press the new bearing(s) into place in the crankcase by hand until it seats completely. Do not hammer it in. If the bearing will not seat, remove it and cool it again. Reheat the crankcase and install the bearing again.

NOTE
Always install bearings with the manufacturer's mark or number facing outward or so that after the crankcase is assembled you can still see these marks.

NOTE
Pack all crankcase oil seals with a heat durable grease before installation.

9. Oil seals can be installed with a suitable size socket and extension (**Figure 42**). When installing oil seals, it is important to drive the seal in squarely. Drive the seals in until they are flush with the case.

10. Align the bearing retainers with the crankcase. Apply Loctite 242 (blue) to the retainer screws and tighten them securely. See **Figure 39** and **Figure 40**.

NOTE
Sometimes a main bearing will come off with the crankshaft instead of staying in the crankcase. If it is necessary to replace a bearing mounted on the crankshaft, a bearing adapter and a hydraulic press will be required.

Crankshaft Inspection

1. Clean the crankshaft thoroughly with solvent. Dry the crankshaft thoroughly. Then lubricate all bearing surfaces with a light coat of two-cycle engine oil.
2. Check the crankshaft journals and crankpin for scratches, heat discoloration or other defects.
3. Check flywheel taper, threads and keyway for damage. If one crankshaft half is damaged, the crankshaft can be disassembled and the damaged part replaced as described in this chapter.
4. Check crankshaft oil seal surfaces for grooving, pitting or scratches.

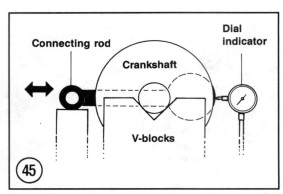

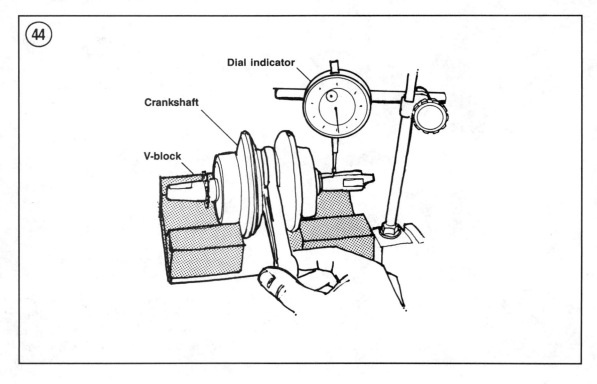

ENGINE LOWER END

5. Check crankshaft bearing surfaces for chatter marks and excessive or uneven wear. Minor cases of chatter mark may be cleaned up with 320 grit carborundum cloth. If 320 cloth is used, clean crankshaft in solvent and check surfaces. If they did not clean up properly, disassemble the crankshaft and replace the damaged part.

6. Slide the connecting rod to one side and check the connecting rod to crankshaft side clearance with a flat feeler gauge (**Figure 43**). Compare to dimensions given in **Table 1**. If the clearance is greater than specified the crankshaft assembly must be disassembled and the connecting rod replaced.

7. Check crankshaft runout with a dial indicator and V-blocks as shown in **Figure 44**. Retrue the crankshaft if the runout exceeds the service limit in **Table 1**.

8. Place the crankshaft in V-blocks and attach a dial indicator to the bottom of the connecting rod big end as shown in **Figure 45**. While holding the crankshaft in position, push the connecting forward and then push it in the opposite direction. The difference in the high and low readings is crankshaft radial clearance. If the radial clearance exceeds the service limit in **Table 1**, replace the connecting rod and rebuild the crankshaft as described in this chapter.

9. If necessary, overhaul the crankshaft as described in this chapter.

Crankshaft Overhaul

Crankshaft overhaul requires a hydraulic press of 30 to 32 tons capacity, holding jigs, crankshaft alignment jig and dial indicators. If you don't have this equipment, have the crankshaft overhauled by a qualified shop. A typical crankshaft is shown in **Figure 46**.

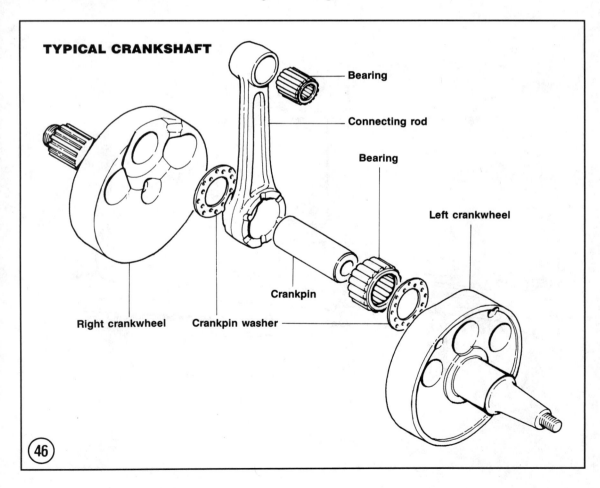

1. Measure the crank wheel width with a micrometer or vernier caliper (**Figure 47**). Record the measurement so that it can be duplicated during crankshaft reassembly.
2. Use a machinist's square and scribe a line across both crank halves. This line will be used for preliminary alignment during reassembly.
3. Place the crankshaft assembly in a suitable jig. Then press out the crankpin. Use an adapter between the press and crankpin. See **Figure 48**. Make sure to catch the lower crank half and crankpin assembly.
4. Remove the spacers, connecting rod and lower end bearing (**Figure 49**).
5. Press out the crankpin (**Figure 50**).
6. Wash the crank halves thoroughly in solvent.

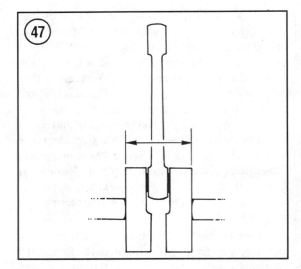

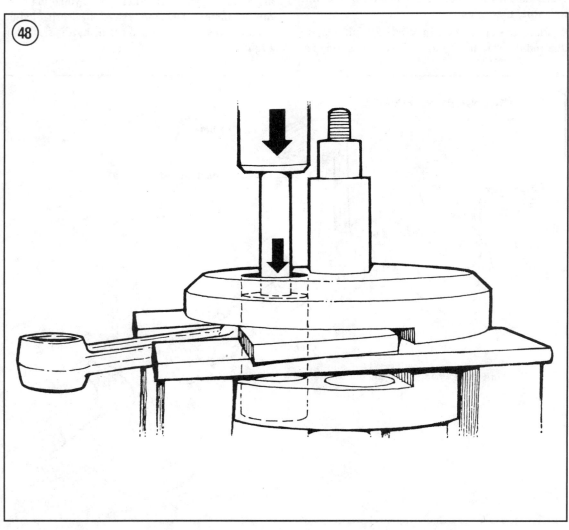

ENGINE LOWER END 111

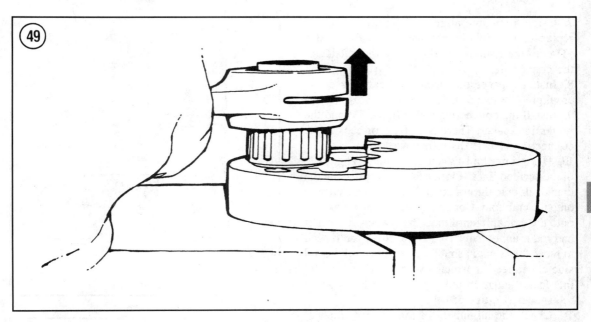

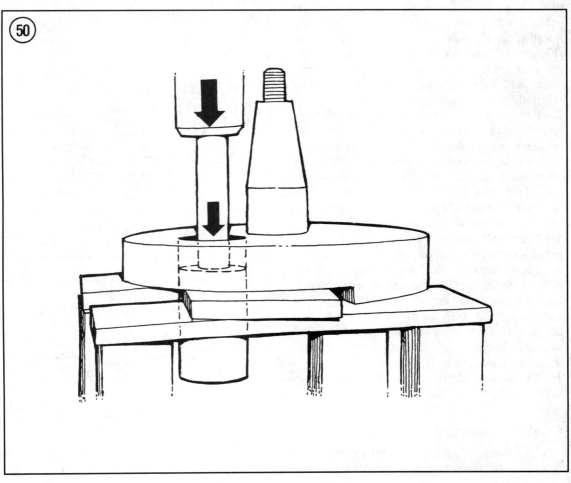

7. Using a suitable alignment fixture, press the replacement crankpin into one crank half (**Figure 51**) until the crankpin is flush with the outside of the crank half.
8. Install a spacer and the needle bearing over the crankpin (**Figure 52**).
9. Install the connecting rod (**Figure 53**) and the remaining spacer. There is no front or back to the connecting rod; it fits either way.
10. Using a machinist's square for initial alignment of the scribed lines (**Figure 54**), start pressing the crank half onto the crankpin. Press it about halfway onto the crankpin. Continue pressing the crank half onto the crankpin until the gap between crank half and rod is about 5 mm (0.20 in.). Now, you'll need to move the crank in small increments until the rod side clearance is correct. Insert a 0.45 mm (0.018 in.) feeler gauge in the gap between the rod and the spacer (**Figure 55**).
11. Check the alignment of the scribed lines. If they are misaligned, remove the crank from the press. Using a brass hammer, hit the partially installed crank half to correct the alignment (**Figure 56**). Recheck alignment. If misalignment has increased, you hit the crank in the wrong direction. After the scribed lines are aligned, reinstall the crank into the press.
12. Apply a slight amount of hydraulic force—enough to register on the press gauge but not enough to move the crank. Now, hit the press table with a metal hammer. This sharp blow will cause the crank to move a small amount. Repeat this procedure until the feeler gauge is a snug fit between the rod and spacer. Refer to connecting rod clearance in **Table 1** for clearance.
13. Release all pressure from the press. The feeler gauge should then slip out easily.
14. Measure crank wheel width (**Figure 47**) and compare to the specifications recorded in Step 1. Use this measurement as a guide only. The connecting rod side clearance should be the determining factor when assembling the crankshaft assembly, but the crank width must not be greater than the measurement in Step 1.
15. Check and adjust crankshaft alignment as described in this chapter.

Crankshaft Alignment

After overhauling the crankshaft or when disassembling the engine, it is important to check

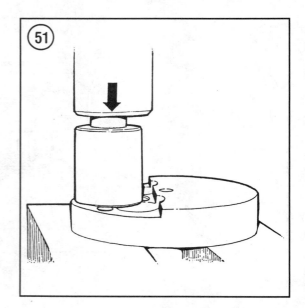

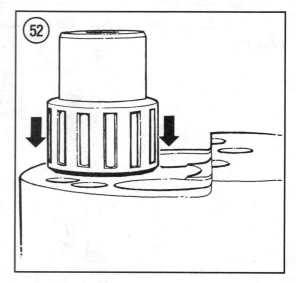

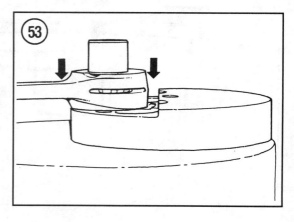

ENGINE LOWER END

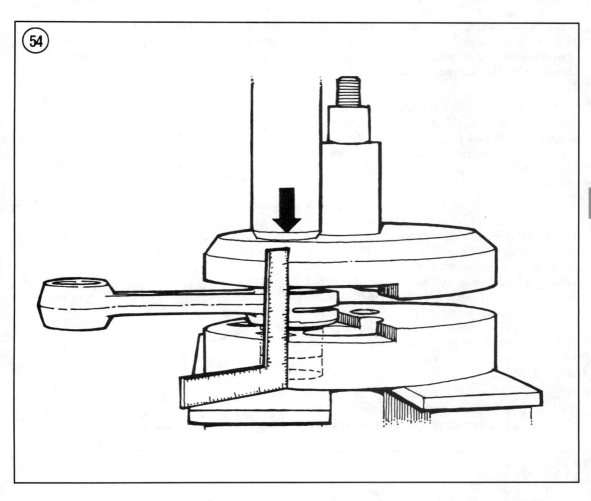

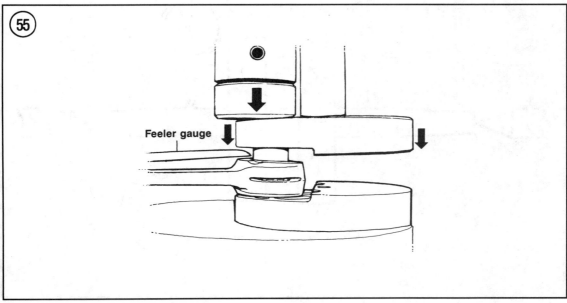

crankshaft alignment and adjust as required so that both crank halves and the shafts extending from them all rotate on a common center. The crankshaft should be checked for runout and wheel deflection as follows.

Mount the assembled crankshaft in a suitable fixture or on V-blocks using 2 dial indicators (**Figure 57**). Slowly rotate the crankshaft through one or more complete turns and observe both dial indicators. One of several conditions will be observed:

1. *Runout:* Neither dial indicator needle begins its swing at the same time, and the needles will move in opposite direction during part of the crankshaft rotation cycle. Each needle will probably indicate a different amount of total travel. This condition is caused by eccentricity (both crank wheels not being on the same center), as shown in **Figure 57**. To correct, slowly rotate the crankshaft assembly until the drive side dial gauge indicates its maximum. Mark the rim of the drive side crank wheel at the point in line with the plungers on both dial indicators.

Remove the crankshaft assembly. Then, while holding one side of the crankshaft, strike the chalk mark a sharp blow with a brass hammer (**Figure 56**). Recheck alignment after each blow, and continue this procedure until both dial gauges begin and end their swings at the same time.

CAUTION
Make sure that only a brass-faced hammer is used to strike the crankshaft wheels. A steel hammer will damage the crankshaft wheels, requiring replacement.

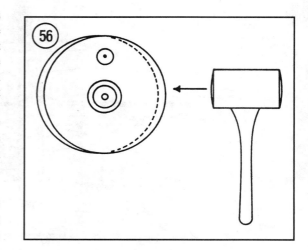

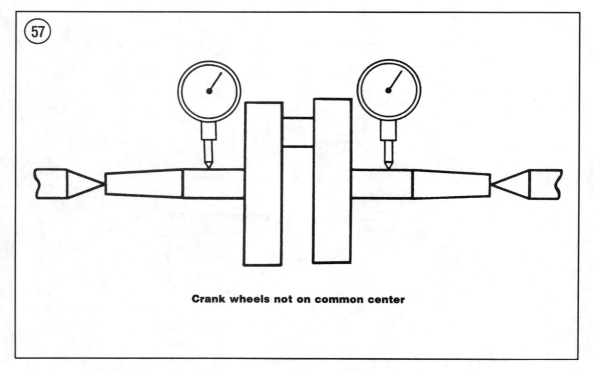

Crank wheels not on common center

ENGINE LOWER END

2. *Wheel deflection:* The crank wheels can become pinched or spread. This condition can be checked by measuring crank wheel width (**Figure 47**) at various spots or by checking runout with 2 dial indicators (**Figure 58** and **Figure 59**). When checking in an alignment jig, both dial indicators will indicate maximum travel when the crankpin is toward the dial gauges if the crank wheels are pinched. Correct the condition by removing the crankshaft assembly from the fixture. Then drive a wedge or chisel between the two crank wheels at a point opposite maximum dial gauge indication. Recheck alignment after each adjustment. Continue until the dial gauges indicate no more than 0.01 mm (0.0004 in.) runout.

If the dial gauges indicated their maximum when the crankpin was on the side of the alignment jig away from the dial gauges, the crank wheels are spread. Correct this condition by tapping the outside of one of the wheels toward the other with a brass hammer. Recheck alignment after each blow. Continue adjustment until runout is within 0.01 mm (0.0004 in.) runout.

NOTE
When adjusting wheel deflection, it will be necessary to check and adjust runout as required.

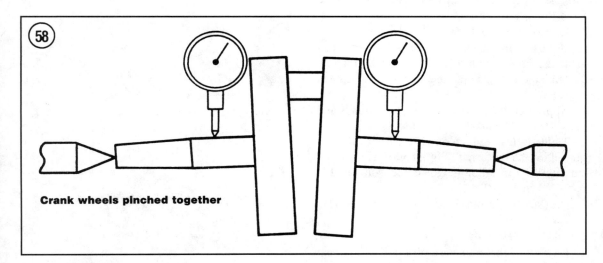

Crank wheels pinched together

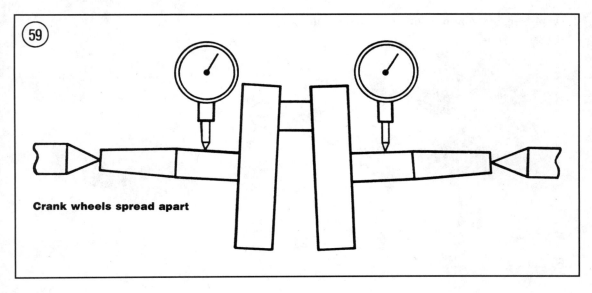

Crank wheels spread apart

Crankcase Stud Replacement

Damaged crankcase studs (**Figure 60**) can cause loss of engine performance and eventual engine damage from compression loss. The crankcase studs can be replaced with 2 wrenches, 2 nuts and a tube of Loctite 271 (red). See **Figure 61**.

1. Measure the distance from the crankcase to the top of the stud. The new studs should be installed to this length.
2. Thread 2 nuts onto the stud being removed (**Figure 62**).
3. Tighten the 2 nuts together as shown in **Figure 63**.
4. Using a wrench on the inner nut (**Figure 64**), turn the nut counterclockwise and remove the stud from the crankcase.
5. Remove the 2 nuts from the old stud.
6. Use a bottom tap and chase the stud hole. Then clean the threads with solvent and dry thoroughly.
7. Thread the 2 nuts onto the new stud and tighten together.
8. Apply Loctite 271 (red) to the stud threads and install the stud into the crankcase.
9. Tighten the stud clockwise with a wrench placed on the outer nut (**Figure 65**). Tighten the stud until its installed height is the same as that recorded in Step 1.
10. Loosen and remove the 2 nuts (**Figure 62**).

Crankcase Assembly

1. Pack all of the crankcase oil seals with a heat durable grease.
2. Apply engine oil to both crankshaft main bearings.

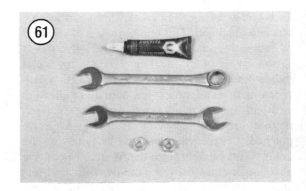

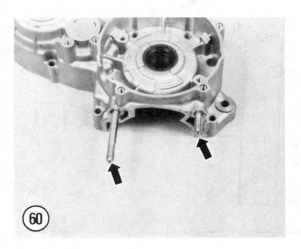
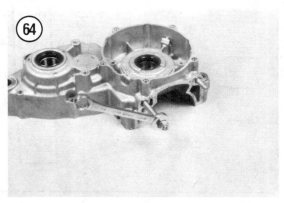

ENGINE LOWER END

3. If the crankshaft was removed, use a press and install it into the right-hand crankcase (**Figure 66**).

CAUTION
If you do not have access to a press, have the crankshaft installed by a dealer or machine shop. Do not drive the crankshaft into the bearing. Do not drive the crankshaft into the crankcase with a hammer.

4. Place the crankcase assembly onto wood blocks as shown in **Figure 67**.
5. Apply transmission oil to the inner race of all bearings (**Figure 68**) in the right-hand crankcase half.
6A. *1983-1985:* Install the transmission as follows:
   a. Coat all sliding surfaces with transmission oil.
   b. Install the mainshaft (A) and countershaft (B) into the right-hand crankcase. See **Figure 69**.
   c. See **Figure 70**. Insert the shift-drum into the right-hand crankcase. Secure the shift drum with the holder. Apply Loctite 242 (blue) onto the holder mounting screws and tighten the screws securely.
   d. **Figure 71** identifies the shift forks. Engage each shift fork with the correct transmission gear. Then fit the pin in the end of each shift fork into the correct shift drum groove.
   e. Install the shift fork shafts. Make sure the shafts engage the shaft holes in the right-hand crankcase.
6B. *1986-on:* Install the transmission as follows:
   a. Coat all sliding surfaces with transmission oil.

b. Install the mainshaft (A) and countershaft (B) into the right-hand crankcase. See **Figure 69**.
c. **Figure 72** identifies the shift forks.
d. Install the first/fourth gear shift fork (**Figure 73**). See A, **Figure 72**.
e. Install the second/third gear shift fork (**Figure 74**). See B, **Figure 72**.
f. Install the fifth/sixth gear shift fork (**Figure 75**). See C, **Figure 72**.
g. Install the shift drum (**Figure 76**).
h. Engage the shift fork pins with the correct shift drum grooves (**Figure 77**).
i. Install the shift fork shafts (**Figure 78**). Make sure the shafts engage the shaft holes in the right-hand crankcase.

NOTE
Step 7 is best done with the aid of a helper as the assemblies are loose and don't want to spin very easily. Have the helper spin the transmission shaft while you turn the shift drum through all the gears.

7. Spin the transmission shafts and shift through the gears using the shift drum. Make sure you can

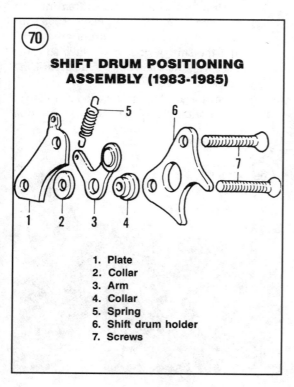

SHIFT DRUM POSITIONING ASSEMBLY (1983-1985)

1. Plate
2. Collar
3. Arm
4. Collar
5. Spring
6. Shift drum holder
7. Screws

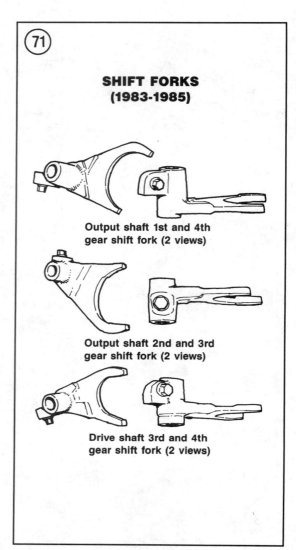

SHIFT FORKS (1983-1985)

Output shaft 1st and 4th gear shift fork (2 views)

Output shaft 2nd and 3rd gear shift fork (2 views)

Drive shaft 3rd and 4th gear shift fork (2 views)

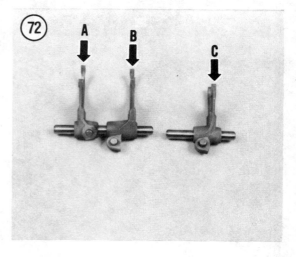

ENGINE LOWER END

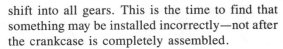

shift into all gears. This is the time to find that something may be installed incorrectly—not after the crankcase is completely assembled.

8. Shift the transmission assembly into NEUTRAL.

9. Set the crankcase assembly on 2 wood blocks or a wood holding fixture shown in **Figure 79**.

10. Install the 2 locating dowels (**Figure 79**).

11. Install the breather grommet (**Figure 80**) into the left-hand crankcase.

12. Apply a light coat of *non-hardening liquid gasket* such as Three Bond or equivalent to the mating surfaces of both crankcase halves.

NOTE
Make sure the mating surfaces are clean and free of all old gasket material. This will ensure a good seal.

13. Set the upper crankcase half over the one on the blocks. Push it down squarely into place until it reaches the crankshaft bearing, usually with about 1/2 inch left to go.
14. Use a press and press the upper crankcase half over the main bearing. A crankcase assembly tool can be used as shown in **Figure 81**. After the cases are assembled make sure each shaft rotates smoothly.

CAUTION
Crankcase halves should fit together without force. If the crankcase halves do not fit together completely, do not attempt to pull them together with the crankcase screws. Separate the crankcase halves and investigate the cause of the interference. If the transmission shafts were disassembled, recheck to make sure that a gear is not installed backwards. Also check that the shift drum neutral detent is not installed—it must be removed during this procedure. Crankcase halves are a matched set and are very expensive. Do not risk damage by trying to force the cases together.

15. Install all the crankcase screws (**Figure 82**) and tighten only finger-tight at first. Place any clips under the screws in the locations recorded during disassembly.
16. Securely tighten the screws in 2 stages in a crisscross pattern until they are firmly hand-tight.
17. After the crankcase halves are completely assembled, rotate the crankshaft and transmission shafts to make sure there is no binding. If any is present, disassemble the crankcase and correct the problem.
18. Install a new O-ring over the countershaft as shown in **Figure 83**.
19. Install all exterior engine assemblies as described in this chapter and other related chapters.

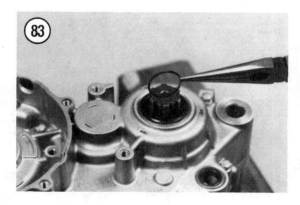

ENGINE LOWER END

Table 1 CRANKSHAFT SPECIFICATIONS

	Standard mm (in.)	Wear limit mm (in.)
Runout	0-0.03 (0-0.001)	0.10 (0.004)
Connecting rod side clearance	0.40-0.50 (0.016-0.020)	0.70 (0.028)
Crankshaft radial clearance	0.026-0.043 (0.0010-0.0017)	0.10 (0.004)

Table 2 ENGINE LOWER END TIGHTENING TORQUES

	N·m	ft.-lb.
Rotor bolt		
1983-1985	22	16
1986-on	27	20
Primary gear nut		
1983-1985	47	35
1986-on	59	43
Shift drum plate bolt		
1986-on	22	16
Engine drain bolt	20	14.5

CHAPTER SIX

CLUTCH, KICKSTARTER AND EXTERNAL SHIFT MECHANISM

This chapter describes removal, inspection and installation of the clutch, external shift mechanism, exhaust advancer system and kickstarter. These sub-assemblies can be removed with the engine in the frame. Clutch specifications are listed in **Table 1**. Clutch tightening torques are listed in **Table 2**. **Table 1** and **Table 2** are at the end of the chapter.

CLUTCH COVER
(1983-1985)

Removal/Installation

1. Drain the clutch/transmission oil as described in Chapter Three.
2. Place a motocross workstand or wood block(s) under the frame to support the bike securely.
3. Remove the rear brake pedal as follows:
   a. Loosen the rear brake rod wing nut (**Figure 1**).
   b. See **Figure 2**. Remove the rear brake pedal pivot bolt (A) and remove the brake pedal.
   c. Remove the return spring.
4. Remove the kickstarter lever nut (B, **Figure 2**) and pull the kickstarter lever off of the shaft.

NOTE
The kickstarter lever can be difficult to remove if rust forms between the lever

CLUTCH, KICKSTARTER AND EXTERNAL SHIFT MECHANISM

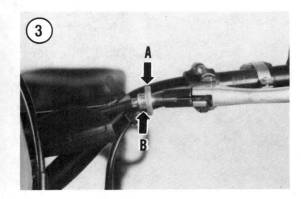

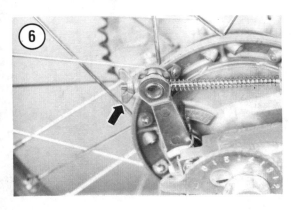

and the kickstarter shaft. If the kickstarter lever is tight, use a 2-jaw puller to remove it.

5. If it is necessary to disconnect the clutch cable from the clutch cover, perform the following:
   a. See **Figure 3**. Loosen the clutch cable adjuster locknut (A) and loosen the adjuster (B).
   b. Loosen the clutch cable adjuster locknuts at the engine (**Figure 4**) and disconnect the clutch cable at the release lever.
6. Remove the clutch cover mounting screws and remove the clutch cover (**Figure 5**).
7. Remove the 2 dowel pins and gasket.
8. Check the clutch cover oil seal for damage. If necessary, replace the seal by prying it out of the cover with a screwdriver. Install a new seal by driving it into the cover with a suitable size socket. Install the seal so that it is flush with the cover.
9. Installation is the reverse of these steps. Note the following.
10. Make sure to install the 2 dowel pins and a new cover gasket.
11. Refill the clutch/transmission oil as described in Chapter Three.
12. Adjust the clutch as described in Chapter Three.

CLUTCH COVER (1986-ON)

Removal/Installation

1. Drain the clutch/transmission oil as described in Chapter Three.
2. Place a motocross workstand or wood block(s) under the frame to support the bike securely.
3. Remove the rear brake pedal as follows:
   a. Loosen the rear brake rod wing nut (**Figure 6**).
   b. See **Figure 7**. Remove the rear brake pedal cover (A).
   c. Remove the rear brake pedal cover pivot bolt and remove the rear brake pedal (B).
   d. Remove the return spring.
4. Remove the kickstarter lever nut (C, **Figure 7**) and pull the kickstarter lever off of the shaft.

NOTE
The kickstarter lever can be difficult to remove if rust forms between the lever

and the kickstarter shaft. If the kickstarter lever is tight, use a 2-jaw puller to remove it.

5. If it is necessary to disconnect the clutch cable from the clutch cover, perform the following:
   a. See **Figure 3**. Loosen the clutch cable adjuster locknut (A) and loosen the adjuster (B).
   b. Disconnect the clutch cable (**Figure 8**) at the clutch cover.
6. Disconnect the exhaust valve lever as follows:
   a. Remove the right-hand lever cover (**Figure 9**).
   b. Remove the lever bolt (**Figure 10**).
   c. Lift the lever (**Figure 11**) up and remove it from the cylinder.
7. Remove the clutch cover mounting screws and remove the clutch cover (**Figure 12**).

CLUTCH, KICKSTARTER AND EXTERNAL SHIFT MECHANISM

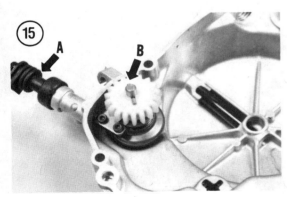

8. Remove the 2 dowel pins (**Figure 13**) and gasket.

9. The exhaust advancer assembly is installed in the clutch cover. If necessary, service it as described in this chapter.

10. Check the kickstarter shaft oil seal (**Figure 14**) for damage. If necessary, replace the seal by prying it out of the cover with a screwdriver. Install the new seal by driving it into the cover with a suitable size socket. Install the seal so that it is flush with the cover.

11. Installation is the reverse of these steps. Note the following.

12. Make sure to install the 2 dowel pins and a new cover gasket.

13. Refill the clutch/transmission oil as described in Chapter Three.

14. Adjust the clutch as described in Chapter Three.

Exhaust Advancer Assembly Removal/Installation

1. Remove the clutch cover as described in this chapter.

2. Turn the advancer lever (A, **Figure 15**) to the right and lift the exhaust advancer assembly (B, **Figure 15**) out of the clutch cover.

3. Remove the Allen bolts (A, **Figure 16**) and remove the advancer lever (B, **Figure 16**).

4. Remove the Phillips screw (A, **Figure 17**) and pull the advancer shaft (B, **Figure 17**) out of the cover.

5. Installation is the reverse of these steps. When installing the advancer assembly, align the

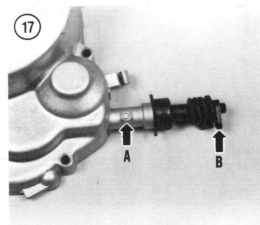

advancer lever (**Figure 18**) with the groove (**Figure 19**) in the assembly. See **Figure 20**. Tighten all bolts securely.

**Advancer Assembly
Disassembly/Inspection/Assembly**

Refer to **Figure 21**.

*NOTE
The advancer assembly is composed of a number of parts. Make sure to store parts in their order of removal to ease assembly. Figure 22 shows a discarded egg carton used to hold the components as they were removed.*

1. Compress the gear assembly and remove the pin (**Figure 23**).
2. Remove the gear (**Figure 24**).
3. Remove the spring (**Figure 25**).
4. Remove the spring seat (**Figure 26**).

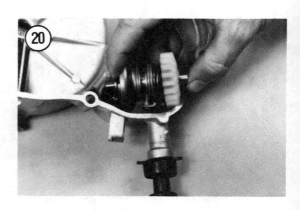

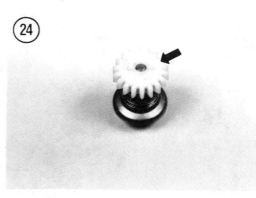

CLUTCH, KICKSTARTER AND EXTERNAL SHIFT MECHANISM

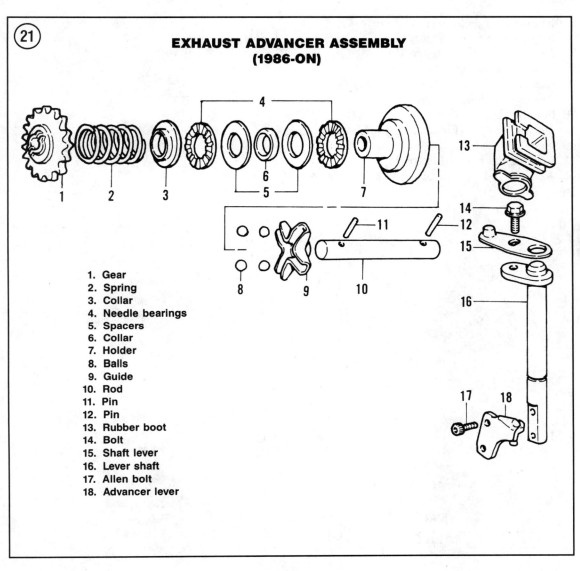

EXHAUST ADVANCER ASSEMBLY (1986-ON)

1. Gear
2. Spring
3. Collar
4. Needle bearings
5. Spacers
6. Collar
7. Holder
8. Balls
9. Guide
10. Rod
11. Pin
12. Pin
13. Rubber boot
14. Bolt
15. Shaft lever
16. Lever shaft
17. Allen bolt
18. Advancer lever

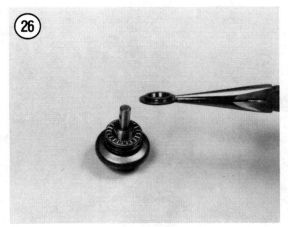

5. Remove the needle bearing (**Figure 27**).
6. Remove the spacer (**Figure 28**).
7. Remove the collar (**Figure 29**).
8. Remove the spacer (**Figure 30**).
9. Remove the needle bearing (**Figure 31**).
10. Remove the holder (**Figure 32**).
11. Remove the 4 steel balls (**Figure 33**).
12. Remove the pin (**Figure 34**) at the bottom of the guide.
13. Remove the guide (**Figure 35**).
14. Remove and discard the O-ring (A, **Figure 36**).

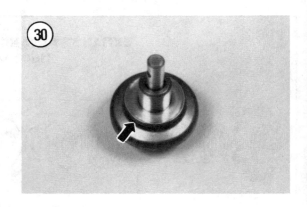

CLUTCH, KICKSTARTER AND EXTERNAL SHIFT MECHANISM

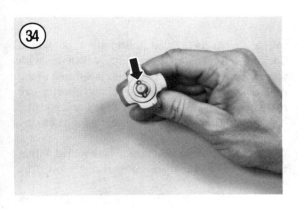

15. Clean all parts in solvent and thoroughly dry.
16. Check the shaft (B, **Figure 36**) for scoring or deep wear marks.
17. Check the needle bearings (**Figure 37**) for loose needles or other damage.
18. Check the gear (**Figure 38**) for worn or broken teeth. Check the pin slot in the gear for damage.
19. Check the guide (**Figure 39**) for deep scoring or other damage.
20. Check the holder (**Figure 40**) for deep scoring or other damage.

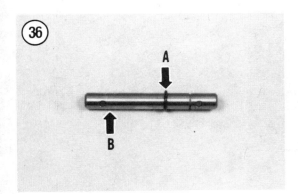

21. Replace worn or damaged parts.
22. Install a new O-ring (A, **Figure 36**) onto the shaft.
23. Slide the guide (**Figure 35**) onto the shaft. Secure the guide to the shaft with the pin (**Figure 34**).
24. Set the assembly upright so that the guide faces as shown in **Figure 41**.
25. Install the 4 steel balls into the guide (**Figure 33**).
26. Install the holder (**Figure 32**) over the guide/ball assembly.
27. Install the needle bearing (**Figure 31**).
28. Install the spacer (**Figure 30**).
29. Install the collar (**Figure 29**).
30. Install the spacer (**Figure 28**).
31. Install the needle bearing (**Figure 27**).
32. Install the spring seat (**Figure 26**).
33. Install the spring (**Figure 25**).
34. Install the gear (**Figure 24**) so that the pin slot faces up.
35. Compress the gear and install the pin (**Figure 23**).

CLUTCH

The clutch is a wet multiplate type which operates immersed in the oil supply it shares with the transmission. The clutch hub is splined to the transmission mainshaft and the clutch housing can rotate freely on the main shaft. The clutch housing is geared to the primary drive gear attached to the crankshaft.

The clutch release mechanism is mounted within the right-hand crankcase cover directly over the clutch mechanism.

The clutch can be removed with the engine in the frame.

Removal/Disassembly

Refer to **Figure 42** for this procedure.
1. Remove the clutch cover as described in this chapter.
2. Remove the pusher rod, washer, bearing and pusher plate (**Figure 43**) from the spring plate. See **Figure 44**.

CLUTCH, KICKSTARTER AND EXTERNAL SHIFT MECHANISM

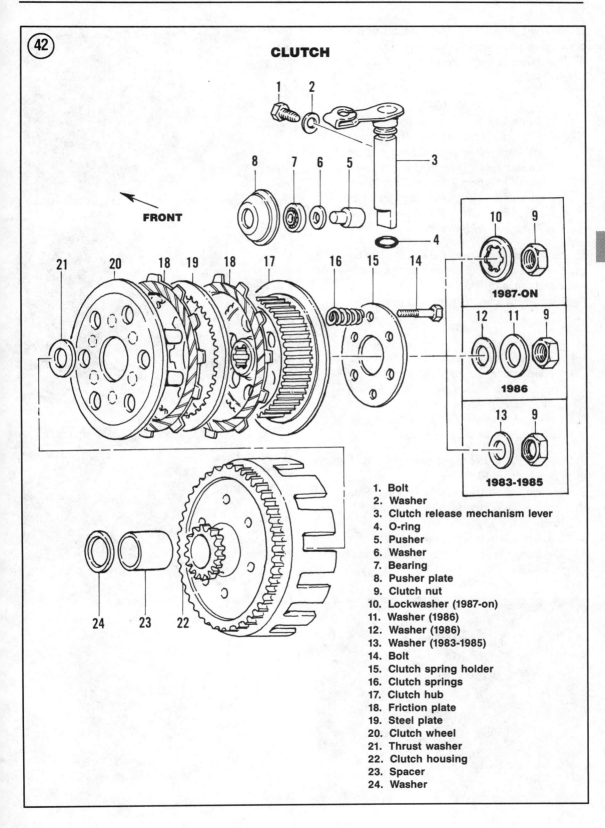

CLUTCH

1. Bolt
2. Washer
3. Clutch release mechanism lever
4. O-ring
5. Pusher
6. Washer
7. Bearing
8. Pusher plate
9. Clutch nut
10. Lockwasher (1987-on)
11. Washer (1986)
12. Washer (1986)
13. Washer (1983-1985)
14. Bolt
15. Clutch spring holder
16. Clutch springs
17. Clutch hub
18. Friction plate
19. Steel plate
20. Clutch wheel
21. Thrust washer
22. Clutch housing
23. Spacer
24. Washer

3. *1987-on:* Flatten the bent-up portion of the clutch hub nut lockplate (**Figure 42**).

4. Loosen and remove the clutch nut and washers (**Figure 45**).

> *NOTE*
> *You can lock the clutch by one of three different methods: shifting the transmission into gear and stepping on the brake pedal; inserting a soft piece of metal (copper) between the primary gear and the clutch housing ring gear teeth; by holding the rotor with a holding tool (**Figure 46**).*

5. See **Figure 47**. Loosen the spring plate bolts (A) gradually in a crisscross pattern, then remove the bolts and spring plate (B).

6. Remove the clutch springs (**Figure 48**).

> *NOTE*
> *If it is not necessary to disassemble the clutch hub/plate assembly, install one clutch spring, a large washer and one spring plate bolt as shown in A, **Figure 49**. The bolt will allow you to remove the hub assembly without having to align the plates during assembly.*

7. Remove the clutch/plate assembly (B, **Figure 49**). See **Figure 50**.
8. Remove the thrust washer (**Figure 51**).
9. Remove the clutch housing (**Figure 52**).
10. Remove the spacer (**Figure 53**).
11. Remove the washer (**Figure 54**).
12. Disassemble the clutch hub/plate assembly (**Figure 42**).

CLUTCH, KICKSTARTER AND EXTERNAL SHIFT MECHANISM

Inspection

Clutch service specifications and wear limits are listed in **Table 1**.

1. Clean all parts in a petroleum based solvent such as kerosene and thoroughly dry with compressed air.
2. Measure the free length of each clutch spring (**Figure 55**) with a vernier caliper. Replace any springs that are too short.
3. **Table 1** lists the number of stock friction discs (**Figure 56**) used in each model. The friction material is made of cork that is bonded onto an aluminum plate for warp resistance and durability. Measure the thickness of each friction plate at several places around the disc (**Figure 57**) with a vernier caliper. Replace all friction plates if any one is found too thin. Do not replace only 1 or 2 plates.

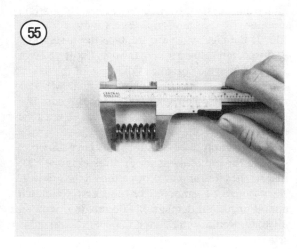

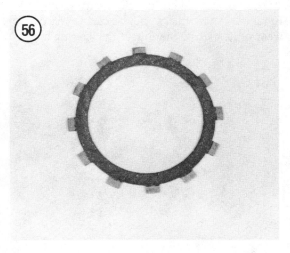

4. Place each friction plate on a surface plate or a thick piece of glass and check for warpage with a feeler gauge (**Figure 58**). If any plate is warped more than specified, replace the entire set of plates. Do not replace only 1 or 2 plates.

5. **Table 1** lists the number of stock clutch metal plates (**Figure 59**) used in each model. Place each clutch metal plate on a surface plate or a thick piece of glass and check for warpage with a feeler gauge (**Figure 60**). If any plate is warped more than specified, replace the entire set of plates. Do not replace only 1 or 2 plates.

6. The clutch metal plate inner teeth (**Figure 59**) mesh with the clutch hub splines (A, **Figure 61**). Check the splines for cracks or galling. They must be smooth for chatter-free clutch operation. If the clutch hub splines are worn, check the clutch metal plate teeth for wear or damage.

7. Inspect the shaft splines (B, **Figure 61**) in the clutch hub assembly. If damage is only a slight amount, remove any small burrs with a fine cut file. If damage is severe, replace the assembly.

8. Inspect the clutch spring towers (**Figure 62**) for thread damage or cracks at the base of the studs. Thread damage may be repaired with an M6 × 1 metric tap. Use kerosene on the tap threads. If a bolt stud is cracked, the clutch wheel must be replaced.

9. The friction plates (**Figure 56**) have tabs that slide in the clutch housing grooves (**Figure 63**). Inspect the tabs for cracks or galling in the grooves. They must be smooth for chatter-free clutch operation. Light damage can be repaired with an oilstone. Replace the clutch housing if damage is severe.

10. Check the clutch housing bearing bore (A, **Figure 64**) for cracks, deep scoring, excessive wear or heat discoloration. If the bearing bore is

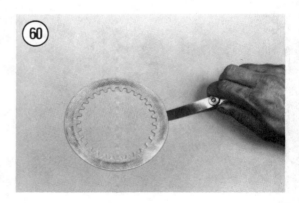

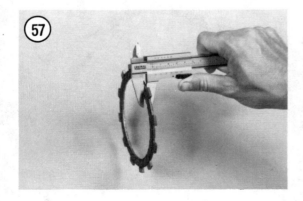

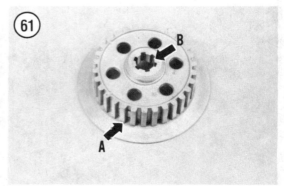

CLUTCH, KICKSTARTER AND EXTERNAL SHIFT MECHANISM

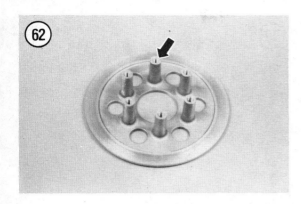

damaged, also check the mainshaft for damage. Replace worn or damaged parts.

11. Check the clutch housing gear teeth (B, **Figure 64**) for tooth wear, damage or cracks. Replace the clutch housing if necessary.

NOTE
If the clutch housing gear teeth are damaged, the gear teeth on the primary drive gear and the kickstarter idler gear may also be damaged.

12. Check the bearing in the pusher plate (**Figure 65**) for roughness or damage. Replace the bearing if necessary.

Assembly/Installation

Refer to **Figure 42** for this procedure.

1. Coat all clutch parts with transmission oil before reassembly.
2. Assemble the clutch hub/plate assembly as follows:
   a. Place the clutch hub onto the workbench so that it faces as shown in **Figure 61**.
   b. Install a friction plate (**Figure 66**) and then a steel plate (**Figure 67**). Alternate until all

of the clutch plates are installed. The last plate installed should be a friction plate (**Figure 68**).

c. Position the friction plates so that all of the plate tabs align as shown in **Figure 69**.
d. Install the clutch wheel (**Figure 70**).
e. Install a clutch spring bolt, spring and washer as shown in **Figure 71**. The bolt will hold the assembly together during installation.

3. Slide the washer (**Figure 54**) onto the mainshaft.
4. Install the spacer (**Figure 53**) onto the mainshaft.
5. Install the clutch housing (**Figure 52**).
6. Install the thrust washer (**Figure 51**).
7. Align the clutch hub/plate assembly with the clutch housing and install the hub assembly (**Figure 72**).
8. Remove the bolt, spring and washer installed in sub-step 2e.
9. Install the clutch springs (**Figure 73**).
10. Install the clutch spring holder (B, **Figure 74**) and the clutch spring bolts (A, **Figure 74**). Tighten the bolts in a crisscross pattern.
11. Referring to **Figure 42**, install the clutch nut and washers.

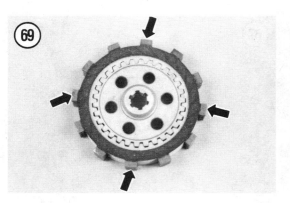

CLUTCH, KICKSTARTER AND EXTERNAL SHIFT MECHANISM

12. Secure the clutch housing with the same tool used during removal. Tighten the clutch nut to the torque specification in **Table 2**.
13. *1986-on:* Bend the lockwasher tab to lock the washer against the clutch nut.
14. Install the washer onto the pusher (**Figure 75**). Then insert the pusher/washer into the pusher holder (**Figure 76**).
15. Install the pusher plate assembly (**Figure 77**).
16. Install the clutch cover as described in this chapter.

PRIMARY DRIVE GEAR

The primary drive gear is part of the primary drive gear system, which transmits power from the crankshaft to the transmission.

Removal/Installation

Removal of the primary drive gear is not required except for replacement, crankcase disassembly or when checking the right-hand crankshaft oil seal during a pressure test.

1. Remove the clutch cover as described in this chapter.
2. Place a piece of copper between the pinion gear and the clutch housing drive gear (A, **Figure 78**).
3. Loosen the primary drive gear nut (B, **Figure 78**).
4. Remove the clutch as described in this chapter.
5. Remove the primary drive gear nut (**Figure 79**).
6. Remove the washer (**Figure 80**).
7. Slide the primary drive gear off of the crankshaft (**Figure 81**).
8. Installation is the reverse of these steps. Note the following:
   a. Do not attempt to tighten the primary drive gear nut until the clutch is installed.

b. Use the same tool to lock the clutch housing when tightening the primary drive gear nut. If you are using a piece of copper to lock the gears, place it underneath the gears at the point indicated in C, **Figure 78**.
c. Tighten the primary drive gear nut to the tightening torque in **Table 2**.
d. Install the clutch cover as described in this chapter.

CLUTCH CABLE

Replacement

In time the clutch cable will stretch to the point that it is no longer useful and will have to be replaced.

1. Remove the fuel tank.

NOTE
Some of the following figures are shown with the engine partially disassembled for clarity. It is not necessary to remove these components for cable replacement.

2. Pull the protective boot away from the clutch lever and loosen the locknut (A, **Figure 82**) and adjusting barrel (B, **Figure 82**).
3. Slip the cable end out of the hand lever.
4. Disconnect the clutch cable at the clutch release mechanism on the right-hand side of the engine.

NOTE
Prior to removing the cable make a drawing (or take a Polaroid picture) of the cable routing through the frame. It is very easy to forget its routing after it has been removed. Replace the cable exactly as it was, avoiding any

CLUTCH, KICKSTARTER AND EXTERNAL SHIFT MECHANISM

5. Pull the cable out of any retaining clips on the frame.
6. Remove the cable and replace it with a new one.
7. Install by reversing these removal steps. Make sure it is correctly routed with no sharp turns. Adjust the clutch cable as described in Chapter Three.

CLUTCH RELEASE MECHANISM

Removal/Installation

1. Remove the clutch cover as described in this chapter.
2. Remove the bolt and washer (A, **Figure 83**) and pull the release mechanism lever (B, **Figure 83**) out of the clutch cover.
3. Discard the O-ring.
4. Install by reversing these steps. Adjust the clutch as described in Chapter Three.

KICKSTARTER

Refer to **Figure 84** when servicing the kickstarter assembly.

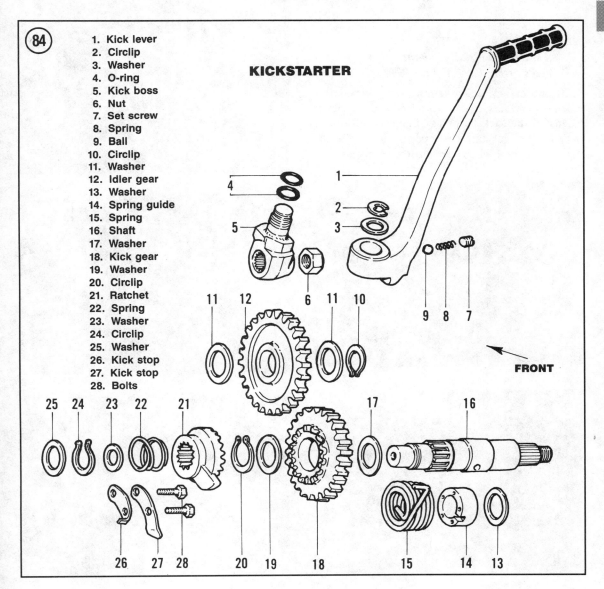

1. Kick lever
2. Circlip
3. Washer
4. O-ring
5. Kick boss
6. Nut
7. Set screw
8. Spring
9. Ball
10. Circlip
11. Washer
12. Idler gear
13. Washer
14. Spring guide
15. Spring
16. Shaft
17. Washer
18. Kick gear
19. Washer
20. Circlip
21. Ratchet
22. Spring
23. Washer
24. Circlip
25. Washer
26. Kick stop
27. Kick stop
28. Bolts

Removal/Installation

1. Remove the clutch as described in this chapter.
2. Remove the idler gear as follows:
   a. Remove the circlip (**Figure 85**).
   b. Remove the washer (**Figure 86**).
   c. Remove the idler gear (**Figure 87**).
   d. Remove the washer (**Figure 88**).
3. Using a pair of needlenose pliers, remove the kickstarter return spring from its post position in the crankcase (A, **Figure 89**). Release the spring and allow it to relax. Then rotate the kickstarter (B, **Figure 89**) assembly counterclockwise by hand and remove it from the crankcase. See **Figure 90**.

NOTE
*A washer is installed on the end of the kickstarter shaft (**Figure 90**).*

4. If necessary, disassemble the kickstarter assembly and service it as described in this chapter.
5. Install the kickstarter assembly as follows.
6. With the kickstarter stopper positioned at the top, insert the kickstarter into the crankcase.

CLUTCH, KICKSTARTER AND EXTERNAL SHIFT MECHANISM

7. Using needlenose pliers, hook the return spring into the hole in the crankcase (A, **Figure 89**).
8. Install the idler gear as follows:
   a. Install the washer (**Figure 88**).
   b. Install the idler gear (**Figure 87**).
   c. Install the washer (**Figure 86**).
   d. Install the circlip (**Figure 85**). Make sure the circlip seats in the groove completely.
9. Install the clutch cover as described in this chapter.

Disassembly/Inspection/Assembly

Refer to **Figure 84**.
1. Remove the washer (**Figure 91**).
2. Remove the plastic spring guide (A, **Figure 92**).
3. Remove the return spring (A, **Figure 93**).
4. Remove the washer (A, **Figure 94**).
5. Remove the circlip (B, **Figure 94**).
6. Remove the washer (C, **Figure 94**).
7. Remove the spring (**Figure 95**).
8. Remove the ratchet (**Figure 96**).

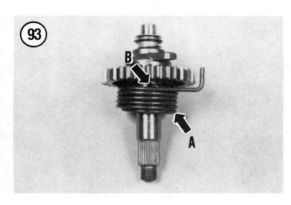

9. Remove the circlip (**Figure 97**).
10. Remove the washer (**Figure 98**).
11. Remove the kick gear (**Figure 99**).
12. Remove the washer (**Figure 100**).
13. Wash all parts thoroughly in solvent.
14. Check for broken, chipped, or missing teeth on the kick gear (**Figure 101**) and ratchet (**Figure 102**).
15. Check the kickstarter shaft (**Figure 103**) as follows:
    a. Check the kickstarter lever splines (A) for damage that would allow the lever to slip when the kickstarter is used.
    b. Check the shaft surface (B) for cracks, deep scoring or other damage.
    c. Check the return spring hole (C) in the shaft for cracks, wear or other conditions that would allow the spring to slip out when using the kickstarter.
    d. Install the kick gear onto the shaft and check that the gear operates smoothly on the shaft. Check the shaft splines (D) for cracks or other damage.
    e. Replace the kickstarter shaft if necessary.
16. Check the return spring (**Figure 104**) for cracks, breakage or other damage. Replace if necessary.
17. Apply assembly oil to the sliding surfaces of all parts.
18. Install the washer (**Figure 100**).
19. Install the kick gear so that the splines face in the direction shown in **Figure 99**.
20. Install the washer (**Figure 98**).
21. Secure the kick gear with the circlip (**Figure 97**).
22. Align the index mark on the shaft with the index mark on the ratchet (**Figure 105**) and install the ratchet. See **Figure 96**.

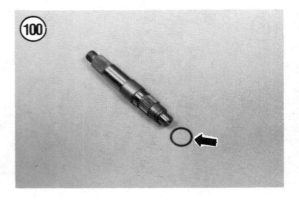

CLUTCH, KICKSTARTER AND EXTERNAL SHIFT MECHANISM

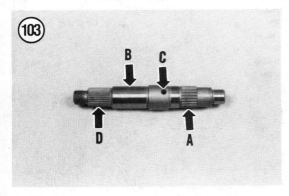

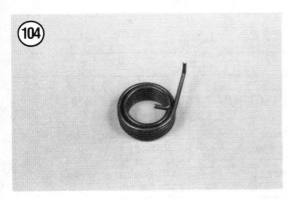

23. Install the spring (**Figure 95**).
24. Install the washer (C, **Figure 94**).
25. Install the circlip (B, **Figure 94**).
26. Install the washer (A, **Figure 94**).
27. Install the return spring onto the kickstarter shaft in the direction shown in A, **Figure 93**. Insert the end of the spring into the hole (B, **Figure 93**) in the shaft.
28. Install the spring guide (A, **Figure 92**) as follows:
    a. Align the notch in the spring guide (B, **Figure 92**) with the portion of the return spring that fits into the shaft and install the spring guide.
    b. Push the spring guide all the way down until it bottoms (**Figure 106**).
29. Install the washer (**Figure 91**).

EXTERNAL SHIFT MECHANISM

The external shift mechanism is located on the same side of the crankcase as the clutch assembly and can be removed with the engine in the frame. To remove the shift drum and shift forks it is necessary to remove the engine and split the crankcases.

The gearshift lever is subject to a lot of abuse under race conditions. If the motorcycle has been in a hard spill, the gearshift lever may have been hit and the shaft may have been bent.

CAUTION
If the shaft is bent, it is very hard to straighten without subjecting the crankcase to abnormal stress where the shaft enters the case. If is much cheaper in the long run to replace the

shaft than risk damaging a set of expensive crankcases.

If the shaft is bent enough to prevent it from being withdrawn from the crankcase, there is little recourse but to cut the shaft off with a hacksaw very close to the crankcase. After cutting off the end of the shaft, use a file or rotary grinder to remove all burrs from the shaft before removing it.

Removal/Installation

Refer to **Figure 107** (1983) or **Figure 108** (1984-on) for this procedure.

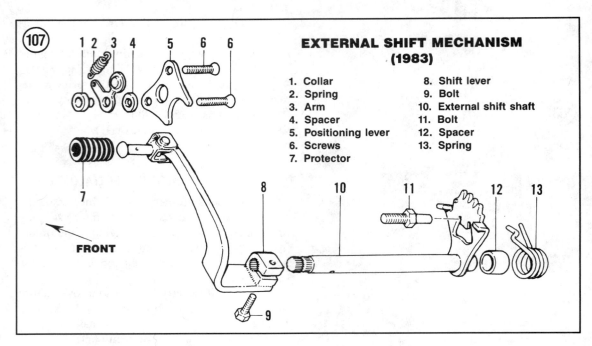

EXTERNAL SHIFT MECHANISM (1983)

1. Collar
2. Spring
3. Arm
4. Spacer
5. Positioning lever
6. Screws
7. Protector
8. Shift lever
9. Bolt
10. External shift shaft
11. Bolt
12. Spacer
13. Spring

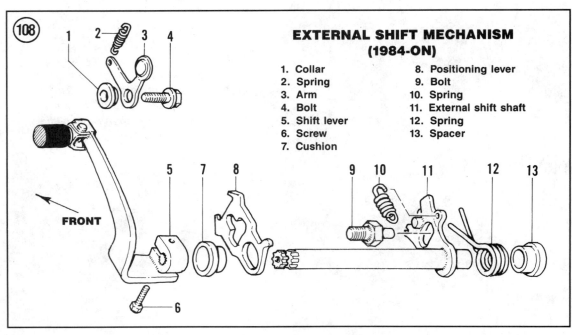

EXTERNAL SHIFT MECHANISM (1984-ON)

1. Collar
2. Spring
3. Arm
4. Bolt
5. Shift lever
6. Screw
7. Cushion
8. Positioning lever
9. Bolt
10. Spring
11. External shift shaft
12. Spring
13. Spacer

CLUTCH, KICKSTARTER AND EXTERNAL SHIFT MECHANISM

109

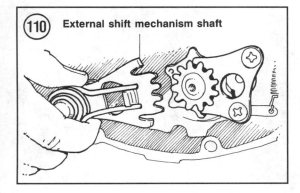

110 External shift mechanism shaft

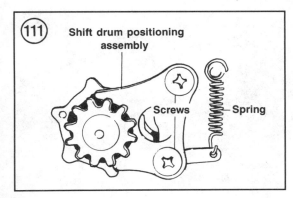

111 Shift drum positioning assembly — Screws — Spring

112

1. Remove the pinch bolt and remove the shift lever (**Figure 109**) from the left-hand side.
2. Remove the clutch as described in this chapter.
3. Remove the idler gear as described under *Kickstarter Removal* in this chapter.
4A. *1983:* Perform the following:
   a. Remove the external shift shaft (**Figure 110**).
   b. Remove the spring (**Figure 111**).
   c. Remove the 2 Phillips screws and remove the shift drum positioning plate (**Figure 111**).

NOTE
The pawls removed in sub-step d are spring loaded. Remove them carefully.

   d. Remove the shift drum ratchet and pawl assembly.
4B. *1984-on:* Perform the following:
   a. Remove the external shift shaft (**Figure 112**).
   b. Disconnect and remove the spring (**Figure 113**).

113

114

c. Remove the bolt and remove the pawl assembly (**Figure 114**).

5. *1986-on:* Remove the shift drum segment as follows:

   a. Remove the bolt (**Figure 115**).
   b. Remove the segment (**Figure 116**).
   c. Remove the pin (**Figure 117**) from the shift drum.

6. Inspect the external shift mechanism assembly as follows. Replace worn or damaged parts.

   a. Check the shift shaft for cracks or bending. Check the splines on the end of the shaft for damage.
   b. Check the return spring on the shift shaft. The return spring arms should be installed on the shaft arm as shown in **Figure 118**. Replace the return spring if it shows signs of fatigue or if it is cracked.
   c. Check the engagement arms on the shift pawl for wear or damage. Damage or severe wear of the engagement arms will cause shifting problems.

7. *1986-on:* Install the shift drum segment as follows:

   a. Insert the pin (**Figure 117**) into the shift drum.
   b. Align the hole in the back of the segment with the pin and install the segment (**Figure 116**).
   c. Apply Loctite 242 (blue) to the bolt (**Figure 115**) and tighten it to the torque specification in **Table 2**.

8A. *1983:* Perform the following:

   a. Install the shift drum ratchet and pawl assembly.
   b. Install the shift drum positioning assembly (**Figure 111**) and secure it with the 2 Phillips screws.
   c. Install the spring (**Figure 111**).
   d. Install the external shift shaft (**Figure 110**).

8B. *1984-on:* Perform the following:

   a. Install the pawl assembly (**Figure 114**) and secure it with the attaching bolt.
   b. Install the spring (**Figure 113**).
   c. Install the external shift shaft (**Figure 112**).

9. Reverse Steps 1-3 to complete installation.

CLUTCH, KICKSTARTER AND EXTERNAL SHIFT MECHANISM

Table 1 CLUTCH SPECIFICATIONS

	Standard mm (in.)	Wear limit mm (in.)
Clutch spring free length	20.6 (0.81)	—
Friction plate thickness	2.92-3.08 (0.115-0.121)	2.8 (0.11)
Friction plate/clutch housing clearance		
1983-1985	0.05-0.45 (0.002-0.018)	0.6 (0.02)
1986-on	0.25-0.55 (0.010-0.022)	0.7 (0.028)
Clutch plate warpage		
1983-1985	0-0.15 (0-0.006)	0.30 (0.012)
1986-on	0-.20 (0-0.008)	0.30 (0.012)
Number of clutch plates 1983-on		
Friction	7	
Steel	6	

Table 2 CLUTCH TIGHTENING TORQUES

	N·m	ft.-lb.
Primary drive gear nut		
1983-1985	47	35
1986-on	59	43
Shift drum segment bolt		
1986-on	22	16
Clutch hub nut		
1983-1985	59	43
1986-on	78	58

CHAPTER SEVEN

TRANSMISSION AND INTERNAL SHIFT MECHANISM

The transmission and internal shift mechanism (shift drum and forks) are basically the same for all models. The transmission on all models is a 6-speed unit. To gain access to the transmission and internal shift mechanism it is necessary to remove the engine and split the crankcase (Chapter Five). Once the crankcase has been split, removal of the transmission and shift drum and forks is a simple task of pulling the assemblies up and out of the crankcase.

Transmission ratios are listed in **Table 1**. Service specifications are listed in **Table 2**. **Table 1** and **Table 2** are at the end of the chapter.

NOTE
If disassembling a used, well run-in transmission for the first time by yourself, pay particular attention to any additional shims that may have been added by a previous owner. These may have been added to take up the tolerance of worn components and must be reinstalled in the same position since the shims have developed a wear pattern. If new parts are going to be installed these shims may be eliminated. This is something you will have to determine upon reassembly.

TRANSMISSION OPERATION

The basic transmission has 6 pairs of constantly meshed gears (**Figure 1**) on the mainshaft (A) and countershaft (B). Each pair of meshed gears gives one gear ratio. In each pair, one of the gears is locked to its shaft and always turns with it. The other gear is not locked to its shaft and can spin freely on it. Next to each free spinning gear is a third gear which is splined to the same shaft, always turning with it. This third gear can slide from side to side along the shaft splines. The side of the sliding gear and the free

TRANSMISSION AND INTERNAL SHIFT MECHANISM

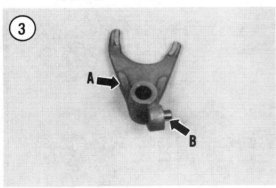

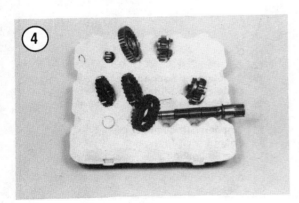

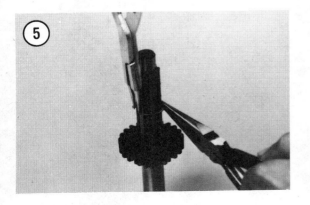

spinning gear have mating "dogs" and slots." When the sliding gear moves up against the free spinning gear, the 2 gears are locked together, locking the free spinning gear to its shaft. Since both meshed mainshaft and countershaft gears are now locked to their shafts, power is transmitted at that gear ratio.

Shift Drum and Forks

Each sliding gear has a deep groove machined around its outside (**Figure 2**). The curved shift fork arm rides in this groove, controlling the side-to-side sliding of the gear, and therefore the selection of different gear ratios. Each shift fork (A, **Figure 3**) slides back and forth on a guide shaft, and has a peg (B, **Figure 3**) that rides in a groove machined in the shift drum. When the shift linkage rotates the shift drum, the zigzag grooves move the shift forks and sliding gears back and forth.

TRANSMISSION TROUBLESHOOTING

Refer to *Transmission* in Chapter Two.

TRANSMISSION OVERHAUL

A 6-speed transmission is used on all 1983 and later KDX200 models.

Removal/Installation

Remove and install the transmission and internal shift mechanism as described under *Crankcase Disassembly/Reassembly* in Chapter Five.

Transmission Service Notes

1. A divided container such as an egg carton (**Figure 4**) can be used to help maintain correct alignment and position of the parts as they are removed from the transmission shafts.
2. The circlips are a tight fit on the transmission shafts. They should all be replaced during reassembly.
3. Circlips will turn and fold over, making removal and installation difficult. To ease replacement, open the circlip with a pair of circlip pliers while at the same time holding the back of the circlip with a pair of pliers and remove it. See **Figure 5**.

CHAPTER SEVEN

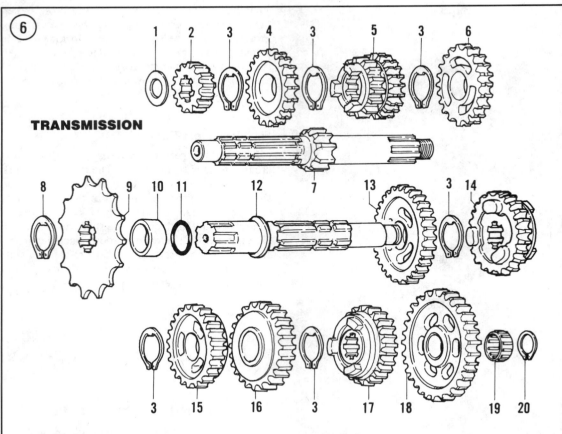

TRANSMISSION

1. Washer
2. Mainshaft second gear
3. Circlip
4. Mainshaft fifth gear
5. Mainshaft third/fourth combination gear
6. Mainshaft sixth gear
7. Mainshaft
8. Circlip
9. Countershaft sprocket
10. Spacer
11. O-ring
12. Countershaft
13. Countershaft second gear
14. Countershaft fifth gear
15. Countershaft third gear
16. Countershaft fourth gear
17. Countershaft sixth gear
18. Countershaft first gear
19. Needle bearing
20. Circlip

TRANSMISSION AND INTERNAL SHIFT MECHANISM

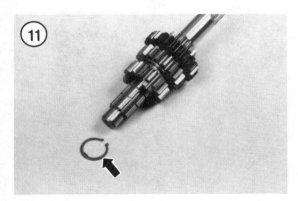

Mainshaft
Disassembly/Assembly

Refer to **Figure 6** for this procedure.
1. Place the assembled shaft into a large can or plastic bucket and thoroughly clean with solvent and stiff brush. Dry with compressed air or let sit on rags to drip dry.
2. Remove the washer (**Figure 7**).
3. Remove second gear (**Figure 8**).
4. Remove the circlip (**Figure 9**).
5. Remove fifth gear (**Figure 10**).
6. Remove the circlip (**Figure 11**).
7. Remove third/fourth combination gear (**Figure 12**).
8. Remove the circlip (**Figure 13**).
9. Remove sixth gear (**Figure 14**).
10. Inspect the mainshaft parts as described under *Transmission Inspection* in this chapter.

NOTE
*When installing the circlips during main shaft assembly, make sure to align the notch in the bottom of each circlip (**Figure 15**) with a shaft groove.*

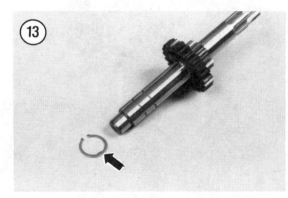

11. Slide on sixth gear (**Figure 14**) and install the circlip into the groove next to the gear.

12. Slide on third/fourth combination gear in the direction shown in **Figure 12**.

13. Install the circlip into the groove closest to the third/fourth combination gear (**Figure 16**).

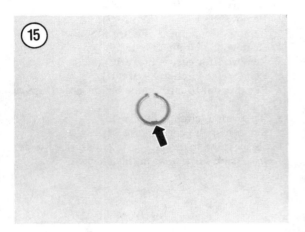

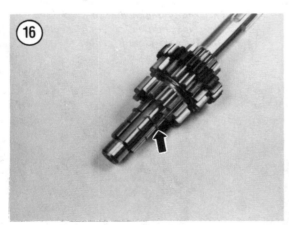

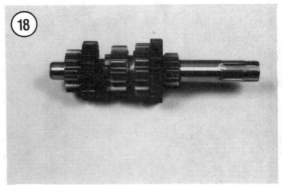

TRANSMISSION AND INTERNAL SHIFT MECHANISM

14. Slide on fifth gear (**Figure 10**).
15. Install the circlip (**Figure 17**).
16. Slide on second gear (**Figure 8**).
17. Install the washer (**Figure 7**).
18. After assembly is complete refer to **Figure 18** for the correct placement of all gears.

Countershaft
Disassembly/Assembly

Refer to **Figure 6** for this procedure.
1. Place the assembled shaft into a large can or plastic bucket and thoroughly clean with solvent and a stiff brush. Dry with compressed air or let it sit on rags to drip dry.
2. Remove the circlip (**Figure 19**).
3. Remove the needle bearing (**Figure 20**).
4. Remove first gear (**Figure 21**).
5. Remove sixth gear (**Figure 22**).
6. Remove the circlip (**Figure 23**).
7. Remove fourth gear (**Figure 24**).
8. Remove third gear (**Figure 25**).
9. Remove the circlip (**Figure 26**).
10. Remove fifth gear (**Figure 27**).
11. Remove the circlip (**Figure 28**).
12. Remove second gear (**Figure 29**).

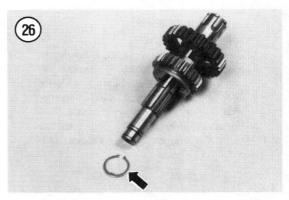

13. Check the countershaft assembly as described under *Transmission Inspection* in this chapter.

NOTE
When installing the circlips during countershaft assembly, make sure to align the notch in the bottom of each circlip (Figure 15) with a shaft groove.

14. Install second gear (**Figure 29**) and install the circlip in the groove next to the gear.
15. Install fifth gear (**Figure 27**).
16. Install the circlip in the groove closest to fifth gear (**Figure 30**).
17. Install third gear (**Figure 25**).
18. Install fourth gear (**Figure 24**).
19. Install the circlip in the groove next to fourth gear (**Figure 31**).
20. Install sixth gear (**Figure 22**).
21. Install first gear (**Figure 19**).
22. Install the needle bearing (**Figure 20**).
23. Install the circlip so that it fits into the groove next to the needle bearing (**Figure 32**).
24. After assembly is complete refer to **Figure 33** for the correct placement of all gears. Make sure all circlips are seated correctly in the countershaft grooves.

NOTE
After both transmission shafts have been assembled, mesh the 2 assemblies together in the correct position (Figure 34). Check that all gears meet correctly. This is your last check prior to installing the assemblies into the crankcase to make sure they are correctly assembled.

TRANSMISSION AND INTERNAL SHIFT MECHANISM

Transmission Inspection

1. Check each gear for excessive wear, burrs, pitting, or chipped or missing teeth.
2. Make sure the lugs (dogs) on the gears are in good condition. See **Figure 35**.
3. Check each stationary gear dog slot (**Figure 36**) for cracks, rounding or other damage.
4. Measure each sliding gear groove width (**Figure 37**) with a vernier caliper and compare to the wear limit specification in **Table 2**.
5. Make sure that all gears slide on their respective shafts smoothly.

NOTE
Defective gears should be replaced, and it is a good idea to replace the mating gear even though it may not show as much wear or damage.

6. Check the mainshaft (**Figure 38**) and countershaft (**Figure 39**) splines for wear, cracks or other damage. Also check the mainshaft first gear (**Figure 38**). If the gear is damaged, replace the mainshaft assembly.
7. Replace all circlips during reassembly. In addition, check the washers for burn marks, scoring or cracks. Replace if necessary.

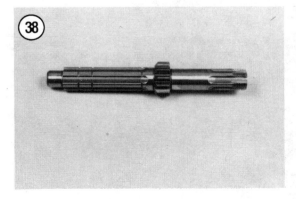

INTERNAL SHIFT MECHANISM

Removal/Installation

Remove and install the transmission and internal shift mechanism as described under *Crankcase Disassembly/Reassembly* in Chapter Five.

Inspection

Refer to **Figure 40** (1983-1985) or **Figure 41** (1986-on) for this procedure.

1. Inspect each shift fork (A, **Figure 42**) for signs of wear or cracking. Examine the shift forks at the points where they contact the slider gear (B, **Figure 42**). This surface should be smooth with no signs of wear or damage. Make sure the forks slide smoothly on their shaft (**Figure 43**). Make sure the shaft is not bent. This can be checked by removing the shift forks from the shaft and rolling the shaft on a piece of glass. Any clicking noise detected indicates that the shaft is bent.
2. Check for any arc-shaped wear or burn marks on the shift forks. This indicates that the shift fork has come in contact with the gear. The fork fingers have become excessively worn and the fork must be replaced.
3. Measure the diameter of each shift fork guide pin with a vernier caliper (**Figure 44**) and compare to the wear limit in **Table 2**.
4. Measure the width of each shift fork finger with a vernier caliper (**Figure 45**) and compare to the wear limit in **Table 2**.
5. Check grooves in the shift drum (**Figure 46**) for wear or roughness. Then measure each groove width with a vernier caliper (**Figure 47**) and compare to the wear limit in **Table 2**.
6. Replace worn or damaged parts.

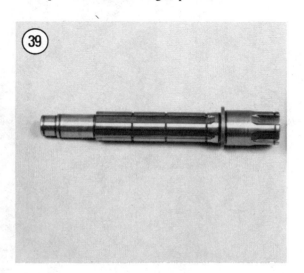

INTERNAL SHIFT MECHANISM (1983-1985)

1. Shift fork
2. Screw
3. Shaft
4. Shift drum
5. Plate
6. Bearing
7. Segment
8. Shaft
9. Shift fork
10. Shift fork

TRANSMISSION AND INTERNAL SHIFT MECHANISM

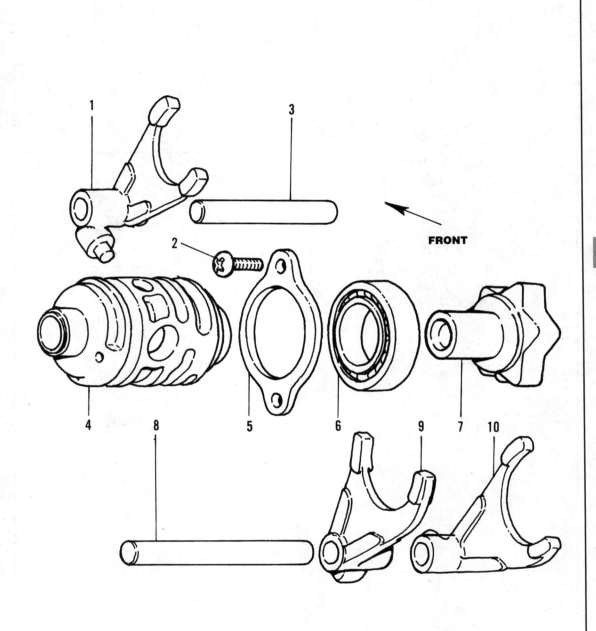

CHAPTER SEVEN

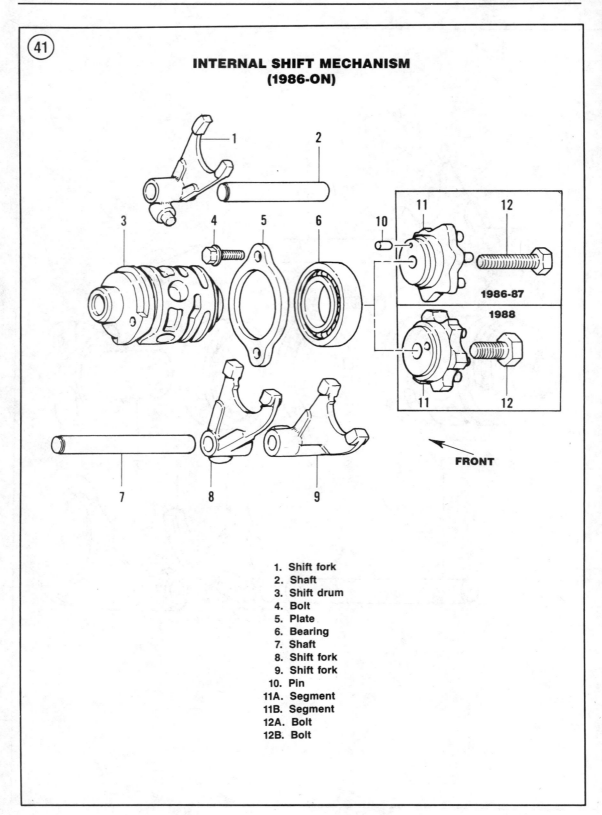

INTERNAL SHIFT MECHANISM
(1986-ON)

1. Shift fork
2. Shaft
3. Shift drum
4. Bolt
5. Plate
6. Bearing
7. Shaft
8. Shift fork
9. Shift fork
10. Pin
11A. Segment
11B. Segment
12A. Bolt
12B. Bolt

TRANSMISSION AND INTERNAL SHIFT MECHANISM

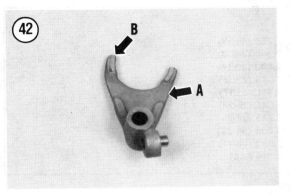

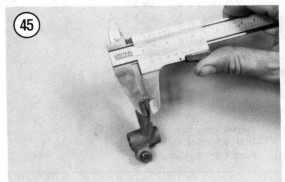

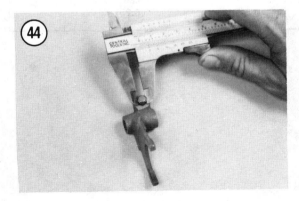

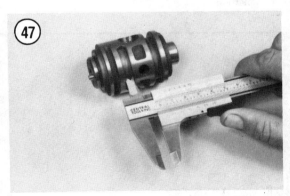

Tables are on the next page.

Table 1 TRANSMISSION GEAR RATIOS

Gear ratio	
1st	
1983-1985	2.769 (36/13)
1986-on	2.692 (35/13)
2nd	2.000 (28/14)
3rd	1.533 (23/15)
4th	1.235 (21/17)
5th	1.041 (25/24)
6th	0.869 (20/23)
Primary reduction ratio	2.863 (63/22)
Final reduction ratio	3.692 (48/13)
Overall drive ratio	9.194 (top)

Table 2 SHIFT FORK/SHIFT DRUM SERVICE SPECIFICATIONS

	Standard mm (in.)	Wear limit mm (in.)
Shift fork finger thickness	3.9-4.0 (0.153-0.157)	3.7 (0.146)
Sliding gear groove width	4.05-4.15 (0.159-0.163)	4.25 (0.167)
Shift drum groove width	6.05-6.20 (0.238-0.244)	6.25 (0.246)
Shift fork guide pin diameter		
1983-1985	5.975-5.994 (0.2352-0.2360)	5.85 (0.23)
1986-on	5.90-6.00 (0.232-0.236)	5.85 (0.23)

CHAPTER EIGHT

FUEL AND EXHAUST SYSTEMS

The fuel system consists of the fuel tank, shutoff valve, and a single Mikuni carburetor (1983-1987) or Keihin carburetor (1988) and air cleaner. There are slight differences among the various models and they are noted in the procedures.

The exhaust system consists of an exhaust pipe assembly and a silencer.

This chapter includes service procedures for all parts of the fuel system and exhaust system.

Carburetor specifications are listed in **Table 1** (end of chapter).

AIR CLEANER

The air cleaner must be cleaned frequently. Refer to Chapter Three for specific procedures and service intervals.

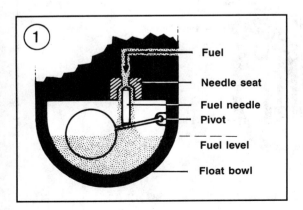

CARBURETOR OPERATION

For proper operation, a gasoline engine must be supplied with fuel and air mixed in proper proportions by weight. A mixture in which there is an excess of fuel is said to be rich. A lean mixture is one which contains insufficient fuel. A properly adjusted carburetor supplies the proper mixture to the engine under all operating conditions.

The carburetors installed on KDX200 models consist of several major systems. A float and float valve mechanism maintain a constant fuel level in the float bowl. The pilot system supplies fuel at low speeds. The main fuel system supplies fuel at medium and high speeds. Finally a starter (choke) system supplies a rich mixture needed to start a cold engine.

Float Mechanism

To assure a steady supply of fuel, the carburetor is equipped with a float valve through which fuel flows by gravity from the gas tank into the float bowl (**Figure 1**). Inside the bowl is a combined float assembly that moves up and down with the fuel level. Resting on the float arm is a float needle, which rides inside the float valve. The float valve regulates fuel flow into the float bowl. The float needle and float valve contact surfaces are machined very accurately to insure correct fuel flow calibration. As the float rises, the float needle rises inside the float valve and blocks it, so that when the fuel has reached the required level in the float bowl, no more fuel can enter.

Pilot and Main Fuel Systems

The carburetor's purpose is to supply atomized fuel and mix it in correct proportions with air that is drawn in through the air intake. At small throttle openings (from idle to 1/8 throttle) a small amount of fuel is siphoned through the pilot jet by suction from the incoming air (**Figure 2**). As the throttle is opened further, the air stream begins to siphon fuel through the main jet and needle jet. The tapered needle increases the effective flow capacity of the needle jet as it rises with the throttle slide, in that it occupies progressively less of the area of the needle jet (**Figure 3**). In addition, the amount of cutaway in the leading edge of the throttle slide aids in controlling the fuel/air mixture during partial throttle openings.

At full throttle, the carburetor venturi is fully open and the needle is lifted far enough to permit the main jet to flow at full capacity. See **Figure 4** and **Figure 5**.

Starting System

The starting system consists of a starter plunger, mixing tube, starter jet and air passage. When the plunger valve is lifted, it opens the air passage permitting air to flow through the passage where it siphons fuel through the starter jet, into the mixing tube and then into the air passage where it is mixed (fuel-rich) and discharged into the throttle bore.

CARBURETOR SERVICE
(1983-1987)

Carburetor removal and cleaning should be performed after every race on competition bikes. On non-competition bikes, service should be performed whenever the engine is decarbonized or when poor engine performance, hesitation, and little or no response to mixture adjustment is observed. The service interval time will become natural to you after owning and running the bike for a period of time.

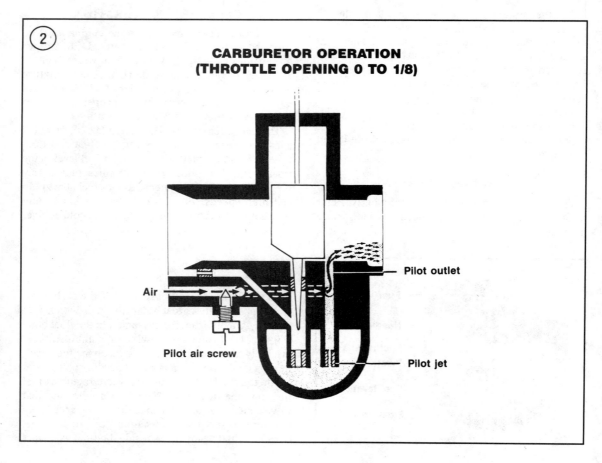

FUEL AND EXHAUST SYSTEMS

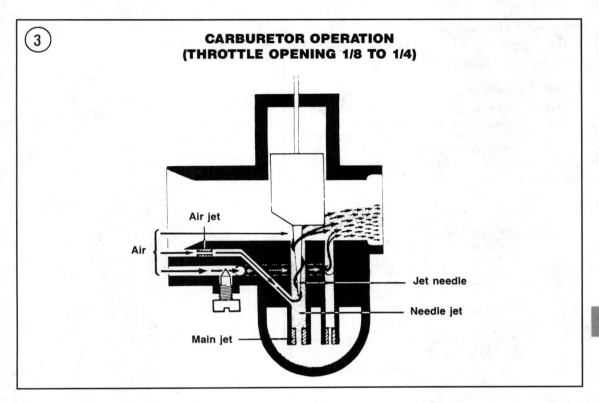

CARBURETOR OPERATION (THROTTLE OPENING 1/8 TO 1/4)

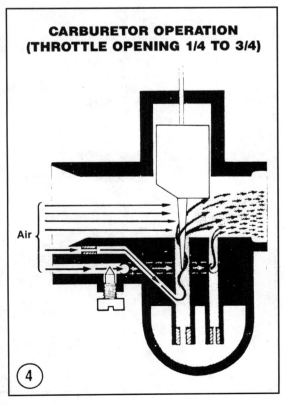

CARBURETOR OPERATION (THROTTLE OPENING 1/4 TO 3/4)

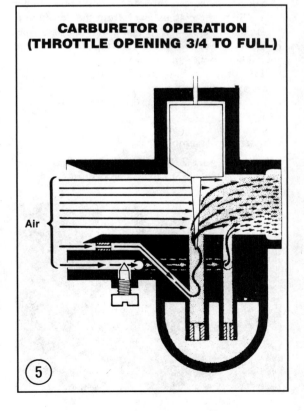

CARBURETOR OPERATION (THROTTLE OPENING 3/4 TO FULL)

Carburetor Identification

Refer to **Table 1** at the end of this chapter for carburetor specifications.

Removal/Installation

1. Place a motocross workstand or wood block(s) under the motorcycle to support it securely.
2. Turn the fuel shutoff valve to the OFF position and remove the fuel line to the carburetor.
3. If necessary, remove the fuel tank as described in this chapter.

NOTE
Prior to removing the top cap, thoroughly clean the area around it so no dirt will fall into the carburetor.

4. Unscrew the carburetor top cap and pull the throttle valve assembly up and out of the carburetor.

NOTE
If the top cover and throttle valve assembly are not going to be removed for cleaning, wrap them in a clean shop cloth or place them in a plastic bag to help keep them clean.

5. Loosen the screws on both clamps on the rubber boots. Slide the clamps away from the carburetor.
6. Make sure all overflow and drain tubes are free.
7. Carefully work the carburetor (**Figure 6**) free from the rubber boots and remove it.
8. Take the carburetor to a workbench for disassembly and cleaning.
9. Install by reversing these removal steps.

Disassembly/Assembly

Refer to **Figure 7** (1983-1984), **Figure 8** (1985) or **Figure 9** (1986-1987) for this procedure.

CARBURETOR (1983-1984)

1. Cable adjuster
2. Locknut
3. Cap
4. Spring
5. Cover
6. Screw
7. Washer
8. Connector
9. Clip
10. Jet needle
11. Throttle valve
12. Seal
13. Guide
14. Clamp
15. Nut
16. O-ring
17. Spring
18. Choke plunger
19. Housing
20. Hose
21. Hose
22. Idle speed screw
23. Spring
24. Pilot jet
25. Main jet
26. Main jet holder
27. Needle jet
28. Pivot pin
29. Float arm
30. Screw
31. Plate
32. Float valve
33. Float valve seat
34. O-ring
35. Cover
36. Floats
37. Gasket
38. Float bowl
39. Hose guide
40. Washer
41. Screw
42. Hose
43. O-ring
44. Drain plug

FUEL AND EXHAUST SYSTEMS

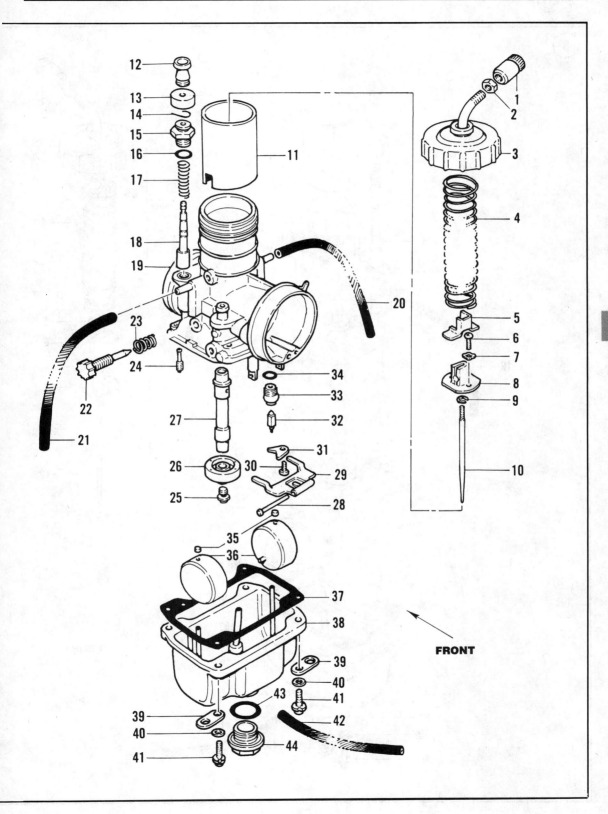

FRONT

166 CHAPTER EIGHT

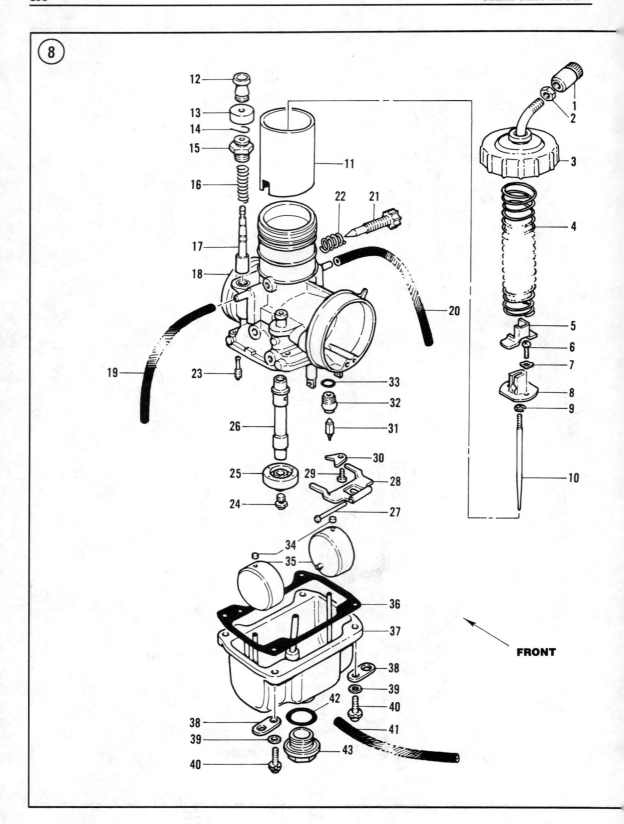

FUEL AND EXHAUST SYSTEMS

CARBURETOR
(1985)

1. Cable adjuster
2. Locknut
3. Cap
4. Spring
5. Cover
6. Screw
7. Washer
8. Connector
9. Clip
10. Jet needle
11. Throttle valve
12. Seal
13. Guide
14. Clamp
15. Nut
16. Spring
17. Choke plunger
18. Housing
19. Hose
20. Hose
21. Idle speed screw
22. Spring
23. Pilot jet
24. Main jet
25. Main jet holder
26. Needle jet
27. Pivot pin
28. Float arm
29. Screw
30. Plate
31. Float valve
32. Float valve seat
33. O-ring
34. Cover
35. Floats
36. Gasket
37. Float bowl
38. Hose guide
39. Washer
40. Screw
41. Hose
42. O-ring
43. Drain plug

CHAPTER EIGHT

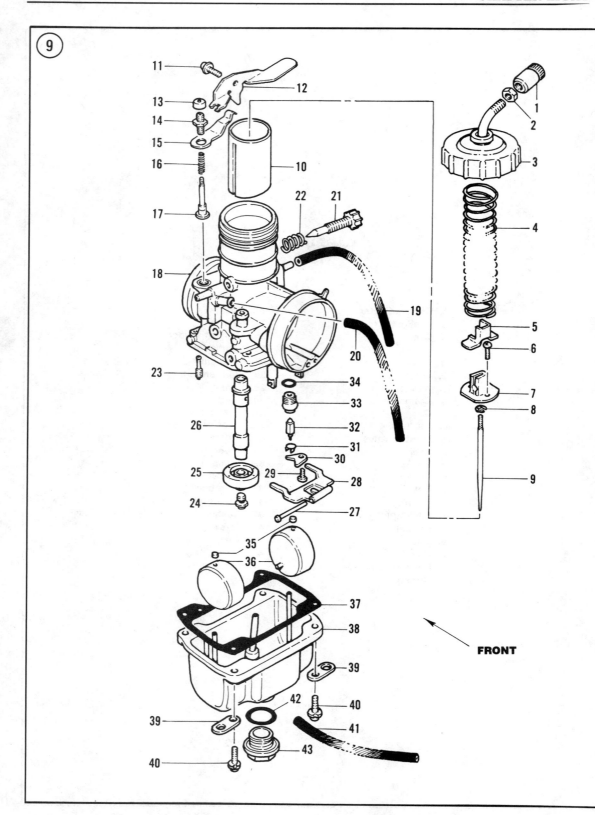

FUEL AND EXHAUST SYSTEMS

CARBURETOR
(1986-1987)

1. Cable adjuster
2. Locknut
3. Cap
4. Spring
5. Cover
6. Screw
7. Connector
8. Clip
9. Jet needle
10. Throttle valve
11. Screw
12. Lever (upper)
13. Seal
14. Bolt
15. Lever (lower)
16. Spring
17. Choke plunger
18. Housing
19. Hose
20. Hose
21. Idle speed screw
22. Spring
23. Pilot jet
24. Main jet
25. Main jet holder
26. Needle jet
27. Pivot pin
28. Float arm
29. Screw
30. Plate
31. Hook
32. Float valve
33. Float valve seat
34. O-ring
35. Cover
36. Floats
37. Gasket
38. Float bowl
39. Hose guide
40. Screw
41. Hose
42. O-ring
43. Drain plug

The carburetors are basically the same even though minor variations exist between different models. Where differences occur they are identified.

1. Remove the fuel line and all drain and overflow tubes.

2A. *1983-1985:* Unscrew the nut and remove the choke assembly (**Figure 10**).

2B. *1986-1987:* Referring to **Figure 9**, remove the screw securing the choke lever. Then remove the choke plunger cap and remove the spring and plunger.

3. Remove the screws securing the float bowl (**Figure 11**) and remove it.

4. Unscrew and remove the main jet (**Figure 12**).

5. Lift the needle jet holder (**Figure 13**) off of the needle jet.

6. Remove the float pin (**Figure 14**).

7. Remove the float valve Phillips screw (**Figure 15**). Then remove the holder and the float valve assembly (**Figure 16**).

8. Push the jet needle down (**Figure 17**) and remove it through the top of the carburetor (**Figure 18**).

9. Unscrew and remove the pilot jet (**Figure 19**).

10. Remove the float bowl gasket (A, **Figure 20**).

11. Unscrew and remove the idle speed screw (B, **Figure 20**).

FUEL AND EXHAUST SYSTEMS

12. Clean and inspect the carburetor components as described in this chapter.
13. After all parts have been cleaned and dried, reverse these steps to assemble the carburetor. Note the following.
14. Check the float height and adjust if necessary. Refer to *Float Adjustment* in this chapter.
15. When installing the jet needle, align the slot in the side of the jet needle with the pin in the carburetor bore (**Figure 21**).
16. After the carburetor has been assembled, adjust the idle speed. Refer to *Idle Speed Adjustment* in Chapter Three.

Cleaning/Inspection

1. Clean all parts, except rubber or plastic parts, in a good grade of spray carburetor cleaner. This spray cleaner is available at most automotive or motorcycle supply stores for just a few dollars. Follow the manufacturer's instructions for cleaning procedure.
2. Blow out the jets with compressed air. *Do not* use a piece of wire to clean them as minor gouges in the jet can alter flow rate and upset the fuel/air mixture.
3. Be sure to clean out the float bowl overflow tube from both ends.

4. Inspect the tip of the float valve (**Figure 22**) for wear or damage. Replace the valve and seat as a set.
5. O-ring seals tend to become hardened after prolonged use and therefore lose their ability to seal properly. Inspect all O-rings and replace if necessary.
6. Check the floats (**Figure 23**) for leaks. Fill the float bowl with water and try to push the floats down. There should be no bubbles. Replace the floats if they leak.
7. Check the idle speed screw for tip wear or thread damage. Replace the screw and/or spring as required.
8. If necessary, disassemble the throttle valve assembly (**Figure 24**). Replace worn or damaged parts. Especially check the slide (**Figure 25**) for scratches or other damage that would allow it to stick open during engine operation.
9. Check all of the choke components for excessive wear or damage. **Figure 26** shows the choke for 1983-1985 models.

CARBURETOR SERVICE
(1988)

Carburetor removal and cleaning should be performed after every race on competition bikes. On a bike that is used for fun on weekends, it should be performed whenever the engine is decarbonized or when poor engine performance, hesitation, and little or no response to mixture adjustment is observed. The service interval time will become natural to you after owning and running the bike for a period of time.

Carburetor Identification

Refer to **Table 1** at the end of this chapter for carburetor specifications.

Removal/Installation

1. Place a motocross workstand or wood block(s) under the motorcycle to support it securely.
2. Turn the fuel shutoff valve to the OFF position and remove the fuel line to the carburetor.
3. If necessary, remove the fuel tank as described in this chapter.

NOTE
Prior to removing the top cap, thoroughly clean the area around it so no dirt will fall into the carburetor.

4. Unscrew the carburetor top cap (**Figure 27**) and pull the throttle valve assembly up and out of the carburetor.

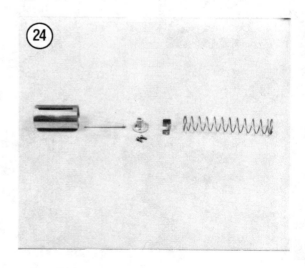

FUEL AND EXHAUST SYSTEMS

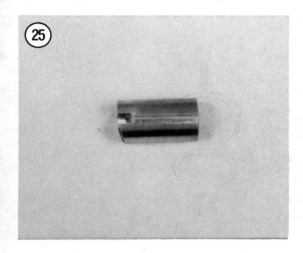

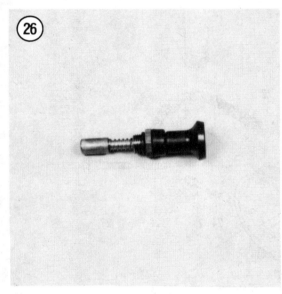

NOTE
If the top cover and throttle valve assembly are not going to be removed for cleaning, wrap them in a clean shop cloth or place them in a plastic bag to help keep them clean.

5. Loosen the screws on both clamps on the rubber boots. Slide the clamps away from the carburetor.
6. Make sure all overflow and drain tubes are free.
7. Carefully work the carburetor free from the rubber boots and remove it.
8. Take the carburetor to a workbench for disassembly and cleaning.
9. Install by reversing these removal steps.

Disassembly/Reassembly (1988)

Refer to **Figure 28** for this procedure.
1. Remove the fuel line and all drain and overflow tubes.
2. Remove the choke lever as follows:
   a. Remove the Phillips screw and washer (**Figure 29**).
   b. Remove the washer (**Figure 30**).
   c. Remove the choke lever (**Figure 31**).
   d. Remove the spacer (**Figure 32**).
   e. Loosen the choke nut (**Figure 33**) and pull the choke knob assembly (**Figure 34**) out of the carburetor housing.
3. Remove the idle speed screw and spring (A, **Figure 35**).
4. Remove the pilot adjust screw and spring (B, **Figure 35**).
5. Remove the screws securing the float bowl and remove it (**Figure 36**).
6. Remove the float pin (**Figure 37**) and lift the float assembly (**Figure 38**) out of the housing.
7. Unscrew and remove the main jet (**Figure 39**).
8. Unscrew and remove the pilot jet (**Figure 40**).

NOTE
*The needle jet (**Figure 41**) is pressed into the carburetor housing and cannot be removed.*

9. Remove the carburetor float bowl O-ring (**Figure 42**).
10. Clean and inspect the carburetor components as described in this chapter.
11. After all parts have been cleaned and dried, reverse these steps to assemble the carburetor. Note the following.

174 CHAPTER EIGHT

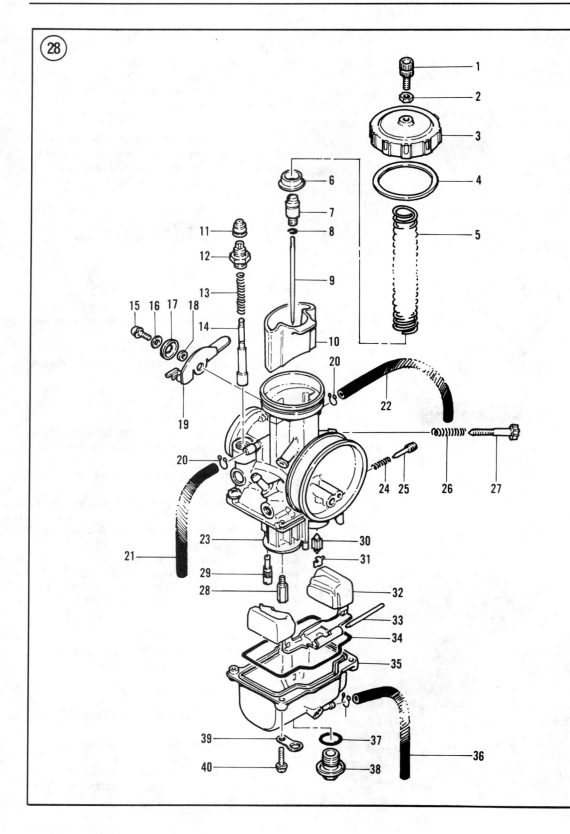

FUEL AND EXHAUST SYSTEMS

CARBURETOR
(1988)

1. Cable adjuster
2. Locknut
3. Cap
4. Gasket
5. Spring
6. Spring seat
7. Cable connector
8. Clip
9. Jet needle
10. Throttle valve
11. Seal
12. Nut
13. Spring
14. Choke plunger
15. Screw
16. Washer
17. Cover
18. Spacer
19. Lever
20. Clamp
21. Hose
22. Hose
23. Housing
24. Spring
25. Pilot adjust screw
26. Spring
27. Idle speed screw
28. Main jet
29. Pilot jet
30. Float valve
31. Hook
32. Floats
33. Pivot pin
34. O-ring
35. Float bowl
36. Hose
37. O-ring
38. Drain plug
39. Hose guide
40. Screw

176　　　　　　　　　　　　　　　　　　　　　　　　　　　　　　　　　　CHAPTER EIGHT

FUEL AND EXHAUST SYSTEMS

12. Check the float height and adjust if necessary. Refer to *Float Adjustment* in this chapter.
13. After the carburetor has been assembled, adjust the idle speed and the pilot air screw. Refer to Chapter Three.

Cleaning/Inspection

1. Clean all parts, except rubber or plastic parts, in a good grade of spray carburetor cleaner. This spray cleaner is available at most automotive or motorcycle supply stores for just a few dollars. Follow the manufacturer's instructions for correct cleaning procedures.
2. Blow out the jets with compressed air. *Do not* use a piece of wire to clean them as minor gouges in the jet can alter flow rate and upset the fuel/air mixture.
3. Be sure to clean out the float bowl overflow tube from both ends.

4. Inspect the tip of the float valve (**Figure 22**) for wear or damage. Replace the valve and seat as a set.
5. O-ring seals tend to become hardened after prolonged use and therefore lose their ability to seal properly. Inspect all O-rings and replace if necessary.
6. Check the floats (**Figure 43**) for leaks. Fill the float bowl with water and try to push the floats down. There should be no bubbles. Replace the floats if they leak.
7. Disassemble the choke valve assembly (**Figure 44**). Check the parts for wear or damage. Assemble the choke valve assembly (**Figure 45**) and check that the plunger works smoothly.
8. Check the idle speed screw for tip wear or thread damage. Replace the screw and/or spring as required.
9. If necessary, disassemble the throttle valve assembly (**Figure 46**). Replace worn or damaged parts. Check the slide (**Figure 47**) for scratches or other damage that would allow it to stick open during engine operation.

CARBURETOR FUEL LEVEL ADJUSTMENT

Float/Arm Height Adjustment

The fuel level in the carburetor float bowl is critical to proper performance. The fuel flow rate from the bowl up to the carburetor bore depends not only on the vacuum in the throttle bore and the size of the jets, but also upon the fuel level. Kawasaki gives a specification of actual *fuel level*, measured from the top edge of the float bowl with the carburetor held level (**Figure 48**).

The measurement is more useful than a simple float height measurement because actual fuel level can vary from bike to bike, even when their floats are set at the same height. However, fuel level inspection requires a special fitting that screws into the bottom of the carburetor. You can get the proper fitting at

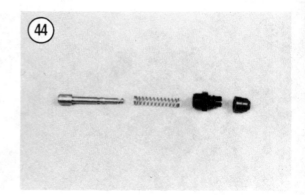

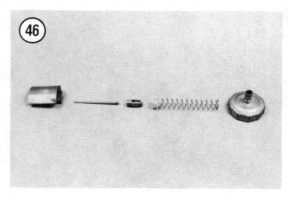

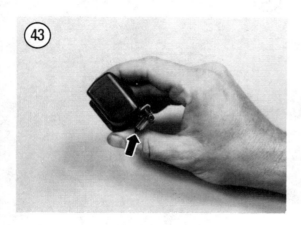

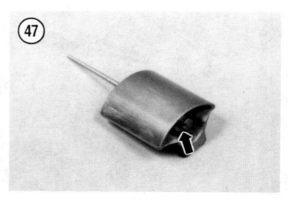

FUEL AND EXHAUST SYSTEMS

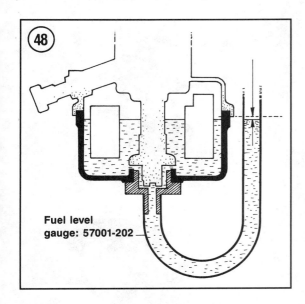

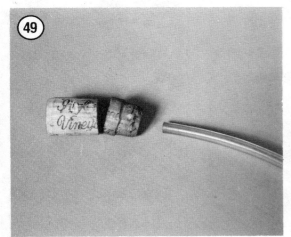

your Kawasaki dealer (part No. 57001-202), or you can improvise one from a piece of plastic tubing and a cork (**Figure 49**).

The fuel level is adjusted by bending the float arm tang.

Fuel Level Inspection

1. Turn the fuel valve off and remove the carburetor from its mounts so that it can be held level. Leave the fuel line connected.
2. Remove the drain plug (**Figure 50**) from the bottom of the float bowl and insert a fitting with a transparent hose (**Figure 51**). The hose should have an inside diameter not less than 1/4 in. (6 mm) so that capillary action will not draw the fuel up inside, giving a false reading.
3. Hold the clear tube against the carburetor body and turn the fuel tap on. With the carburetor level to the ground, check the fuel level in the tube. See **Figure 48** or **Figure 52**. See **Table 1** for your bike's fuel level specification.

NOTE
Take your readings just after the fuel level has risen to its maximum in the

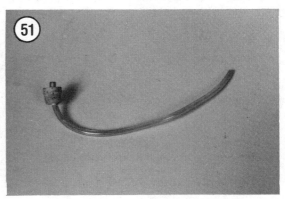

tube. *If you raise the tube (and the fuel drops in the tube) you'll probably get a faulty level reading. Try it again, forcing the fuel level to rise against surface tension within the tube.*

4. If the fuel level is incorrect, adjust the float/arm height setting as described in Step 5 for your model. Then recheck the fuel level. Readjust if necessary.

NOTE
A larger arm height measurement (1983-1987) raises the fuel level. A larger float height (1988) lowers the fuel level.

5A. *1983-1987:* Adjust the float arm as follows:
   a. Remove the float bowl.
   b. Adjust the float arm by bending the tang (**Figure 53**) with a screwdriver.
   c. Reinstall the float bowl.
5B. *1988:* Adjust the float arm as follows:
   a. Remove the float bowl.
   b. Remove the pivot pin (**Figure 54**) and lift the float assembly (**Figure 55**) out of the housing.
   c. Remove the fuel valve (**Figure 56**) from the float.
   d. Adjust the float by bending the tang (**Figure 57**) with a screwdriver.

Needle Jet Adjustment

The position of the needle jet can be adjusted to affect the fuel/air mixture for medium throttle openings.

The top of the carburetor must be removed for this adjustment. It is easier to perform this procedure with the fuel tank removed but it can be accomplished with it in place.

1. If necessary, loosen the carburetor clamp screws and turn the carburetor to gain access to the carburetor cap.

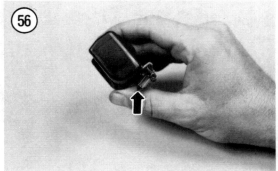

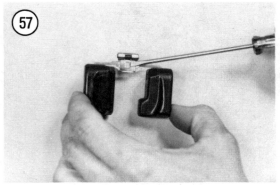

FUEL AND EXHAUST SYSTEMS

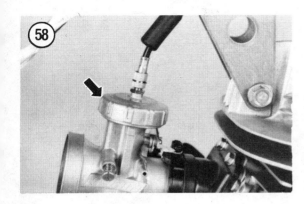

NOTE
Prior to removing the top cap, thoroughly clean the area around it so no dirt will fall into the carburetor.

2. Unscrew the carburetor top cap (**Figure 58**) and pull the throttle valve assembly (**Figure 59**) up and out of the carburetor.
3. At the end of the throttle cable, push up on the throttle valve spring.
4A. *1983-1987:* Perform the following:
   a. Remove the clip (**Figure 60**) securing the throttle cable in the throttle valve assembly.
   b. Remove the throttle cable from the throttle valve assembly (**Figure 61**) and remove the assembly.
   c. Remove the 2 screws (**Figure 62**) securing the jet needle into the throttle valve assembly and disassemble it. Remove the jet needle.
4B. *1988:* Perform the following:
   a. Move the throttle cable end over to the larger hole in the throttle valve and withdraw the cable out through the top and remove it. See **Figure 63**.

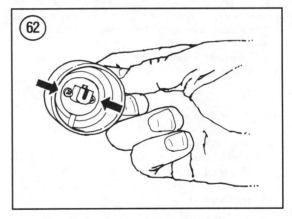

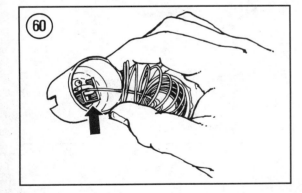

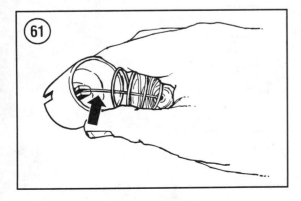

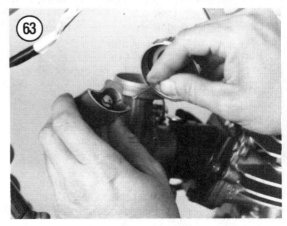

b. Unscrew the jet needle plug (**Figure 64**) and remove the jet needle (**Figure 65**).

5. Note the position of the clip. Raising the needle (lowering the clip) will enrich the mixture during mid-throttle opening, while lowering it (raising the clip) will lean the mixture. Refer to **Figure 66**.

6. Refer to **Table 1** at the end of the chapter for standard clip position for all models.

7. Installation is the reverse of these steps.

Pilot Screw and Idle Speed Adjustment

Refer to Chapter Three.

High Altitude Adjustment (Main Jet Replacement)

If the bike is going to be raced or ridden for any sustained period of time in high elevations (above 5,000 ft.; 1,500 m), the main jet should be changed to a one-step smaller jet. Never change the jet by more than one size at a time without test riding the bike and running a spark plug test. Refer to *Reading Spark Plugs* in Chapter Three.

The carburetor is set with the standard jet for normal sea level conditions. But if the bike is run at higher altitudes or under heavy load—deep sand or mud—the main jet should be replaced. High altitude requires leaner jetting while deep sand and mud at low altitude requires richer jetting.

> **CAUTION**
> *If the bike has been rejetted for high altitude operation (smaller jet), it must be changed back to the standard main jet if ridden at altitudes below 5,000 ft. (1,500 m). Engine overheating and piston seizure will occur if the engine runs too lean with the smaller jet.*

Refer to **Table 1**, at the end of this chapter, for standard main jet sizes.

1. Turn the fuel shutoff valve to the OFF position and disconnect the fuel line from the carburetor.
2. Loosen the main jet cover (float bowl plug) and drain out all fuel in the bowl. See **Figure 50**.

> **WARNING**
> *Place a metal container under the cover to catch the fuel that will flow out. Do not let it drain out onto the engine or the bike's frame as it presents a real fire danger. **Do not** perform this procedure with a hot engine. Dispose of the fuel properly; wipe up any that may have spilled on the bike and the floor.*

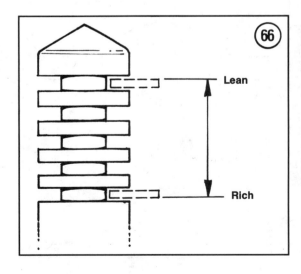

FUEL AND EXHAUST SYSTEMS

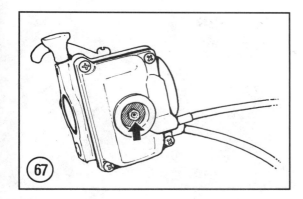

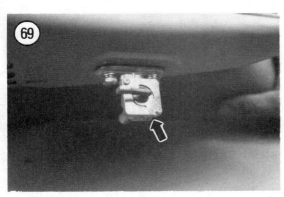

3. The main jet is directly under the cover (**Figure 67**). Remove it and replace it with a different one. Remember, change only one jet size at a time.
4. Install the main jet cover; tighten it securely.

FUEL TANK

Removal/Installation

1. Place a motocross workstand or wood block(s) under the motorcycle to support it securely.
2. Turn the fuel shutoff valve to the OFF position (**Figure 68**) and remove the fuel line to the carburetor.
3. Remove the seat.
4. Pull the fuel cap vent tube free from the steering head area.
5. Remove the bolts and strap securing the fuel tank and remove it.
6. Install by reversing these removal steps.

FUEL SHUTOFF VALVE

Removal/Installation

1. Remove the fuel tank as described in this chapter.
2. Drain the fuel into a fuel storage container.
3. Remove the bolts and remove the fuel shutoff valve (**Figure 69**).
4. Remove the screw above the handle or on the handle and disassemble the valve. Clean all parts in solvent with a medium soft toothbrush, then dry. Check the small O-ring within the valve and the O-ring gasket; replace if they are starting to deteriorate or get hard. Make sure the spring is not broken or getting soft; replace if necessary.
5. Reassemble the valve and install it on the tank. Don't forget the O-ring gasket between the valve and the tank.

EXHAUST SYSTEM

This section provides service procedures for the exhaust system. The exhaust advancer system is covered in the *Clutch* section of Chapter Six.

The exhaust system (**Figure 70**), which is called an expansion chamber on a 2-stroke motorcycle engine is much more than a means of routing the exhaust gases to the rear of the bike. It's a vital performance component and frequently, because of its design, it is a vulnerable piece of equipment.

Check the exhaust system for deep dents and fractures and repair them as described under *Exhaust System Repairs* at the end of this chapter. Check the expansion chamber mounting flanges for fractures and loose bolts and bushings. Check the cylinder mounting flange or collar for tightness. A loose headpipe connection will not only rob the engine of power, it could also damage the piston and cylinder.

The exhaust system consists of an exhaust pipe assembly (head pipe and expansion chamber) and a silencer. This system varies slightly with different models and years. All attachments are basically the same but they all vary a little.

Removal/Installation

1. Remove the seat, fuel tank and both side cover/number plates.
2. Place the bike on a sturdy crate or wood blocks to support it securely.
3. Remove the bolts securing the silencer (**Figure 71**). Also loosen the clamping band and remove the silencer.
4. Use a pair of Vise Grips or a spring removal tool and disconnect the springs at the front of the exhaust pipe (**Figure 72**).
5. Remove the bolts securing the exhaust pipe (**Figure 73**) and remove the exhaust pipe.
6. Installation is the reverse of these steps. Note the following:
    a. Replace the special sealing ring at the head pipe and apply grease from the edge of the pipe to the ring (**Figure 74**). If the joint leaks in spite of a good ring and grease, clean the surfaces with solvent and use high temperature silicone sealant to seat the joint.
    b. Make sure the spark plug wire, fuel line, and throttle cable protection spring are properly positioned to prevent damage from a hot exhaust pipe (**Figure 75**).

EXHAUST SYSTEM DECARBONIZING

Refer to Chapter Three for complete details on engine and exhaust system decarbonization.

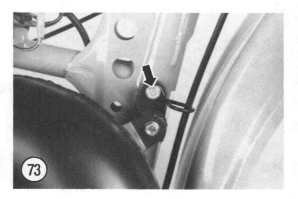
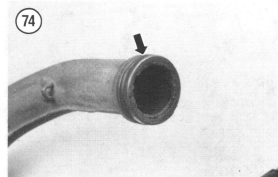

FUEL AND EXHAUST SYSTEMS

EXHAUST SYSTEM REPAIR

A dent in the headpipe or expansion chamber of a 2-stroke exhaust system can alter the system's flow characteristics and degrade performance. Minor damage can be easily repaired if you have welding equipment, some simple body tools, and a slide hammer.

Small Dents

1. Drill a small hole in the center of the dent. Screw the end of the slide hammer into the hole.
2. Heat the area around the dent evenly with a torch.
3. When the dent is heated to a uniform orange-red color, operate the slide hammer to raise the dent.
4. When the dent is removed, unscrew the slide hammer and weld or braze the drilled hole closed.

Large Dents

Large dents that are not crimped can be removed with heat and a slide hammer as previously described. However, several holes must be drilled along the center of the dent so that it can be pulled out evenly.

If the dent is sharply crimped along the edges, the affected section should be cut out with a hacksaw, straightened with a body dolly and hammer and welded back into place.

Before cutting the exhaust pipe apart, scribe alignment marks over the area where the cuts will be made to aid correct alignment when the pipe is rewelded.

After the welding is completed, wire brush and clean up all welds. Paint the entire pipe with a high-temperature paint to prevent rusting.

Table 1 is on the next page.

Table 1 CARBURETOR SPECIFICATIONS

	1983	1984-1985
Type	Mikuni	Mikuni
Size	VM32SS	VM32SS
Main jet	135	260
Jet needle	5FJ57	5FJ57
Clip position	3	3
Needle jet	R-6	R-6
Cutaway	3.0	3.0
Pilot jet	40	40
Bore center	33 mm (1.3 in.)	33 mm (1.3 in.)
Float height	23.8 mm (0.94 in.)	23.8 mm (0.94 in.)
Fuel level	0-2 mm (0-0.08 in.)	0-2 mm (0-0.08 in.)
	1986	**1987**
Type	Mikuni	Mikuni
Size	VM34SS	VM34SS
Main jet	300	320
Jet needle	6FL52	6FL52
Clip position	3	4
Needle jet	R-4	R-2
Cutaway	3.0	3.0
Pilot jet	35	25
Bore center	33 mm (1.3 in.)	33 mm (1.3 in.)
Float height	17.1 mm (0.67 in.)	17.1 mm (0.67 in.)
Fuel level	0-2 mm (0-0.08 in.)	0-2 mm (0-0.08 in.)
	1988	
Type	Keihin	
Size	PWK35	
Main jet	145	
Jet needle	R1368E	
Clip position	3	
Needle jet	2.9	
Cutaway	6.0	
Pilot jet	48	
Bore center	32 mm (1.26 in.)	
Float height	16.0 mm (0.63 in.)	
Fuel level	0-2 mm (0-0.08 in.)	

CHAPTER NINE

ELECTRICAL SYSTEM

This chapter describes service procedures for the ignition and lighting systems. Electrical troubleshooting is described in Chapter Two.

Electrical system test specifications are found in **Table 1**. Tightening torques are listed in **Table 2**. **Table 1** and **Table 2** are at the end of the chapter.

CAPACITOR DISCHARGE IGNITION

All KDX200s are equipped with a capacitor discharge ignition (CDI) system. This solid state system uses no contact breaker points or other moving parts.

Alternating current from the magneto is rectified and used to charge the capacitor. As the piston approaches the firing position, a pulse from the pulser coil is rectified, then triggers the capacitor. This allows the capacitor to discharge quickly into the primary side of the high-voltage ignition coil where it is increased, or stepped up, to a voltage high enough to jump the gap between the spark plug electrodes.

CDI Precautions

Certain measures must be taken to protect the capacitor discharge system. Instantaneous damage to the semiconductors in the system will occur if the following are not observed.

1. Keep all connections between the various units clean and tight. Be sure that the wiring connectors are pushed together firmly.
2. Never disconnect any of the electrical connections while the engine is running.
3. Do not substitute another type of ignition coil.
4. The CDI unit is mounted on a rubber vibration isolator. Always be sure that the CDI unit is mounted correctly.

CDI Troubleshooting

Problems with the capacitor discharge system are usually limited to the production of a weak spark or no spark at all.

1. Untape the electrical connectors and check for moisture and dirt buildup. Clean the connectors with electrical contact cleaner and reconnect. Retape the connectors with electrical tape.
2. Disconnect the kill switch and try to restart the engine. Refer to *Engine Kill Switch* in this chapter.

NOTE
If the engine starts with the kill switch disconnected, use the choke to turn the engine off. As an alternative, apply both brakes, shift the transmission into gear, then slowly let out the clutch—this will turn off the engine.

3. Check to see that the ignition coil high tension wire is connected securely to the ignition coil and spark plug cap.
4. Make sure that all stator plate screws are tight. If not, retighten the screws and time the ignition as described in Chapter Three.
5. Check the crankshaft bearings for excessive wear as this could cause ignition problems. Refer to *Crankcase* in Chapter Five for details.

MAGNETO

Rotor
Removal/Installation

1. Place the bike on a stand to support it securely.
2. Remove the shift lever (**Figure 1**).
3. Remove the left-hand side cover (**Figure 2**).
4. Using a universal magneto holding tool (**Figure 3**) to secure the magneto, loosen the magneto rotor bolt.
5. Remove the bolt and plain washer. On some models, a lockwasher is installed between the bolt and plain washer.

NOTE
*The Kawasaki flywheel puller (part No. 57001-259 and part No. 57001-1099) will be required to remove the rotor (**Figure 4**). In addition, depending on the style of puller used, it may be necessary to make a small spacer that should thread into the crankshaft when removing the rotor. The spacer can be made by cutting an 8 mm × 1.25 bolt with a hacksaw (**Figure 5**). The length of the spacer will depend on the tool used.*

CAUTION
Don't pry or hammer on the rotor in any way. Damage is sure to result, and you may demagnetize the rotor. Use the proper type of puller assembly described.

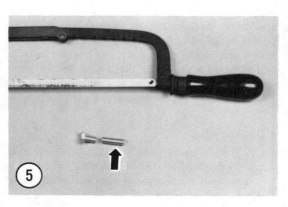

ELECTRICAL SYSTEM

6. Thread the spacer into the end of the crankshaft (**Figure 6**).

7. Bolt one half of the flywheel puller onto the rotor as shown in **Figure 7**. Thread the pressure bolt into the flywheel puller (**Figure 8**). Then screw in the pressure bolt (**Figure 9**) to pull the rotor off. You may have to tap on the pressure bolt sharply with a hammer and tighten the bolt some more, but don't hit the rotor.

CAUTION
If normal rotor removal attempts fail, do not force the puller as the threads may be stripped out of the rotor, causing expensive damage. Take it to a dealer and have it removed.

8. Remove the rotor and puller. Don't lose the Woodruff key (**Figure 10**) on the crankshaft.

CAUTION
*Carefully inspect the inside of the rotor (**Figure 11**) for small bolts, washers or other metal "trash" that may have been picked up by the magnets. These small metal bits can cause severe damage to the magneto stator plate components.*

CHAPTER NINE

9. Install by reversing these removal steps, noting the following:
   a. Make sure the Woodruff key (**Figure 10**) is in place on the crankshaft and align the keyway in the rotor with the key when installing the rotor.
   b. Install and tighten the rotor bolt to the torque specification in **Table 2**. To keep the rotor from turning, hold it with the same tool used during removal. See **Figure 12**.

Stator Assembly
Removal/Installation

1. Remove the magneto rotor as described under *Rotor Removal/Installation* in this chapter.
2. Remove the fuel tank as described in Chapter Eight.
3. Disconnect the electrical wire connectors from the magneto to the CDI unit. See **Figure 13** or **Figure 14**.
4. Note the timing marks on the stator plate and on the crankcase. These must be realigned during installation. If necessary, make a mark on the stator plate at the centerline of the left-hand attachment screw (A, **Figure 15**).
5. Remove the screws securing the stator plate.
6. Carefully pull the electrical harness out along with the rubber grommet from the crankcase and any holding clips on the engine.
7. Remove the stator assembly (B, **Figure 15**).
8. Install by reversing these removal steps, noting the following.
9. Route the electrical wires in the same way they were. Make sure to keep them away from the exhaust system.
10. Realign the stator plate and crankcase timing marks for preliminary ignition timing.
11. Check and adjust the ignition timing as described in Chapter Three.

Stator Coil Testing

The stator coils can be inspected for continuity without removing them from the bike. With the engine off, disconnect the connector from the magneto and measure the resistance between the pairs of leads listed in **Table 1**.

If the resistance is zero (short circuit) or infinite (open circuit), check the wiring to the coils, and replace the coils if the wiring is okay.

CAPACITOR DISCHARGE IGNITION UNIT

Removal/Installation

1. Support the bike on the sidestand.
2. Remove the seat and fuel tank.
3. Disconnect the CDI electrical connector.

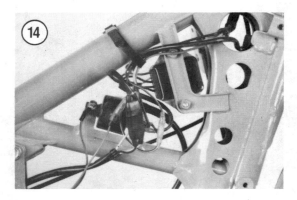

ELECTRICAL SYSTEM

4. Remove the CDI mounting bolts and remove the CDI unit. See **Figure 16** (1983-1985) or A, **Figure 17** (1986-on).
5. Installation is the reverse of these steps.

Testing

The capacitor discharge ignition unit can only be tested with special electrical equipment. Refer all testing to a Kawasaki dealer.

IGNITION COIL

Removal/Installation

1. Support the bike on the sidestand.
2. Remove the seat and fuel tank.
3. Disconnect the electrical wires to the ignition coil.
4. Remove the screws securing the ignition coil to the frame and remove it. See **Figure 18** (1983-1985) or B, **Figure 17** (1986-on).
5. Install by reversing these removal steps. Make sure all electrical connectors are tight and free of corrosion. Make sure the ground wire is secured tightly.

Testing

If the functional condition of the coil is in doubt, there are several checks which should be made. Disconnect the coil wires before testing.

1. Measure the coil primary resistance using an ohmmeter set at R × 1 (**Figure 19A**). Measure the resistance between the primary terminal and the mounting flange. See **Table 1** for test specifications.
2. Measure the secondary resistance using an ohmmeter set at R × 1,000 (**Figure 19A**). Measure the resistance between the secondary lead (spark plug lead) and the mounting flange. See **Table 1** for test specifications.
3. If the meter indicates an open circuit (no continuity) in Step 2, unplug the high-tension lead from the coil and test it again with the meter lead connected directly to the contact pin in the coil cap. If there is continuity, the trouble is in the high-tension lead. It may be a bad connection at the spark plug or an internal break in the wire. Make sure the connection is good and check the lead for continuity. If an open circuit is still indicated, replace the high-tension lead.
4. If the high tension lead has continuity, but there is no continuity in Step 2, the coil itself is defective and must be replaced.

NOTE
Continuity in both the primary and secondary windings in the coil is not a guarantee that the unit is in top working order; only an operational test can tell if a coil is producing an adequate spark from the input voltage. Your motorcycle dealer or auto electrical repair shop may have the equipment to test the coil's output. If not, substitute a known good coil to see if the problem goes away.

SPARK PLUG

The spark plugs recommended by the factory are usually the most suitable for your machine. If riding conditions are mild, it may be advisable to go to spark plugs one step hotter than normal. Unusually severe riding conditions may require slightly colder plugs. See Chapter Three for details.

ENGINE KILL SWITCH

Testing

1. Remove the fuel tank as described in Chapter Eight.
2. Disconnect the black kill switch connector at the CDI unit.
3. Use an ohmmeter set at R × 1 and connect the 2 leads of the ohmmeter to the 2 electrical wires of the switch.
4. Push the kill switch button—if the switch is good there will be continuity (resistance).
5. If the needle does not move (no continuity) the switch is faulty and must be replaced.
6. Remove the screw securing the switch (**Figure 19B**) and remove it. Reverse to install a new switch.

LIGHTING SYSTEM

The KDX200 models have simple lighting systems using alternating current taken directly from the magneto.

Headlight Bulb
Replacement

1. Remove the screws securing the headlight housing (**Figure 20**) and pull the housing away from the front forks.
2. Disconnect the connector at the bulb and remove the bulb (**Figure 21**).
3. Installation is the reverse of these steps.

Headlight Aim

The headlight should be aimed so that the beam is slightly below horizontal. Turning the headlight adjustment screw (**Figure 22**) counterclockwise points the headlight beam downward.

Taillight Bulb
Replacement

Remove the taillight lens (**Figure 23**) and remove the bulb from the bulb holder (**Figure 24**). Reverse to install.

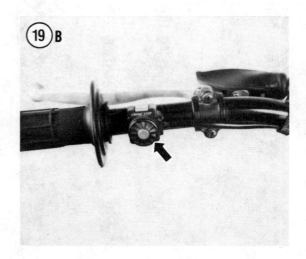

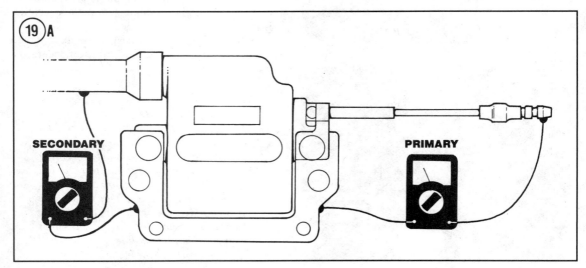

ELECTRICAL SYSTEM

Headlight Switch Testing/Replacement

The headlight switch (**Figure 25**) is mounted either in front of the handlebar or on the right-hand side of the handlebar. Use a continuity tester or ohmmeter to check out the headlight switch. Disconnect the wires at the switch (A, **Figure 26**). If continuity is shown when the switch is pulled out (ON), the switch is good.

Replace the switch by removing it from its mounting bracket. Reverse to install.

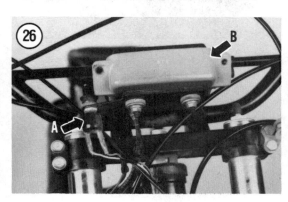

ENDURO TIMER CASE

The timer case (**Figure 27**) batteries should be replaced when the display becomes pale in color.
1. Turn the timer case power switch off.
2. Remove the bolts securing the headlight housing and remove it (**Figure 20**).
3A. *1983-1985:* Remove the 2 bolts and remove the timer case unit (B, **Figure 26**).
3B. *1986-on:* Remove the rubber strap (**Figure 28**) and remove the timer case unit.
4. Open the timer case unit (**Figure 29**) and replace the batteries.

CAUTION
*Do not reverse battery polarity when installing new batteries. Battery polarity is labeled on the timer case (**Figure 30**). Installing the batteries incorrectly will damage the timer case.*

5. Reverse to install. Make sure all battery contacts are free of corrosion.

WIRING DIAGRAMS

Wiring diagrams for all models are located at the end of this book.

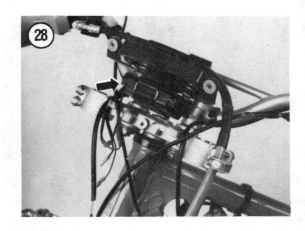
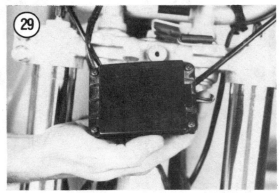

ELECTRICAL SYSTEM

Table 1 IGNITION SYSTEM TEST SPECIFICATIONS

Item	Ohm reading*
Ignition coil	
Primary	0.22
Secondary	7.2 K
Stator coil	
1983-1986	
Black to blue	104
Black to white/red	38
Blue to white/red	142
Black to yellow	0.54
1987-on	
Black to white/red	54.5
Black to yellow	0.53

* All test readings ±20%.

Table 2 TIGHTENING TORQUES

	N·m	ft.-lb.
Rotor bolt		
1983-1985	22	16
1986-on	27	20

CHAPTER TEN

FRONT SUSPENSION AND STEERING

This chapter describes repair and maintenance on the front wheel, forks and steering components.

Front suspension specifications are listed in **Table 1**. Front suspension tightening torques are listed in **Table 2**. **Table 1** and **Table 2** are at the end of the chapter.

FRONT WHEEL

Removal/Installation (1983-1985)

WARNING
When removing the wheels or working on the brakes, wear a protective mask to keep from inhaling any dust from the brake linings. The brake linings contain asbestos fiber; asbestos has been connected with lung scarring and cancer. Do not use compressed air to clean the brake drums or linings; dump any dust onto a newspaper and dispose of it according to local regulations for hazardous waste. Wash your hands after handling the brake parts.

1. Support the motorcycle with the front wheel off the ground.
2. Disconnect the front brake cable at the wheel as follows:
   a. Remove the cotter pin from the clevis pin (**Figure 1**).

FRONT SUSPENSION AND STEERING

b. Remove the washer (**Figure 2**).
c. Remove the clevis pin (**Figure 3**).
d. Loosen the brake cable adjuster (**Figure 4**) at the front hub and disconnect the cable from the hub. See **Figure 5**.

3. Loosen and remove the front axle nut (**Figure 6**).

4. Remove the front axle (A, **Figure 7**) from the right-hand side. Then pull the wheel forward and pull the speedometer drive housing (B, **Figure 7**) out of the front wheel.

5. Pull the brake hub (**Figure 8**) out of the front wheel.

6. To install the front wheel, reverse the removal steps. Note the following:
   a. When installing the speedometer housing, align the tabs in the speedometer housing (**Figure 9**) with the slots in the front hub (**Figure 10**).
   b. When installing the wheel in the forks, make sure the anchor boss on the left-hand fork leg (**Figure 11**) fits between the lugs cast into the brake panel (**Figure 12**).

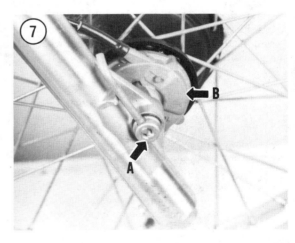

c. Clean the axle and axle spacers in solvent and thoroughly dry. Make sure all axle contact surfaces are clean and free of dirt and old grease prior to installation. If these surfaces are not cleaned, the axle may be difficult to remove later on.
d. Apply a light coat of grease to the axle, bearings and grease seals.
e. To center the brake shoes in the drum, tighten the axle nut lightly, spin the wheel and apply the brake forcefully, then tighten the axle nut.
f. Tighten the axle nut to the torque specification in **Table 2**.
g. Install a new cotter pin (**Figure 1**) when securing the brake cable clevis pin.
h. Adjust brake cable play. Refer to Chapter Three.

**Removal/Installation
(1986-on)**

1. Support the motorcycle with the front wheel off the ground.
2. Loosen and remove the front axle nut (**Figure 13**).
3. Slide the axle (A, **Figure 14**) out from the right-hand side and lower the front wheel. Disconnect the speedometer drive housing from the front wheel (B, **Figure 14**).

NOTE
After removing the front wheel, insert a piece of wood or hose in the caliper between the brake pads. That way, if the brake lever is accidentally squeezed, the piston will not be forced out of the brake caliper cylinder. If the brake lever is squeezed and the piston comes out, the caliper might have to be disassembled to reseat the piston and the system will have to be bled.

4. Remove the left-hand axle spacer (**Figure 15**).

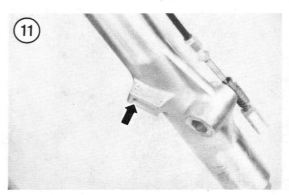

FRONT SUSPENSION AND STEERING

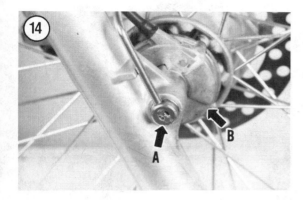

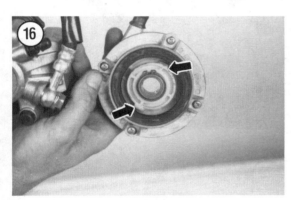

5. Install the axle spacers, washers and axle nut on the axle to prevent their loss when servicing the wheel.
6. To install the front wheel, reverse the removal steps. Note the following:
   a. When installing the speedometer housing, align the tabs in the speedometer housing (**Figure 16**) with the slots in the front hub (**Figure 17**).
   b. Clean the axle and axle spacers in solvent and thoroughly dry. Make sure all axle contact surfaces are clean and free of dirt and old grease prior to installation. If these surfaces are not cleaned, the axle may be difficult to remove later on.
   c. Apply a light coat of grease to the axle, bearings and
      grease seals.
   d. Carefully insert the disc between the brake pads when installing the wheel.
   e. Install the axle nut (**Figure 13**). Tighten the axle to the torque specification in **Table 2**.
   f. After the wheel is completely installed, rotate the front wheel and apply the brake. Do this a couple of times to make sure the front wheel and brake are operating correctly.

Inspection

Spokes loosen with use and should be checked prior to each race or weekend ride. The "tuning fork" method for checking spoke tightness is simple and works well. Tap each spoke with a spoke wrench or the shank of a screwdriver and listen for a tone. A tightened spoke will emit a clear, ringing tone, and a loose spoke will sound flat. All the spokes in a correctly tightened wheel will emit tones of similar pitch but not necessarily the same precise tone.

Bent, stripped or broken spokes should be replaced as soon as they are detected, as they can cause the destruction of an expensive hub. Unscrew the nipple from the spoke and depress the nipple into the rim far enough to free the end of the spoke, taking care not to push the nipple all the way in. Remove the damaged spoke from the hub and use it to match a new spoke of identical length. If necessary, trim the new spoke to match the original and dress the end of the threads with a thread die. Install the new spoke in the hub and screw on the nipple; tighten it until the spoke's tone is similar to the tone of the other spokes in the wheel. Periodically check the new spoke; it will stretch and must be retightened several times before it takes its final set.

Wheel rim runout is the amount of "wobble" a wheel shows as it rotates. You can check runout with the wheels on the bike by simply supporting the wheel off the ground and turning the wheel slowly while you hold a pointer solidly against a fork leg or the swing arm (**Figure 18**). Just make sure any wobble you observe isn't caused by your own hand.

Off the motorcycle, runout can be checked with the wheel installed on a truing stand (**Figure 19**).

The maximum allowable axial (side-to-side) and radial (up and down) play is listed in **Table 1**. Tighten or replace any bent or loose spokes.

1. Draw the high point of the rim toward the centerline of the wheel by tightening the spokes in the area of the high point and on the same side as the high point, and loosening the spokes on the side opposite the high point.
2. Rotate the wheel and check runout. Continue adjusting until the runout is within specification. Be patient and thorough, adjusting the position of the rim a little at a time. If you tighten 2 spokes at the high point 1/2 turn, tighten the adjacent spokes 1/4 turn. Loosen the spokes on the opposite side equivalent amounts.

FRONT HUB

Refer to **Figure 20** (1983-1985) or **Figure 21** (1986-on) for this procedure.

Disassembly/Reassembly

Do not remove bearings for periodic inspection as bearing removal normally damages the first bearing removed. Always replace bearings as a set.

1. Remove the front wheel as described under *Front Wheel Removal* in this chapter.
2. *1986-on:* Remove the left-hand oil seal (**Figure 22**) by carefully prying it out of the hub with a long screwdriver. Prop a piece of wood or rag underneath the screwdriver to prevent it from damaging the hub.

NOTE
If the seal is tight, work the screwdriver around the seal every few degrees until the seal pops out of the hub.

3. Remove the circlip (**Figure 23**) from the left-hand side.
4. Remove the left- and right-hand bearings (**Figure 24**) and distance collar. To remove them, insert a soft aluminum or brass drift into one side of the hub. Push the distance collar over to one side and place the drift on the inner race of the lower bearing (**Figure 25**). Tap the bearing out of the hub with a hammer, working around the perimeter of the inner race.

FRONT SUSPENSION AND STEERING

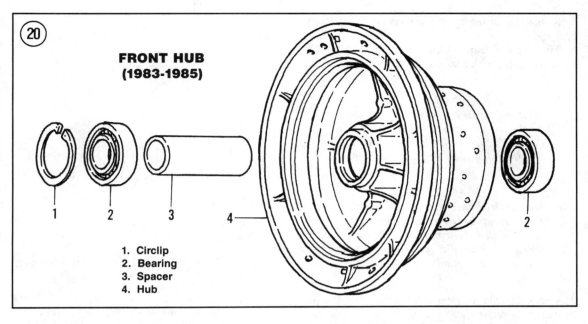

20

**FRONT HUB
(1983-1985)**

1. Circlip
2. Bearing
3. Spacer
4. Hub

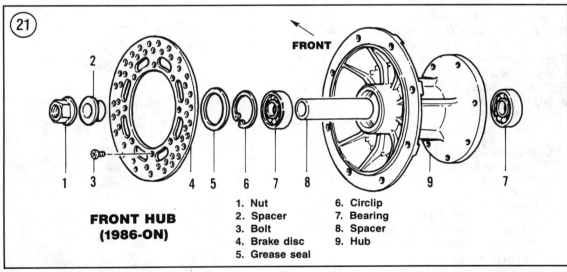

21

**FRONT HUB
(1986-ON)**

1. Nut
2. Spacer
3. Bolt
4. Brake disc
5. Grease seal
6. Circlip
7. Bearing
8. Spacer
9. Hub

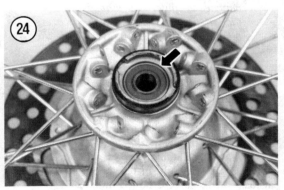

5. Remove the distance collar and tap out the opposite bearing.
6. Thoroughly clean out the inside of the hub with solvent and dry with compressed air or a shop cloth.

NOTE
Avoid getting any greasy solvent residue on the brake drum (1983-1985) during this procedure. If this happens, clean it off with a shop cloth and lacquer thinner.

NOTE
Fully sealed bearings are available from many good bearing specialty shops. Fully sealed bearings provide better protection from dirt and moisture that may get into the hub.

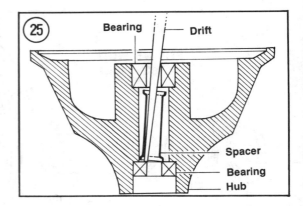

7. Check the axle for wear and straightness. Use V-blocks and a dial indicator. If the runout is 0.2 mm (0.008 in.) or greater, the axle should be replaced.
8. Pack non-sealed bearings with good quality bearing grease. Work the grease in between the balls thoroughly. Turn the bearing by hand a couple of times to make sure the grease is distributed evenly inside the bearing.
9. Pack the wheel hub and distance collar with multipurpose grease.

NOTE
If a bearing has only one sealed side, install the bearing with the sealed side facing out.

CAUTION
When installing the bearings in the following procedures, tap the bearings squarely into place and tap on the outer race only. Use a socket (Figure 26) that matches the outer race diameter. Do not tap on the inner race or the bearing might be damaged. Be sure that the bearings are completely seated.

10. Install the left-hand bearing.
11. Install the distance collar.
12. Install the right-hand bearing.
13. Install the left-hand circlip (**Figure 23**).
14. *1986-on:* Install a new left-hand grease seal. Lubricate it with multipurpose grease and tap it squarely into the hub. Install the oil seal until it is at least flush with the hub (**Figure 27**).

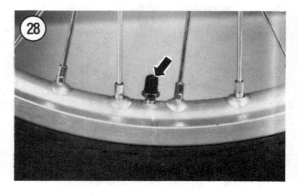

FRONT SUSPENSION AND STEERING

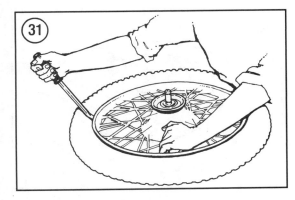

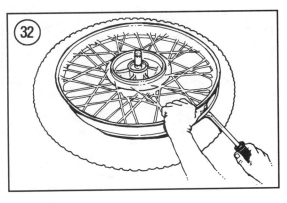

TIRE CHANGING

Removal

1. Remove the valve core (**Figure 28**) and deflate the tire.
2. Loosen the rim lock nuts (**Figure 29**).
3. Press the entire bead on both sides of the tire into the center of the rim.
4. Lubricate the beads with soapy water.

NOTE
*Use only quality tire irons without sharp edges (**Figure 30**). If necessary, file the ends of the tire irons to remove rough edges.*

5. Insert the tire iron under the bead next to the valve (**Figure 31**). Force the bead on the opposite side of tire into the center of the rim and pry the bead over the rim with the tire iron.
6. Insert a second tire iron next to the first to hold the bead over the rim. Then work around the tire with the first tire iron, prying the bead over the rim. Be careful not to pinch the inner tube with the tire irons.
7. Remove the valve from the hole in the rim and remove the tube from the tire.

NOTE
Step 8 is required only if it is necessary to completely remove the tire from the rim, such as for tire replacement.

8. Stand the tire upright. Insert the tire iron between the second bead and the side of the rim that the first bead was pried over (**Figure 32**). Force the bead on the opposite side from the tire iron into the center of the rim. Pry the second bead off of the rim, working around as with the first.

Installation

1. Carefully check the tire for any damage, especially inside. On the front tire carefully check the sidewall as it is very vulnerable to damage from rocks and other rider's footpegs.
2. Check that the spoke ends do not protrude through the nipples into the center of the rim which can puncture the tube. File off any protruding spoke ends.

NOTE
If you are having trouble with water and dirt entering the wheel, remove and discard the rubber rim band. Then wrap the rim center with 2 separate revolutions of duct tape. Punch holes through the tape at the rim lock and valve stem mounting areas.

3. Install the rim lock if removed.
4. If you are using the rubber rim band, be sure the band is in place with the rough side toward the rim. Align the holes in the band with the holes in the rim.
5. Liberally sprinkle the inside tire casing with baby powder. This helps to minimize tube pinching because the powder reduces chafing between the tire and tube.
6. If the tire was removed, lubricate one bead with soapy water. Then align the tire with the rim and push the tire onto the rim (**Figure 33**). Work around the tire in both directions (**Figure 34**).
7. Install the core into the inner tube valve. Put the tube in the tire and insert the valve stem through the hole in the rim. Inflate just enough to round it out. Too much air will make installing it in the tire difficult, and too little will increase the chances of pinching the tube with the tire irons.
8. Lubricate the upper tire bead and rim with soapy water.
9. Press the upper bead into the rim opposite the valve. Pry the bead into the rim on both sides of the initial point with your hands and work around the rim to the valve. If the tire wants to pull up on one side, either use a tire iron or one of your knees to hold the tire in place. The last few inches are usually the toughest to install and are also where most pinched tubes occur. If you can, continue to push the tire into the rim with your hands. Relubricate the bead if necessary. If the tire bead wants to pull out from under the rim, use both of your knees to hold the tire in place. If necessary, use a tire iron for the last few inches (**Figure 35**).
10. Wiggle the valve to be sure the tube is not trapped under the bead. Set the valve squarely in its hole before screwing on the valve nut.

NOTE
*Make sure the valve stem is not cocked in the rim as shown in **Figure 36**.*

11. Check the bead on both sides of the tire for even fit around the rim. Inflate the tire to approximately 25-30 psi to insure the tire bead is seated properly on the rim. If the tire is hard to seat, relubricate both sides of the tire and reinflate.
12. Tighten the rim lock nut (**Figure 29**).
13. Bleed the tire back down to between 10 and 14 psi. Never tighten the valve stem nut against the rim. It should always be installed finger-tight, near the valve stem cap rather than flush against the rim (**Figure 28**).

TIRE REPAIRS

Every dirt rider eventually experiences trouble with a tire or tube. Repairs and replacement are fairly simple, and every rider should know how to patch a tube.

Patching a motorcycle tube is only a temporary fix, especially on a dirt bike. The tire flexes too much and the patch could rub right off.

NOTE
If a regular standard inner tube is used replace it every 10 races. A stronger

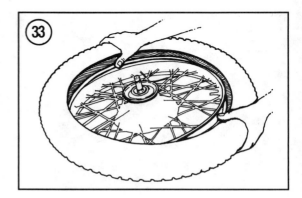

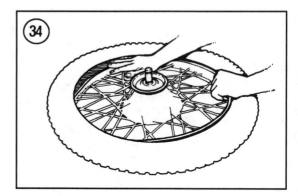

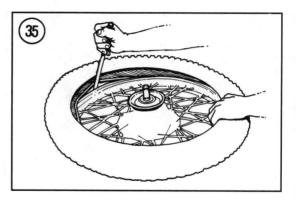

FRONT SUSPENSION AND STEERING

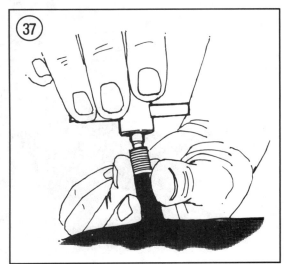

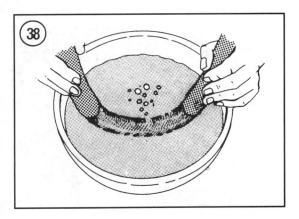

heavy-duty tube will last longer and is not as easy to puncture. The stronger tube weighs more where you least need it (unsprung weight), but the increased durability is worth the weight penalty.

Tire Repair Kits

Tire repair kits can be purchased from motorcycle dealers and some auto supply stores. When buying, specify that the kit you want is for motorcycles.

There are 2 types of tire repair kits:
  a. Hot patch.
  b. Cold patch.

Hot patches are stronger because they actually vulcanize to the tube, becoming part of it. However, they are far too bulky to carry for trail repairs, and the strength is unnecessary for a temporary repair.

Cold patches are not vulcanized to the tube; they are simply glued to it. Though not as strong as hot patches, cold patches are still very durable. Cold patch kits are less bulky than hot and more easily applied out on a dusty trail or in the pits. A cold patch kit contains everything necessary and tucks easily in with your emergency tool kit.

Tube Inspection

1. Remove the tube as described under *Tire Changing* in this chapter.
2. Install the valve core into the valve stem (**Figure 37**) and inflate the tube slightly. Do not overinflate.
3. Immerse the tube in water a section at a time (**Figure 38**). Look carefully for bubbles indicating a hole. Mark each hole and continue checking until you are certain that all holes are discovered and marked. Also make sure that the valve core is not leaking. Tighten it if necessary.

NOTE
If you do not have enough water to immerse sections of the tube, try running your hand over the tube slowly and very close to the surface. If your hand is damp, it works even better. If you suspect a hole anywhere, apply some saliva to the area to verify it.

4. Apply a cold patch using the techniques described under *Cold Patch Repair,* following.
5. Dust the patch area with talcum powder to prevent it from sticking to the tire.
6. Carefully check the inside of the tire casing for small rocks, sand or twigs which may have damaged the tube. If the inside of the tire is split, apply a patch to the area to prevent it from pinching and damaging the tube again.

7. Check the inside of the rim. Make sure the rubber rim band is in place, with no spoke ends protruding, which could puncture the tube.
8. Deflate the tube prior to installation in the tire.

Cold Patch Repairs

1. Remove the tube from the tire as previously described.
2. Roughen an area around the hole slightly larger than the patch, using a cap from the tire repair kit or a pocket knife. Do not scrape too vigorously or you may cause additional damage.
3. Apply a small amount of the special cement from the kit to the puncture and spread it evenly with your finger.
4. Allow the cement to dry until tacky—usually 30 seconds or so is sufficient.
5. Remove the backing from the patch.

CAUTION
Do not touch the newly exposed rubber with your fingers or the patch will not stick firmly.

6. Center the patch over the hole. Hold patch firmly in place for about 30 seconds to allow the cement to set.
7. Dust the patched area with talcum powder to prevent sticking.
8. Install the tube as previously described.

HANDLEBAR

Removal/Installation

1. Remove the plastic straps on the engine kill switch wire.
2. Remove the kill switch and the clutch lever assembly from the left-hand side. See **Figure 39**.

NOTE
Step 3 describes disassembly and removal of the throttle assembly. If you don't need to disassemble the throttle assembly when removing the handlebar, loosen the throttle screws only. Then when the handlebar bolts and handlebar are removed from the steering stem, slide the throttle assembly off the handlebar.

3. Remove the front brake lever assembly (1983-1985) and remove the switch from the right-hand side (**Figure 40**). Then remove the screws securing the throttle assembly and remove it.

NOTE
Carefully lay the throttle assembly and cable over the front fender, or back over the frame, so the cable does not get crimped or damaged.

4. *Disc brake models:* Remove the bolts securing the master cylinder to the handlebar and remove the master cylinder. Support the master cylinder so that it does not hang by the hydraulic hose.
5. Remove the bolts (**Figure 41**) securing the handlebar holders and remove the holders.
6. Remove the handlebar.

FRONT SUSPENSION AND STEERING

7. Install by reversing these removal steps, noting the following.

8. To maintain a good grip on the handlebar and to prevent it from slipping down, clean the knurled section of the handlebar with a wire brush. It should be kept rough so it will be held securely by the holders. The holders should also be kept clean and free of any metal that may have been gouged loose by handlebar slippage.

9. Tighten the bolts securing the handlebar to the torque specification listed in **Table 2**.

10. Apply a light coat of light machine oil to the throttle grip area on the handlebar prior to installation.

WARNING
After installation is completed, make sure the brake lever does not come in contact with the throttle grip assembly when it is fully applied.

11. Adjust the front brake (1983-1985) and clutch as described in Chapter Three.

WARNING
Make sure the front brake and clutch operate properly before riding the bike.

STEERING HEAD

The steering head on these models uses tapered roller bearings at the top and bottom pivot positions. Refer to **Figure 42** (1983-1985) or **Figure 43** (1986-on) for this procedure.

Disassembly

1. Remove the front wheel as described under *Front Wheel Removal* in this chapter.
2. Remove the front fender.
3. Remove the handlebar as described under *Handlebar Removal/Installation* in this chapter.
4. Remove the front forks as described in this chapter.
5. *1983-1985:* Loosen the upper fork bracket pinch bolt (**Figure 44**).
6. Loosen and remove the steering stem bolt (**Figure 45**). Remove the washer (**Figure 42**) on 1983-1985 models.
7. Remove the upper fork bracket (**Figure 46**).
8. *1986-on:* Remove the collar (**Figure 47**).
9. Remove the steering stem adjusting nut (A, **Figure 48**). Use a large drift and hammer or a spanner wrench.
10. Hold onto the steering stem and remove the upper cover (B, **Figure 48**) and bearing (**Figure 49**).
11. Lower and remove the steering stem (**Figure 50**).

Inspection

1. Clean the bearing races in the steering head, the steering stem races, ball bearings and the tapered roller bearing with solvent.
2. Check the welds around the steering head for cracks and fractures. If any are found, have them repaired by a competent frame shop or welding service.
3. Check the balls for pitting, scratches, or discoloration indicating wear or corrosion. Replace them in sets if any are bad.
4. Check the races (**Figure 51**) for pitting or galling and corrosion. If any of these conditions exist, replace the races as described under *Bearing Race Replacement* in this chapter.
5. See **Figure 52**. Check the steering nut (A), adjust nut (B) and the upper bearing cover (C) for cracks or damage. Replace if necessary.
6. Check the steering stem (**Figure 53**) for cracks and damage.
7. Check the tapered roller bearings (**Figure 54** and **Figure 55**) for pitting, scratches or discoloration indicating wear or corrosion. If necessary, replace the lower bearing as follows:
   a. Install a bearing puller onto the steering stem and bearing.
   b. Pull the bearing off of the steering stem.
   c. Clean the steering stem thoroughly in solvent.
   d. Slide a new bearing onto the steering stem until it stops.
   e. Align the bearing with the machined portion of the shaft and slide a long hollow pipe over the steering stem until it seats against the inner bearing race. Drive the bearing onto the shaft until it bottoms.
8. *1986-on:* Check the collar (**Figure 56**) for cracks or damage. Also check the upper fork bracket where the collar rides (**Figure 57**) for cracks or damage. Replace worn or damaged parts.
9. Check the upper (**Figure 58**) and lower fork bracket (**Figure 53**) for cracks or damage, especially where the fork tubes mount.

Steering Head Race Replacement

To remove an upper or lower bearing race (**Figure 51**), insert a soft punch into the head tube (**Figure 59**) and carefully tap the race out from the inside. After it is started, tap around the race so that neither the race nor the head tube is damaged.

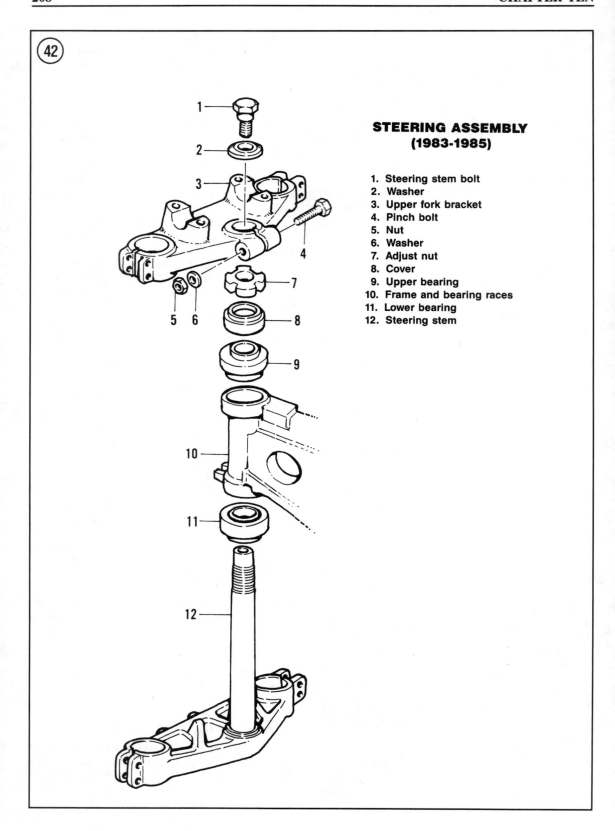

FRONT SUSPENSION AND STEERING

**STEERING ASSEMBLY
(1986-ON)**

1. Steering stem bolt
2. Upper fork bracket
3. Collar
4. Adjust nut
5. Cover
6. Upper bearing
7. Frame and bearing races
8. Lower bearing
9. Steering stem

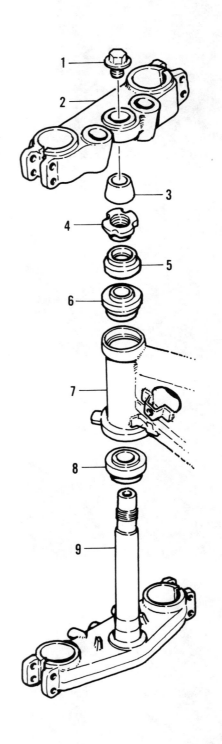

CHAPTER TEN

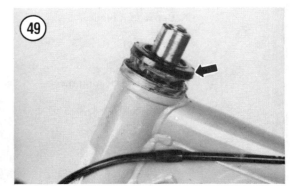

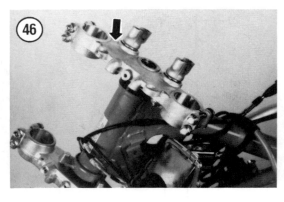

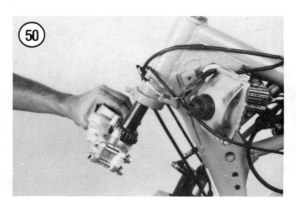

FRONT SUSPENSION AND STEERING

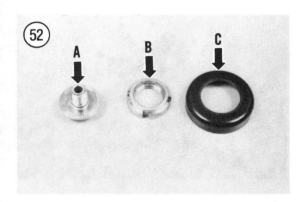

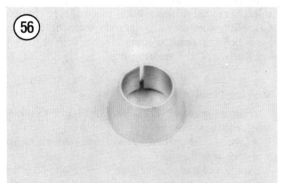

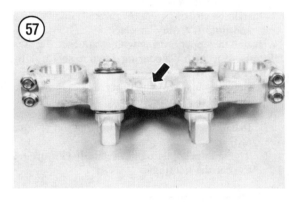

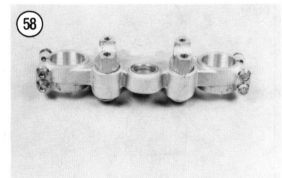

To install the race, tap it in slowly with a block of wood or suitable size socket or piece of pipe (**Figure 60**). Make sure they are squarely seated in the race bores before tapping them in. Tap them in until they are flush with the steering head.

Steering Head Assembly

Refer to **Figure 42** (1983-1985) or **Figure 43** (1986-on) for this procedure.

1. Make sure the steering head and stem races are properly seated.
2. Apply a coat of bearing grease to the tapered roller bearing on the steering stem (**Figure 55**). Carefully work the grease into the rollers.
3. Install the steering stem (**Figure 50**) into the head tube and hold it firmly in place.
4. Install the upper bearing with its attached dust seal (**Figure 49**). Push the bearing down to seat it in the race (**Figure 61**).
5. Install the dust cover (**Figure 62**).
6. Install and tighten the steering stem adjusting nut as follows:
    a. Install the steering stem adjusting nut (**Figure 63**).
    b. Tighten the adjusting nut securely (**Figure 64**) to seat the bearings.

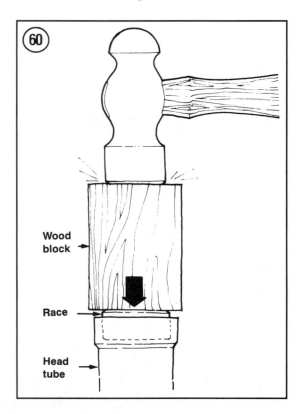

FRONT SUSPENSION AND STEERING

c. Loosen the adjusting nut and check the bearing play. The adjusting nut should be just tight enough to remove play, both horizontal and vertical, yet loose enough so that the assembly will turn to both full lock positions under its own weight after being centered, then pushed in that direction.
7. *1986-on:* Install the collar (**Figure 65**).
8. Install the upper fork bracket (**Figure 66**).
9. Install the steering bolt. On 1983-1985 models, install the washer and bolt.
10. Tighten the steering bolt (**Figure 67**) finger-tight at this time.

NOTE
Steps 11-13 must be performed in this order to assure proper upper and lower fork bracket to fork alignment.

11. Slide both fork tubes into position and tighten the lower fork bracket pinch bolts to the torque specification in **Table 2**.
12. Tighten the steering stem bolt to the torque specification in **Table 2**.
13. Tighten the upper fork bracket pinch bolts to the torque specification in **Table 2**.
14. *1983-1985:* Tighten the upper fork bracket pinch bolt (**Figure 68**) to the torque specification in **Table 2**.
15. Continue assembly by reversing Steps 1-4, *Steering Stem Disassembly*.
16. After a few hours of riding, the bearings have had a chance to seat; readjust the free play in the steering stem with the steering stem adjusting nut.

Steering Adjustment

1. Raise the front wheel off the ground. Support the motorcycle securely under the engine.
2. *1983-1985:* Loosen the upper fork bracket pinch bolt (**Figure 68**).
3. Loosen the lower fork bracket pinch bolts.
4. Loosen the steering stem bolt.
5. Turn the steering stem adjusting nut with a spanner wrench or punch until you just feel the steering play taken up.
6. Tighten all steering bolts to the torque specifications in **Table 2**.
7. Recheck the steering play.

FRONT FORK

The Kawasaki front fork is spring-controlled and hydraulically damped. The damping rate is determined by the viscosity (weight) of the oil used, and the spring rate can be altered by varying the amount of oil used by air pressurization of the forks. See Chapter Three for front fork adjustment.

Before suspecting major trouble with the front fork, drain the fork oil and refill with the proper type and quantity. If you still have trouble, such as poor damping, tendency to bottom out or top out, or leakage around the fork seals, then follow the service procedures in this section.

To simplify fork service and to prevent the mixing of parts, the legs should be removed, serviced and reinstalled individually.

Each front fork leg consists of the fork tube (inner tube), slider (outer tube), fork spring, damper rod with its damper components and bushings.

Removal/Installation

1. Remove the front wheel as described in this chapter.
2. Disconnect the front brake cable or hose at the left-hand fork tube. See **Figure 69** (1983-1985) or **Figure 70** (1986-on).
3. *1986-on:* Remove the brake caliper as described under *Front Caliper Removal/Installation* in Chapter Twelve.

NOTE
Insert a piece of wood in the caliper in place of the disc. That way, if the brake lever is inadvertently squeezed, the piston will not be forced out of the caliper. If it does happen, the caliper might have to be disassembled to reseat the piston.

WARNING
When performing Step 4, release the air pressure gradually. If released too fast, oil may spurt out with the air. Protect your eyes accordingly.

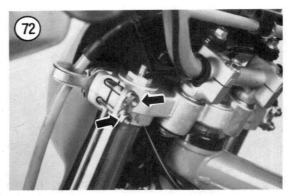

FRONT SUSPENSION AND STEERING

4. Remove the air valve cap and depress the valve (**Figure 71**) to release fork air pressure from both fork tubes.
5. If the fork bracket are going to be disassembled, perform the following before removing them:
   a. Loosen the top fork bracket pinch bolts (**Figure 72**).
   b. Using a speeder bar and socket (**Figure 73**), loosen and remove the fork cap. See **Figure 74**.
   c. Remove the spacer (**Figure 75**).
   d. Remove the spring seat (**Figure 76**).
   e. Remove the fork spring (**Figure 77**).
6. Loosen the lower fork bracket pinch bolts (**Figure 78**). Loosen the fork boot's upper clamp to prevent damaging the boot during fork removal.
7. Twist the fork tube and remove it.
8. Install by reversing these removal steps. Note the following.
9. Tighten the fork bracket pinch bolts to the torque specification in **Table 2**.
10. If the fork spring was removed, reverse Step 5 to assemble the fork spring assembly. Some oil is always lost when the fork springs are removed. Add oil, as necessary, to bring the oil to the correct level. See Tables 3-10.
11. *1986-on:* Install and tighten the brake caliper as described in Chapter Twelve.
12. *1986-on:* After installing the front wheel, squeeze the front brake lever. If the brake lever feels spongy, bleed the brake as described under *Bleeding the System* in Chapter Twelve.
13. Refill the front fork air pressure as described under *Suspension Adjustment* in Chapter Three.

Disassembly

Refer to **Figure 79** (1983-1985) or **Figure 80** (1986-on) for this procedure.

CHAPTER TEN

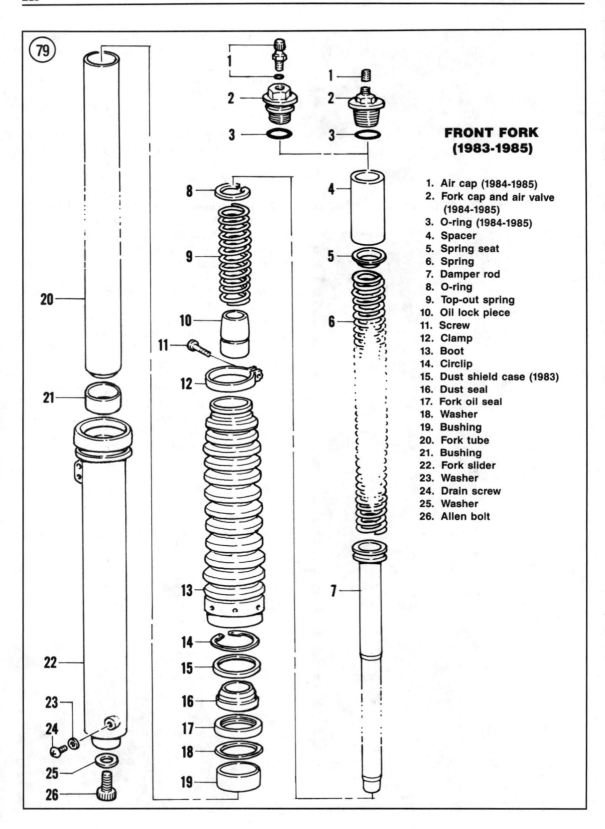

FRONT SUSPENSION AND STEERING

FRONT FORK (1986-ON)

1. Air cap
2. Fork cap/air valve
3. O-ring
4. Spacer
5. Spring seat
6. Fork spring
7. Damper rod
8. Piston ring
9. Spring
10. Oil lock piece
11. Clamp
12. Boot
13. Circlip
14. Fork dust seal
15. Fork seal
16. Washer
17. Bushing
18. Fork tube
19. Bushing
20. Fork slider
21. Washer
22. Drain screw
23. Washer
24. Allen bolt

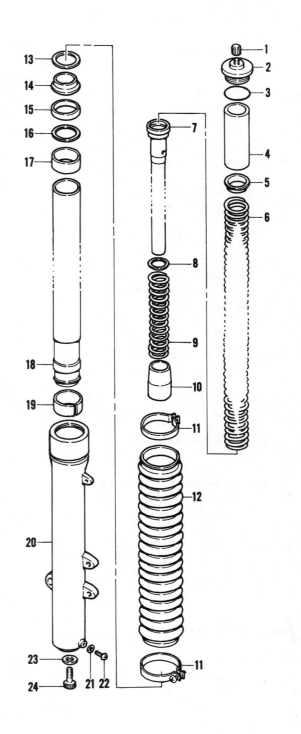

WARNING
When performing Step 1, release the air pressure gradually. If released too fast, oil may spurt out with the air. Protect your eyes accordingly.

1. Depress the air valve(s) to release all fork air pressure.

NOTE
*The fork slider Allen bolt is secured with a thread locking agent and is hard to remove. If a heavy duty air powered impact wrench is available, try that first. If necessary, you may be able to keep the damper rod inside from turning by temporarily installing the fork spring, spring seat, spacer and fork cap, and having an assistant compress the fork while you try to loosen the bottom bolt. It may be easier to attempt this method while the fork tubes are installed on the bike. If these methods are not successful, you will have to keep the damper rod from turning with a special tool. Kawasaki sells a long T-handle (part No. 57001-183) and adapter (part No. 57001-1057). See **Figure 81**. You can substitute the long T-handle with a short T-handle and a number of 3/8 in. drive extensions.*

2. Remove the fork spring assembly as follows:
   a. Loosen the top fork bracket pinch bolts (**Figure 72**).
   b. Using a speeder bar and socket (**Figure 73**), loosen and remove the fork cap. See **Figure 74**.
   c. Remove the spacer (**Figure 75**).
   d. Remove the spring seat (**Figure 76**).
   e. Remove the fork spring (**Figure 77**).

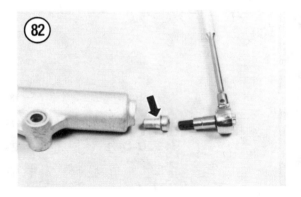
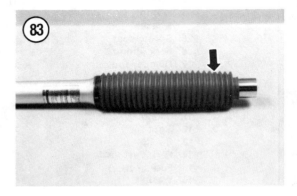
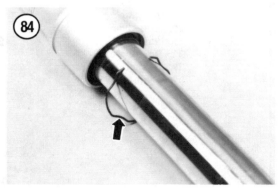
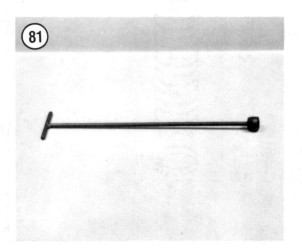

FRONT SUSPENSION AND STEERING

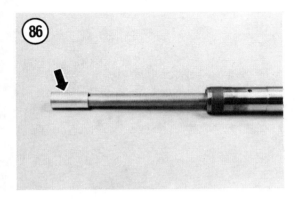

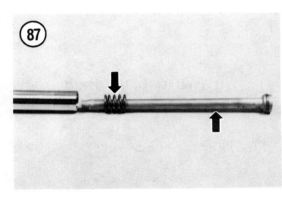

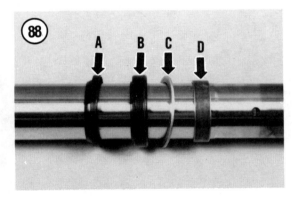

3. Turn the fork tube over and pour out the fork oil.
4. Remove the Allen bolt and gasket from the bottom of the slider (**Figure 82**).
5. Remove the clamps and remove the fork tube boot (**Figure 83**).
6. Remove the snap ring (**Figure 84**) from the slider.
7. There is an interference fit between the bushing in the fork slider and the bushing on the fork tube. In order to remove the slider from the fork tube, pull hard on the slider using quick in-and-out strokes. Doing this will withdraw the oil seal, washer and bushing (**Figure 85**).
8. Remove the oil lock piece from the end of the damper rod (**Figure 86**).
9. Slide the damper rod and top-out spring (**Figure 87**) out of the fork tube.
10. See **Figure 88**. Slide the following parts off of the fork tube:
   a. Dust seal (A).
   b. Oil seal (B).
   c. Washer (C).
   d. Bushing (D).

Inspection

1. Thoroughly clean all parts in solvent and dry them.
2. Check both fork tubes for wear or scratches. Check the fork tube for straightness. If bent, refer service to a Kawasaki dealer.
3. Check the fork tube for chrome flaking or creasing; this condition will damage oil seals. Replace the fork tube if necessary.
4. Check the slider oil seal area (**Figure 89**) for dents or other damage that would allow oil leakage. Replace the fork tube if necessary.
5. Check the damper rod (**Figure 90**) for straightness by rolling it on a surface plate or thick piece of glass. Any clicking noise indicates a bent rod.

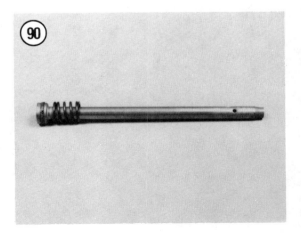

6. Check the damper rod piston ring (**Figure 91**) for cracks or damage.

7. Check the guide bushing on the fork tube (**Figure 92**) for scoring, nicks or damage on its outside surface. Replace if necessary by pulling off the fork tube.

8. Check the mating guide bushing (D, **Figure 88**) for scoring, nicks or damage on its inside surface. Replace if necessary.

9. Measure the uncompressed length of the fork spring (**Figure 93**) with a tape measure and compare to specifications in **Table 1**. If one spring is too short, replace both springs as a set.

10. Replace the fork cap O-ring (**Figure 94**) if damaged.

11. Check the oil and dust seals for wear or damage. Replace if necessary.

NOTE
If the fork seals were replaced recently and they appear okay, it is permissible to reinstall them. If the fork seals have never been replaced, they should be changed now.

Assembly

Refer to **Figure 79** (1983-1985) or **Figure 80** (1986-on) for this procedure.

1. Slide the top-out spring (**Figure 87**) onto the damper rod and insert the damper rod and spring into the fork tube (**Figure 87**).

2. Slide the oil lock piece (**Figure 86**) onto the end of the damper rod.

3. Insert the damper rod/fork tube into the slider (**Figure 95**).

4. Make sure the gasket is on the Allen bolt (**Figure 96**).

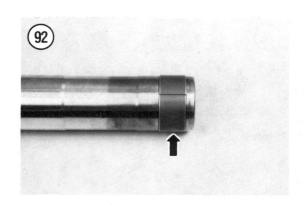
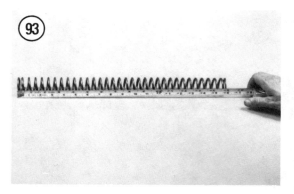
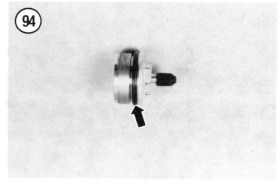
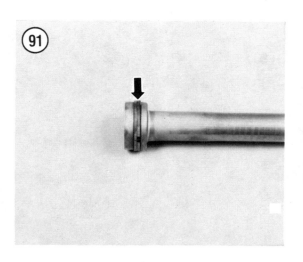
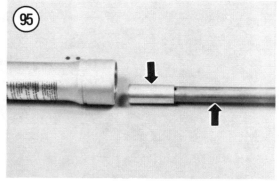

FRONT SUSPENSION AND STEERING

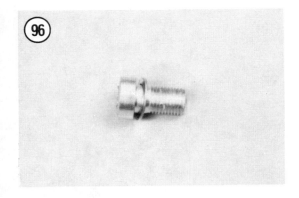

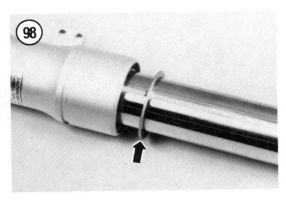

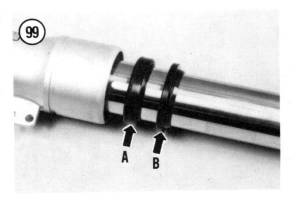

5. Apply Loctite 242 (blue) to the threads on the Allen bolt. Install the Allen bolt (**Figure 82**) and tighten securely.

NOTE
Use the same tool and procedure as during disassembly to prevent the damper rod from turning when tightening the Allen bolt.

NOTE
The guide bushing can be installed with a piece of pipe or other piece of tubing that fits over the fork tube. If both ends of the pipe are threaded, wrap one end with duct tape to prevent the threads from damaging the interior of the lower fork tube.

6. Slide the guide bushing (**Figure 97**) over the fork tube. Tap the guide bushing into the lower fork tube until it bottoms.
7. Slide the washer (**Figure 98**) down the fork tube until it rests against the bushing.
8. Position the oil seal with the marking facing upward and slide down onto the fork tube (A, **Figure 99**). Drive the seal into the lower fork tube with the same tool used in Step 6. Drive the oil seal in until it rests against the washer.
9. Press the dust seal (B, **Figure 99**) into the slider.

NOTE
*Make sure the groove in the lower fork tube can be seen above the dust seal (**Figure 100**). If not, the bushing and oil seal will have to driven farther into the lower fork tube.*

10. Slide the snap ring (**Figure 101**) down the fork tube and seat it in the slider groove. Make sure the snap ring is completely seated in the groove.
11. Fill the fork tube with the correct quantity and weight fork oil as described in Chapter Three. Check the oil level as described in Chapter Three under *Front Fork Oil Change*.
12. Install the fork tubes onto the motorcycle as described in this chapter. Reverse Step 2 of *Disassembly* to install the spring assembly. Install the fork spring so that the closer wound coils face toward the top of the fork tube.

CHAPTER TEN

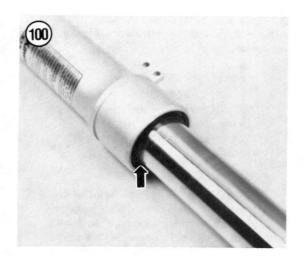

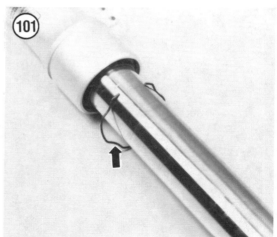

FRONT SUSPENSION AND STEERING

Table 1 FRONT SUSPENSION SPECIFICATIONS

Caster	
1983-1985	28°
1986	26.5°
1987-on	27.5°
Trail	
1983-1985	121 mm (4.76 in.)
1986-on	135 mm (5.3 in.)
Front wheel travel	
1983-1985	260 mm (10.24 in.)
1986-on	270 mm (10.60 in.)
Front wheel tire size	
1983-1985	3.00 × 21 (4PR)
1986-on	80/100 × 21 51M
Front fork spring free length	
1983-1985	
Standard	538.5 mm (21.2 in.)
Service limit	528 mm (20.8 in.)
1986	
Standard	513.5 mm (20.2 in.)
Service limit	503 mm (19.8 in.)
1987-on	
Standard	453.5 mm (17.9 in.)
Service limit	445 mm (17.5 in.)
Rim runout	
Axial	
Standard	0.5 mm (0.02 in.)
Limit	2.0 mm (0.08 in.)
Radial	
Standard	0.8 mm (0.032 in.)
Limit	2.0 mm (0.08 in.)

Table 2 FRONT SUSPENSION TIGHTENING TORQUES

	N·m	ft.-lb.
Front axle nut		
1983-1985	64	47
1986-on	78	58
Lower fork bracket pinch bolt		
1983-1985	20	14.5
1986-on	20	14.5
Upper fork bracket pinch bolt		
1983-1985	20	14.5
1986-on	20	14.5
Front fork cap bolts	23	16.5
Front fork Allen bolt		
1983-1985	36	27
1986-on	61	45
Handlebar clamp bolts		
1983-1985	14	10
1986-on	18	13
Steering stem bolt	54	40
Steering stem pinch bolt		
1983-1985	20	14.5
1986-on	—	—

CHAPTER ELEVEN

REAR SUSPENSION

This chapter contains repair and replacement procedures for the rear wheel and hub and rear suspension components. Service to the rear suspension consists of periodically checking bolt tightness, replacing swing arm bushings, and checking the condition of the spring/gas shock unit and overhauling it as required.

Rear suspension specifications are listed in **Table 1**. Rear suspension tightening torques are listed in **Table 2** and **Table 3**. **Tables 1-3** are found at the end of the chapter.

REAR WHEEL

Removal/Installation

1. Support the bike so that the rear wheel is off of the ground.
2. Unscrew the rear brake adjusting nut completely from the brake rod (**Figure 1**). Withdraw the brake rod from the brake lever and pivot it down out of the way. Reinstall the adjusting nut to avoid misplacing it.
3. Loosen and remove the axle nut (A, **Figure 2**).
4. Remove the right-hand chain adjuster (B, **Figure 2**).
5. Push the wheel forward to provide as much chain slack as possible. Then turn the rear wheel and slip the drive chain off of the sprocket.
6. Remove the axle and chain adjuster from the right-hand side. See **Figure 3**.

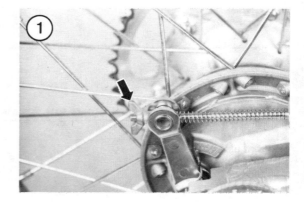

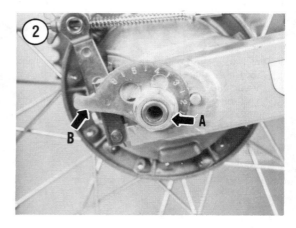

REAR SUSPENSION

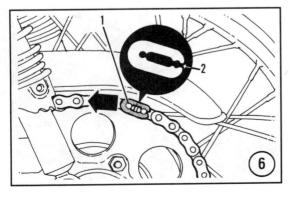

7. Pull the wheel back as required to disconnect the brake panel from the tab welded to the swing arm and remove the rear wheel.
8. Remove the axle spacer (**Figure 4**) from the left-hand side.
9. Remove the brake panel (**Figure 5**) from the right-hand side.
10. Install by reversing these removal steps. Note the following:
   a. Be sure to install the axle spacer on the left-hand side of the wheel (**Figure 4**).
   b. Make sure to align the groove in the brake panel with the tab welded to the swing arm.
   c. If the drive chain was disconnected, install the drive chain master link so that its closed end is facing the direction of chain travel (**Figure 6**).
   d. Install the axle from the left-hand side.
   e. Adjust the drive chain as described in Chapter Three.
   f. Lightly tighten the axle nut, but don't torque it yet.
   g. After the wheel is completely installed, rotate it several times to make sure it rotates smoothly. Apply the brake several times to make sure it operates correctly.

NOTE
Torquing the axle nut with the brake applied properly centers the rear brake assembly.

   h. With the rear brake fully applied, torque the axle nut to the specifications in **Table 2** or **Table 3**.
   i. Adjust the rear brake as described under *Rear Brake Pedal Adjustment* in Chapter Three.

Inspection

Spokes loosen with use and should be checked prior to each race or weekend ride. The "tuning fork" method for checking spoke tightness is simple and works well. Tap each spoke with a spoke wrench or the shank of a screwdriver and listen for a tone. A tightened spoke will emit a clear, ringing tone, and a loose spoke will sound flat. All the spokes of the same length in a correctly tightened wheel will emit tones of similar pitch but not necessarily the same precise tone.

Bent, stripped or broken spokes should be replaced as soon as they are detected, as they can cause the destruction of an expensive hub. Unscrew the nipple from the spoke and depress the nipple into the rim far enough to free the end of the spoke, taking care not to push the nipple all the way in. Remove the damaged spoke from the hub and use it to match a new spoke of identical length. If necessary, trim the new spoke to match the original and dress the end of the threads with a thread die. Install the new spoke in the hub and screw on the nipple; tighten it until the spoke's tone is similar to the tone of the other spokes in the wheel. Periodically check the new spoke; it will stretch and must be retightened several times before it takes its final set.

Wheel rim runout is the amount of "wobble" a wheel shows as it rotates. You can check runout with the wheels on the bike by simply supporting the wheel off the ground and turning the wheel slowly while you hold a pointer solidly against the frame or swing arm (**Figure 7**). Just make sure any wobble you observe isn't caused by your own hand.

Off the motorcycle, runout can be checked with the wheel installed on a truing stand (**Figure 8**).

The maximum allowable axial (side-to-side) and radial (up and down) play is listed in **Table 1**. Tighten or replace any bent or loose spokes.

NOTE
*Make sure to use a spoke wrench of the correct size to prevent damaging the spoke nipple (**Figure 9**).*

1. Draw the high point of the rim toward the centerline of the wheel by tightening the spokes in the area of the high point and on the same side as the high point, and loosening the spokes on the side opposite the high point.
2. Rotate the wheel and check runout. Continue adjusting until the runout is within specification. Be patient and thorough, adjusting the position of the rim a little at a time. If you tighten 2 spokes at the high point 1/2 turn, tighten the adjacent spokes 1/4 turn. Loosen the spokes on the opposite side equivalent amounts.

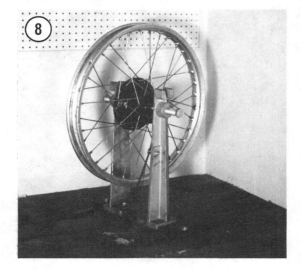

REAR HUB

Refer to **Figure 10** (1983-1985) or **Figure 11** (1986-on) for this procedure.

Disassembly/Reassembly

Do not remove bearings for periodic inspection as bearing removal normally damages the first bearing removed. Always replace bearings as a set.

1. Remove the rear wheel as described under *Rear Wheel Removal/Installation* in this chapter.
2. Remove the axle spacer (**Figure 4**) from the wheel.
3. Pull the brake panel (**Figure 5**) straight up and out of the drum.
4. *1983-1985:* Remove the circlip from the left-hand side (**Figure 10**).

REAR SUSPENSION

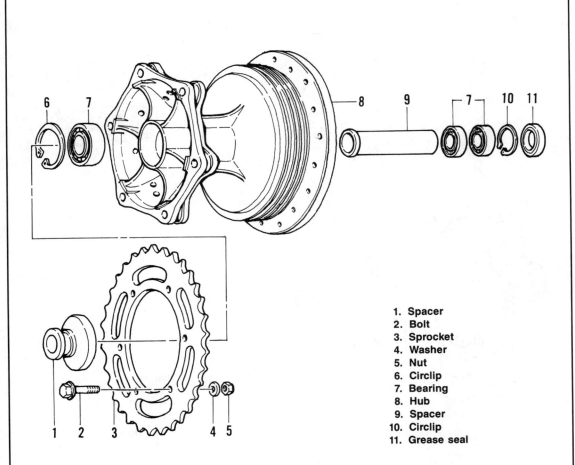

**REAR HUB
(1983-1985)**

1. Spacer
2. Bolt
3. Sprocket
4. Washer
5. Nut
6. Circlip
7. Bearing
8. Hub
9. Spacer
10. Circlip
11. Grease seal

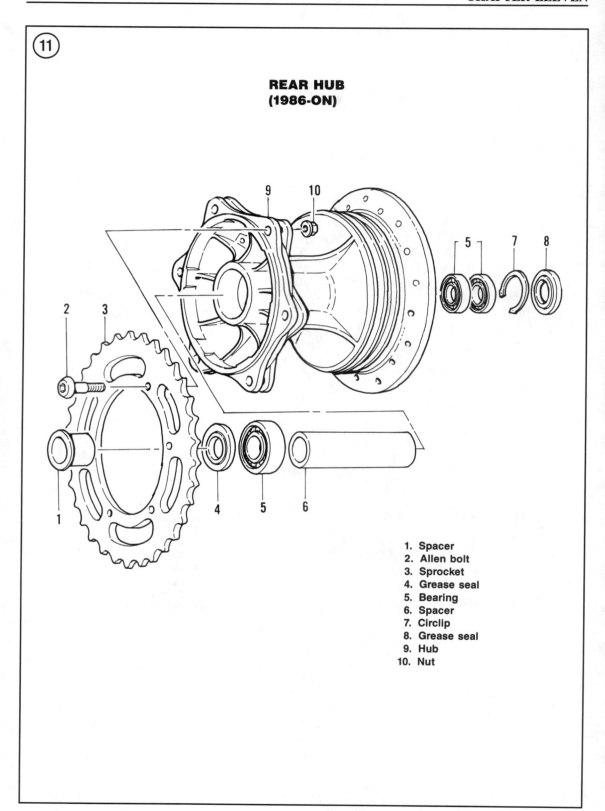

REAR SUSPENSION

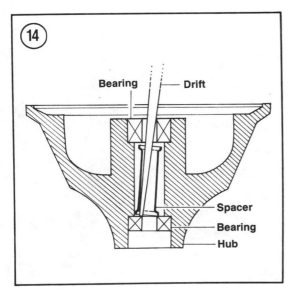

5. Remove the oil seals (**Figure 12**) by carefully prying them out of the hub with a long screwdriver. Prop a piece of wood or rag underneath the screwdriver to prevent damaging the hub.

NOTE
If the seal is tight, work the screwdriver around the seal every few degrees until the seal pops out of the hub.

6. Remove the circlip from the right-hand side (**Figure 13**).
7. Remove the left- and right-hand bearings and distance collar. To remove them, insert a soft aluminum or brass drift into one side of the hub. Push the distance collar over to one side and place the drift on the inner race of the lower bearing (**Figure 14**). Tap the bearing out of the hub with a hammer, working around the perimeter of the inner race.
8. Remove the distance collar and tap out the opposite bearing.
9. Thoroughly clean out the inside of the hub with solvent and dry with compressed air or a shop cloth.

NOTE
Avoid getting any greasy solvent residue on the brake drum during this procedure. If this happens, clean it off with a shop cloth and spray brake cleaner.

NOTE
Fully sealed bearings are available from many good bearing specialty shops. Fully sealed bearings provide better protection from dirt and moisture that may get into the hub.

10. Check the axle for wear and straightness. Use V-blocks and a dial indicator. If the runout is 0.2 mm (0.008 in.) or greater, the axle should be replaced.
11. Pack non-sealed bearings with good quality bearing grease. Work the grease in between the balls thoroughly. Turn the bearing by hand a couple of times to make sure the grease is distributed evenly inside the bearing.
12. Pack the wheel hub and distance collar with multipurpose grease.

NOTE
If a bearing has only one sealed side, install the bearing with the sealed side facing out.

CAUTION
*When installing the bearings in the following procedures, tap the bearings squarely into place and tap on the outer race only. Use a socket (**Figure 15**) that matches the outer race diameter. Do not tap on the inner race or the bearing might be damaged. Be sure that the bearings are completely seated.*

13. Install the 2 right-hand bearings.
14. Install the distance collar.
15. Install the right-hand bearing.
16. Install the right-hand circlip.
17. *1983-1985:* Install the left-hand circlip.
18. Install a new right-hand grease seal. Lubricate it with multipurpose grease and tap it squarely into the hub. Install the oil seal until it is at least flush with the hub (**Figure 16**).
19. *1986-on:* Install the left-hand oil seal as described in Step 18.

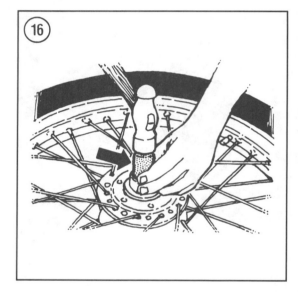

DRIVE SPROCKET

Disassembly/Assembly

1. Remove the rear wheel as described in this chapter.
2A. *1983-1985:* Loosen and remove the bolts and nuts.
2B. *1986-on:* Loosen the nuts at the back of the sprocket. Then remove the nuts, washers and Allen bolts. Do not loosen the Allen bolts by turning the bolt; this will damage the Allen head.
3. Remove the drive sprocket (**Figure 17**).
4. Assemble by reversing these disassembly steps. Tighten nuts and bolts to the torque specification in **Table 2** or **Table 3**.

Inspection

Inspect the sprocket teeth. If they are visibly worn, replace the sprocket.

If the sprocket requires replacement, the drive chain is probably worn also and may need replacement. Refer to *Drive Chain/Cleaning, Inspection and Lubrication* in Chapter Three.

DRIVE CHAIN

Removal/Installation

1. Place a motocross workstand or wood block(s) under the frame so the rear wheel is off the ground.

REAR SUSPENSION

2. Turn the rear wheel and drive chain until the master link is accessible.

3. Remove the master link clip (**Figure 6**) and remove the master link.

4. Slowly rotate the rear wheel and pull the drive chain off the drive sprocket.

5. Install by reversing these removal steps.

6. Install the clip on the master link so that its closed end is facing the direction of chain travel (**Figure 6**).

Service and Inspection

For service and inspection of the drive chain, refer to *Drive Chain/Cleaning, Inspection and Lubrication* in Chapter Three.

TIRE CHANGING AND TIRE REPAIRS

Refer to Chapter Ten.

UNI-TRAK REAR SUSPENSION

All KDX200 models use a single rear shock absorber/spring unit. The single shock controls swing arm movement through a compound linkage system with spherical bearings at both ends of a vertical link and rocking arm (**Figure 18**).

The single shock/spring unit minimizes swing arm flex caused by unequal damping and spring tension between dual shocks. However, several suspension bushings carry a great load in the Uni-Trak system. Frequent lubrication and inspections are necessary to preserve good handling and prevent premature component wear.

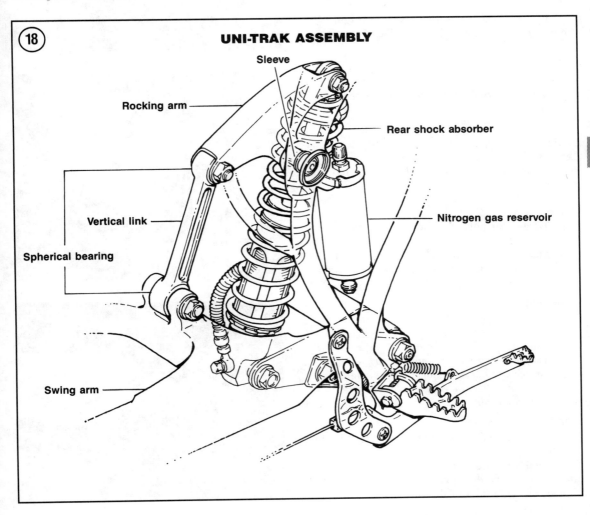

UNI-TRAK SHOCK ABSORBER (1983-1985)

Removal/Installation

1. Support the motorcycle with the rear wheel off the ground.
2. Remove the seat and both side covers.
3. Remove the air cleaner element and air box (**Figure 19**).

> **WARNING**
> Do not disconnect the shock absorber reservoir hose when performing Step 4. In addition, do not drop the reservoir or lay it in a position where it could be damaged. The shock and reservoir are under extreme pressure and eye injury could occur from misuse.

4. Remove the shock absorber reservoir (**Figure 20**) from its mount on the right-hand side of the frame.

> **NOTE**
> It is easier to remove the first shock mounting bolt, if you hold up the rear wheel.

5. Remove the top and bottom shock mounting bolts (**Figure 21**).
6. Remove the shock absorber through the left side of the frame.
7. To install, reverse the removal procedures. Note the following:
    a. Tighten the nuts to the torque specification in **Table 2**.
    b. Make sure the shock reservoir is properly mounted on the right-hand side of the frame.

Disassembly

> **NOTE**
> The angle of the reservoir hose is critical. Mark the shock body and reservoir to ensure that the hose angle is correct after you reassemble the shock and reservoir.

Refer to **Figure 22**.
1. Remove the shock absorber as described in this chapter.
2. Wash the outside of the shock absorber in solvent and allow to dry thoroughly. Especially clean the threads at the bottom of the shock.

3. Secure the bottom shock absorber mount in a vise with soft jaws (**Figure 23**).
4. Using the Kawasaki wrenches (part No. 57001-1101) or equivalent, loosen the locknut (**Figure 23**). Then turn the adjusting nut all the way down to reduce spring preload.
5. Slide the rubber bumper down the shock shaft.

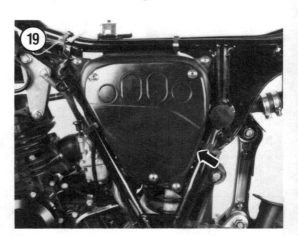

REAR SUSPENSION

REAR SHOCK ABSORBER (1983-1985)

1. Collar
2. O-ring
3. Circlip
4. Bushing
5. Rod/piston assembly
6. Piston ring
7. Circlip
8. Spring seat
9. Spring
10. Adjust nut
11. Locknut
12. Shock body
13. Bushing
14. Washer
15. Banjo bolt
16. Hose
17. O-ring
18. Reservoir
19. Reservoir guard
20. Cap

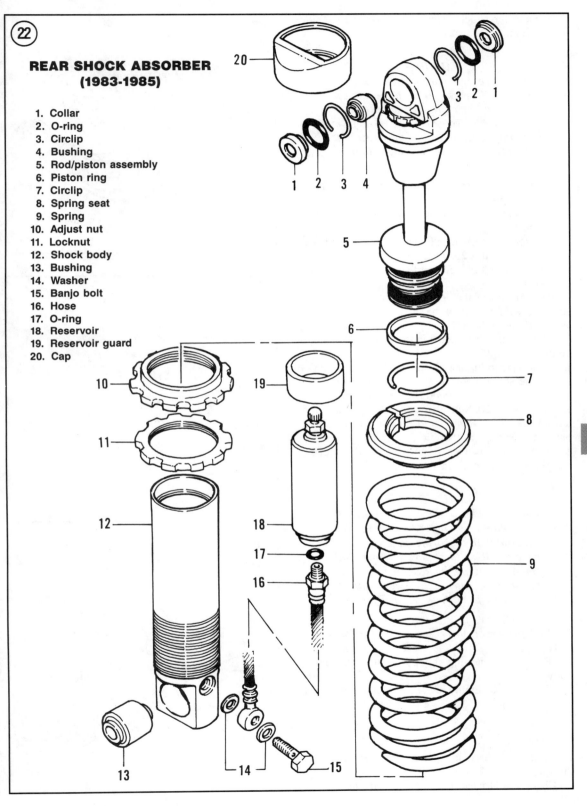

6. Remove the shock absorber through the left side of the frame.

WARNING
When discharging the nitrogen pressure in Step 7, make sure to wear eye protection. In addition, make sure to point the reservoir air valve away from your body or face. Failure to observe this warning may cause severe eye injury.

7. To install, reverse the removal procedures. Note the following:
   a. Tighten the nuts to the torque specification in **Table 3**.
8. Secure the reservoir in a vise (with padded jaws) as shown in **Figure 26**. Then loosen the hose bolt at the reservoir and disconnect the reservoir from the hose.
9. Pour oil out of the reservoir.
10. Secure the bottom of the shock absorber in a vise as described in Step 3.
11. Remove the bolt securing the hose to the shock body.
12. Referring to **Figure 27**, loosen the ring nut at the top of the shock body. Use the Kawasaki ring nut wrench (part No. 57001-1105) or equivalent.
13. See **Figure 28**. Slide the rubber bumper and ring nut up the shock shaft. Hold them up with rubber bands or a wooden clothes pin. Then push the bearing on the pushrod down and remove the circlip securing the pushrod assembly in the shock body.

CAUTION
Check the edge of the circlip groove. If it is flared or burred, remove this material with a bearing knife or emery paper. Failure to remove this material could result in damage to the shock piston ring when the shock shaft is withdrawn from the shock body.

14. Pull the rod/piston assembly out of the shock body.
15. Pour any remaining shock oil out of the shock body.
16. Further disassembly of the shock assembly is not recommended.

Inspection

1. Clean all parts in contact cleaner and dry thoroughly.
2. Check the O-rings for wear or damage.

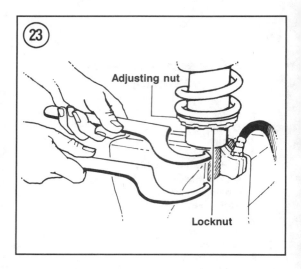

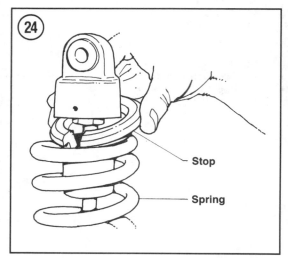

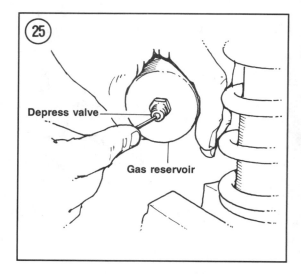

REAR SUSPENSION

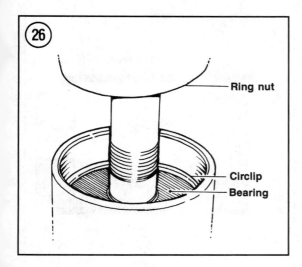

㉖ Ring nut / Circlip / Bearing

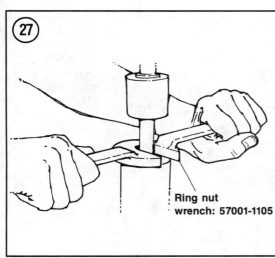

㉗ Ring nut wrench: 57001-1105

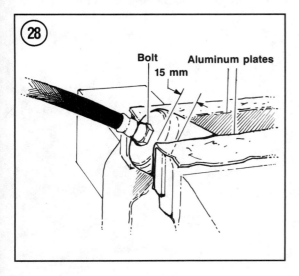

㉘ Bolt / 15 mm / Aluminum plates

3. Check the gas reservoir for dents or other damage that would prevent the internal piston from operating freely.
4. Replace all worn or damaged parts as required.

Assembly

Refer to **Figure 22** for this procedure.
1. Do not assemble the shock assembly until all of the parts have been cleaned and allowed to dry thoroughly.
2. Remove the air valve from the reservoir.
3. Invert the reservoir, then slowly fill it to the top of the hose threads with SAE 5W shock oil.

NOTE
Hold the reservoir up when performing Steps 5 and 6 to prevent oil from leaking out.

4. Make sure there is an O-ring on the end of the hose and attach the hose to the gas reservoir. Hand tighten the hose.
5. Secure the bottom shock mounting boss into a vise with soft jaws. Attach the hose to the shock body. Make sure to install the banjo bolt and the 2 washers as shown in **Figure 22**. Tighten the bolt to 18 N·m (13 ft.-lb.). Do not overtighten the bolt.
6. Pour SAE 5W shock oil into the shock body until it is just below the circlip groove.
7. Soak the piston end of the rod/piston assembly in SAE 5W shock oil. Loosen the hose end at the reservoir.
8. Insert the rod/piston assembly slowly into the shock body, until the piston end is just below the circlip groove. Oil and some air will ooze out of the loosened hose end (at the reservoir). Hand tighten the hose. Slowly pump the rod/piston up and down in gradually increasing strokes—begin with short strokes. This will bleed air from the shock body. Do it about 5 to 10 times. Tiny air bubbles will have come to the surface of the oil. Skim them off with your finger. Then push the bearing down and install the circlip (**Figure 28**) so that it seats in the groove in the shock body. Make sure the circlip seats completely in the groove. Install a new circlip if necessary.
9. Loosen the hose at the reservoir. Push in the reservoir piston until it is 46 mm (1.81 in.) from the ouside end of the reservoir as shown in **Figure 29**. Hold the hose end of the reservoir up when pushing on the piston to promote air bleeding. This will bleed any excess fluid and air from the reservoir and hose. Torque the reservoir hose to 18 N·m (13 ft.-lb.)

10. Use spray contact cleaner to wash excess oil away from the bearing and from the outside of the shock and reservoir

11. Align the ring nut with the top of the shock body and thread it slowly into the body threads. These parts use fine threads and they can strip easily if the parts are not aligned properly. Tighten the ring nut to 54 N·m (40 ft.-lb.).

WARNING
Only nitrogen should be used to pressurize the rear shock gas reservoir. Do not use air or any other type of gas; these may cause rust, wear or become a fire hazard.

WARNING
Working with high pressure is dangerous. Have your shock pressurized by a Kawasaki dealer or qualified suspension specialist.

12. When having your shock pressurized, note the following:
    a. Adjustment range: 10-15 kg/cm² (142-213 psi).
    b. Standard factory pressure: 10 kg/cm² (142 psi).
13. After the shock absorber has been safely pressurized with nitrogen, perform Step 12.
14. Install the spring over the shock rod and install the spring seat and circlip. Adjust the spring preload as described in Chapter Three.

UNI-TRAK SHOCK ABSORBER (1986-ON)

Removal/Installation

1. Support the motorcycle with the rear wheel off the ground.
2. Remove the seat and both side covers.
3. Remove the air cleaner element and air box (**Figure 30**).

WARNING
Do not disconnect the shock absorber reservoir hose when performing Step 4. In addition, do not drop the reservoir and lay it in a position where it could be damaged. The shock and reservoir is under extreme pressure.

4. Remove the shock absorber reservoir (**Figure 31**) from its mount on the right-hand side of the frame.

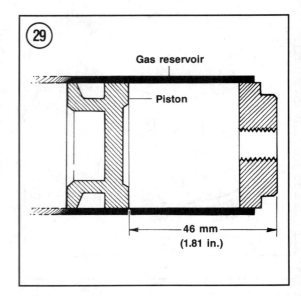

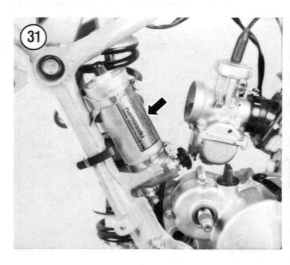

REAR SUSPENSION

5. Remove the top (**Figure 32**) and bottom (**Figure 33**) shock mounting bolts.
6. Remove the shock absorber through the left side of the frame.
7. To install, reverse the removal procedures. Note the following:

   a. Tighten the nuts to the torque specification in **Table 3**.

   b. Make sure the shock reservoir is properly mounted on the right-hand side of the frame.

NOTE
It is easier to remove the first shock mounting bolt if you hold up the rear wheel.

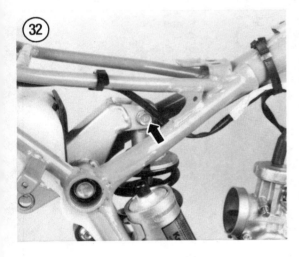

Disassembly

NOTE
The angle of the reservoir hose is critical. Mark the shock body and reservoir to ensure that the hose angle is correct after you reassemble the shock and reservoir.

Refer to **Figure 34**.
1. Remove the shock absorber as described in this chapter.
2. Wash the outside of the shock absorber in solvent and allow to dry thoroughly. Especially clean the threads at the bottom of the shock.
3. Secure the bottom shock absorber mount in a vise with soft jaws (**Figure 23**).
4. Using the Kawasaki wrenches (part No. 57001-1101) or equivalent, loosen the locknut (**Figure 35**). Then turn the adjusting nut all the way down to reduce spring preload.
5. Slide the rubber bumper down the shock shaft.
6. When all of the spring preload is removed, remove the circlip and spring seat at the top of the spring and remove the spring (**Figure 24**).

WARNING
When discharging the nitrogen pressure in Step 7, make sure to wear eye protection. In addition, make sure to point the reservoir air valve away from your body or face. Failure to observe this warning may cause severe eye damage.

7. Remove the air valve cap (A, **Figure 36**) from the air valve on the reservoir. Then depress the air valve with a small screwdriver (**Figure 25**) to release all nitrogen from the shock absorber.
8. Secure the reservoir in a vise (with padded jaws) as shown in **Figure 26**. Then loosen the hose bolt (B, **Figure 36**) at the reservoir and disconnect the reservoir from the hose.
9. Remove the bolt (**Figure 37**) securing the hose to the shock body and disconnect the hose.
10. Pour oil out of the reservoir and the shock body.
11. Secure the bottom of the shock absorber in a vise as described in Step 3.
12. Referring to **Figure 38**, pry up the stop with 2 small punches or screwdrivers until the stop is clear of the shock body. Slide the stop up the shock shaft and out of the way.

238 CHAPTER ELEVEN

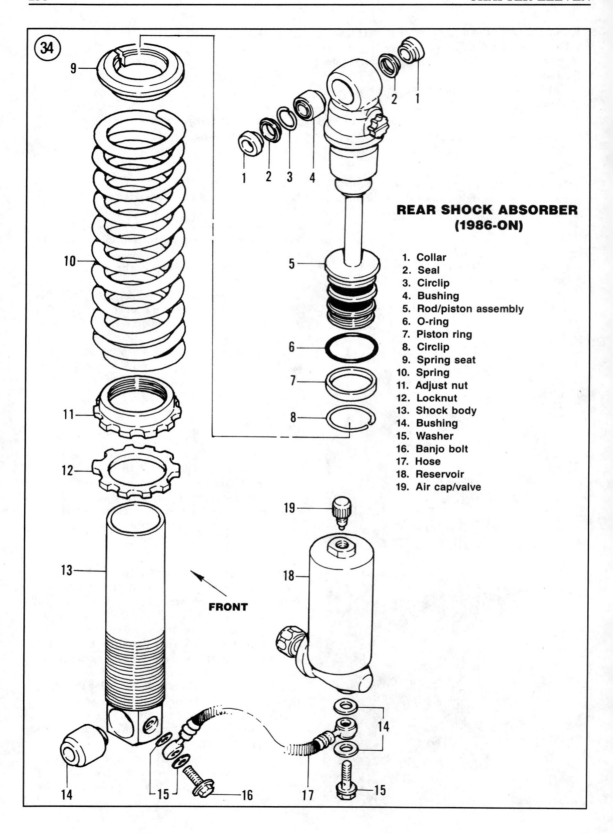

REAR SUSPENSION

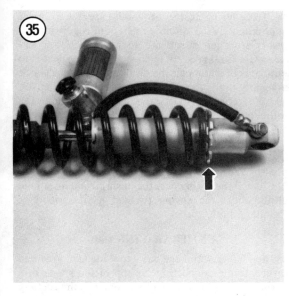

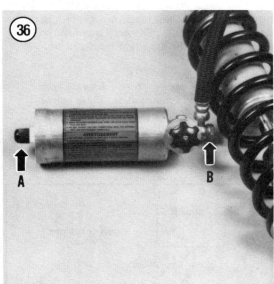

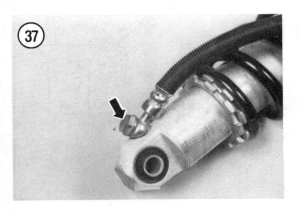

13. A bearing is now visible in the shock body. Lightly tap the bearing downward approximately 20 mm (0.8 in.) or until the circlip in the shock body is exposed.
14. Remove the circlip from the shock body.

CAUTION
Check the edge of the circlip groove. If it is glared or burred, remove this material with a bearing knife or emery paper. Failure to remove this material could result in damage to the shock piston ring when the shock shaft is withdrawn from the shock body.

15. Move the pushrod up and down and carefully and remove it from the shock body.
16. Pour any remaining shock oil out of the shock body.
17. Further disassembly of the shock assembly is not recommended.

Inspection

1. Clean all parts thoroughly in solvent and dry thoroughly.
2. Check the O-rings for wear or damage.
3. Check the gas reservoir for dents or other damage that would prevent the internal piston from operating freely.
4. Replace all worn or damaged parts as required.

Assembly

Refer to **Figure 34** for this procedure.
1. Do not assemble the shock assembly until all of the parts have been cleaned and allowed to dry thoroughly.
2. Mount the shock body in a vise with soft jaws.
3. Turn the gas reservoir dampin adjuster to the number 1 position.

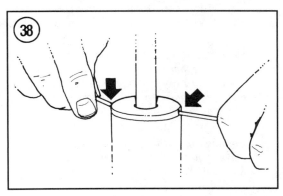

4. If the air valve was removed from the reservoir, apply Loctite 242 (blue) to the valve threads. Install the valve and tighten to 12 N·m (8.5 ft.-lb.).

5. Attach the hose to the shock body and the reservoir. Make sure to install washers on both sides of the hose fitting as shown in **Figure 37**. Only hand tighten the bolts.

6. Fill the shock body with oil until it is just level with the circlip groove.

7. Soak the piston end of the rod/piston assembly in shock oil. Slowly turn it in the oil to allow any air bubbles to escape.

8. Carefully insert the rod/piston assemnbly into the shock body until the bearing is just below the edge of the shock body.

9. Loosen the hose bolt at the reservoir. Compress the shock about 25 mm (1 in.). Excess oil and air will ooze out of the loose hose joint. Tighten the hose joint to 18 N·m (13 ft.-lb.).

10. Repeat Step 9 for the hose joint at the shock body, but tighten its hose bolt by hand.

11. Slowly pump the shock rod up and down. Begin with short strokes and gradually increase stroke length.

12. Push the shock rod into the shock body until the circlip groove is visible. Install the circlip (**Figure 28**). Make sure the circlip seats fully in the groove. Tap the stop over the shock body until it bottoms.

13. Clamp the shock in a vise so the oil bolt on the shock is pointing straight up. Disconnect the oil bolt at the shock. Keep the hose end elevated to avoid losing too much oil.

14. Extend the shock rod to full extension. Pour oil into the oil bolt hole until it is topped-off (**Figure 39**).

15. Carefully reinstall the oil bolt, 2 washers and oil hose. Hand tighten the bolt.

16. Add about 10-15 psi air to the reservoir's air valve. This will allow the diaphragm to assume its normal shape and will also force any excess oil and air from the hand-tightened oil bolt.

17. Stroke the shock rod back-and-forth its full stroke. If all the air has been bled from the shock, resistance will be consistent. If there is still some air in the shock, resistance will be inconsistent.

WARNING
Only nitrogen should be used to pressurize the rear shock gas reservoir. Do not use air or any other type of gases; these may cause rust, wear or become a fire hazard.

WARNING
Working with high pressure is dangerous. Have your shock pressurized by a Kawasaki dealer or qualified suspension specialist.

18. Have your dealer or shock specialist inject approximately 0.5 kg/cm^2 (7 psi) of nitrogen into the reservoir. Then check the shock body, hose and reservoir for leaks. If the shock leaks, bleed the nitrogen out and repair the problem. When the shock assembly holds the nitrogen, proceed with Step 19.

19. When having your shock pressurized, note the following:
   a. Adjustment range: 10-15 kg/cm^2 (142-213 psi).
   b. Standard factory pressure: 10 kg/cm^2 (142 psi).

20. After the shock absorber has been safely pressurized with nitrogen, perform Step 21.

21. Install the spring over the pushrod and install the clip. Adjust the spring preload as described in Chapter Three.

UNI-TRAK LINKAGE

The Uni-Trak linkage has a rocking arm mounted on the frame connecting the top of the shock to a vertical link. The vertical link connects the rocking arm to the swing arm. The bushings at all these joints must be inspected and lubricated according to the maintenance schedule (Chapter Three) and replaced when worn past the specified limits.

NOTE
Grease fittings (zerk fittings) are installed on some models. These can be used to periodically lubricate the bushings. Other models will require disassembly of the Uni-Trak linkage for periodic lubrication.

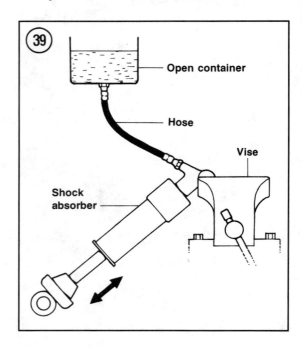

REAR SUSPENSION

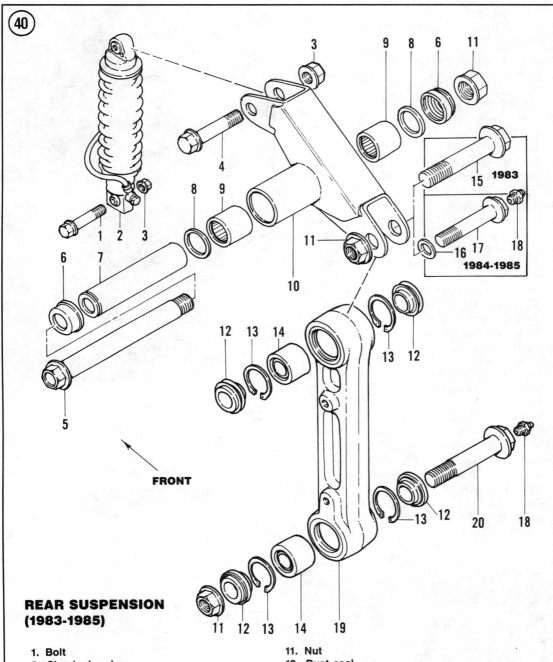

REAR SUSPENSION (1983-1985)

1. Bolt
2. Shock absorber
3. Nut
4. Pivot bolt
5. Pivot bolt
6. Dust seal
7. Sleeve bushing
8. Shim
9. Bearing
10. Rocking arm
11. Nut
12. Dust seal
13. Circlip
14. Ball-joint
15. Pivot bolt (1983)
16. Washer (1984-1985)
17. Pivot bolt (1984-1985)
18. Grease nipple (1984-1985)
19. Vertical link
20. Pivot bolt

Uni-Trak Linkage
Disassembly/Inspection/Lubrication
(1983-1985)

Refer to **Figure 40** for this procedure.
1. Support the motorcycle with the rear wheel off the ground.
2. Remove the seat and side covers.
3. Remove the air cleaner element and box (A, **Figure 41**).
4. Remove the vertical link as follows:
    a. Remove the 2 vertical link bolts (A, **Figure 42**).
    b. Remove the link (B, **Figure 42**) and the 4 end caps.
5. Remove the rocking arm as follows:
    a. Remove the pivot shaft plugs (B, **Figure 41**).
    b. Remove the upper link bolt at the rocking arm (A, **Figure 43**).
    c. Remove the upper shock absorber pivot bolt and shaft (B, **Figure 43**) at the rocking arm.
    d. Remove the rocking arm pivot shaft nut and bolt (C, **Figure 43**) and remove the rocking arm.
6. Inspect the vertical link (**Figure 44**) as follows:
    a. Remove the caps (A, **Figure 45**) and circlips (B, **Figure 45**).
    b. Clean the vertical link assembly in solvent and dry thoroughly.
    c. Inspect the bearings (**Figure 46**) and pivot bolts. Maximum bearing wear is 0.7 mm (0.028 in.). Replace any bearings that show excessive wear. Bearing replacement requires a press. Refer this service to a Kawasaki dealer or machine shop.
7. Inspect the rocking arm (**Figure 47**) as follows:
    a. Remove the caps (A, **Figure 48**) and washers (B, **Figure 48**).
    b. Remove the sleeve bushing (C, **Figure 48**).
    c. Clean the rocking arm assembly (**Figure 49**) in solvent and dry thoroughly.

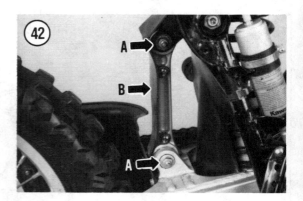

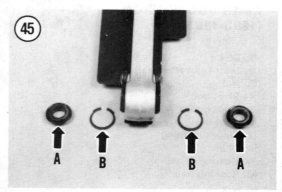

REAR SUSPENSION

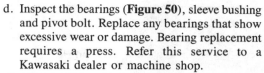

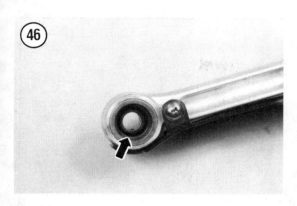

d. Inspect the bearings (**Figure 50**), sleeve bushing and pivot bolt. Replace any bearings that show excessive wear or damage. Bearing replacement requires a press. Refer this service to a Kawasaki dealer or machine shop.

8. Lubricate all bearings, bushings and pivot bolts with molybdenum disulfide grease.

9. To assemble the linkage, reverse the disassembly procedure. Note the following:
   a. Be sure to install the end caps during assembly.
   b. Tighten all pivot bolts to the torque specifications in **Table 2**.

Uni-Trak Linkage Disassembly/Inspection/Lubrication (1986-on)

Refer to **Figure 51** for this procedure.

1. Support the motorcycle with the rear wheel off the ground.
2. Remove the seat and side covers.
3. Remove the air cleaner element and box (**Figure 52**).
4. Remove the vertical link as follows:
   a. Remove the 2 vertical link bolts (A, **Figure 53**).
   b. Remove the link (B, **Figure 53**) and the 4 end caps.
5. Remove the rocking arm as follows:
   a. Remove the pivot shaft plugs (**Figure 54**).
   b. Remove the vertical link.
   c. Remove the shock absorber as described in this chapter.
   d. Remove the rocking arm pivot shaft nut and bolt (A, **Figure 55**) and remove the rocking arm (B, **Figure 55**).
6. Inspect the vertical link (**Figure 56**) as follows:
   a. Remove the end caps.
   b. Clean the vertical link assembly in solvent and dry thoroughly.

CHAPTER ELEVEN

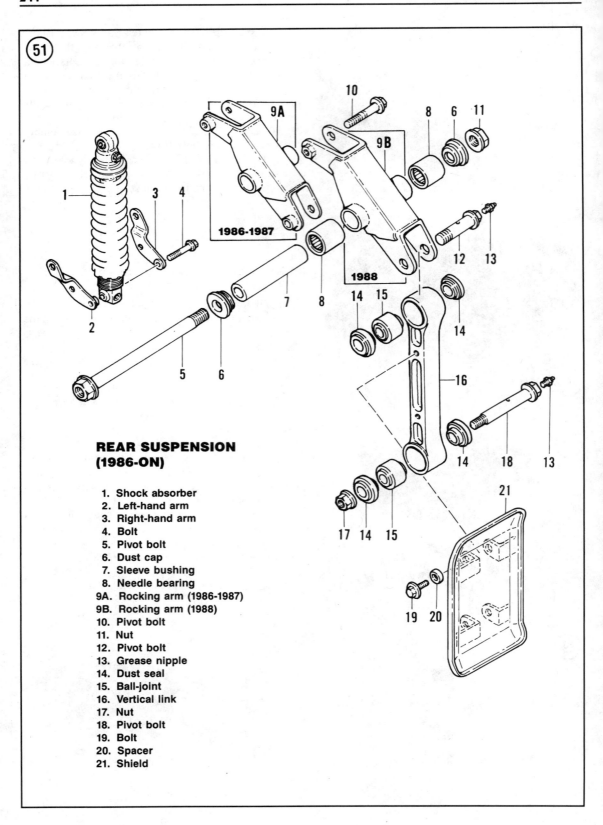

REAR SUSPENSION (1986-ON)

1. Shock absorber
2. Left-hand arm
3. Right-hand arm
4. Bolt
5. Pivot bolt
6. Dust cap
7. Sleeve bushing
8. Needle bearing
9A. Rocking arm (1986-1987)
9B. Rocking arm (1988)
10. Pivot bolt
11. Nut
12. Pivot bolt
13. Grease nipple
14. Dust seal
15. Ball-joint
16. Vertical link
17. Nut
18. Pivot bolt
19. Bolt
20. Spacer
21. Shield

REAR SUSPENSION

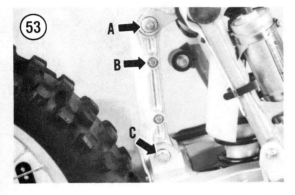

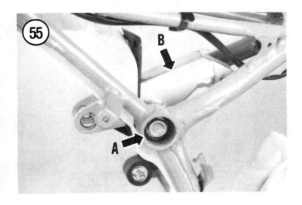

c. Inspect the bearings (**Figure 51**) and pivot bolts. Maximum bearing wear is 0.7 mm (0.028 in.). Replace any bearings that show excessive wear. Bearing replacement requires a press. Refer this service to a Kawasaki dealer or machine shop.

7. Inspect the rocking arm (**Figure 57**) as follows:
   a. Remove the end caps.
   b. Remove the sleeve bushing (**Figure 51**).
   c. Clean the rocking arm assembly in solvent and dry thoroughly.
   d. Inspect the bearings (**Figure 51**), sleeve bushing and pivot bolt. Replace any bearings that show excessive wear or damage. Bearing replacement requires a press. Refer this service to a Kawasaki dealer or machine shop.

8. Lubricate all bearings, bushings and pivot bolts with molybdenum disulfide grease.

9. To assemble the linkage, reverse the disassembly procedure. Note the following:
   a. Be sure to install the end caps during assembly.
   b. Tighten all pivot bolts to the torque specifications in **Table 3**.

SWING ARM

In time the bearings will wear beyond service limits and must be replaced. The condition of the bearings

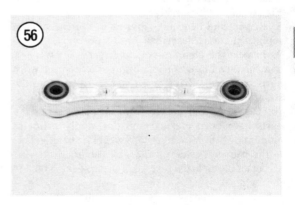

can greatly affect handling performance and if not replaced they can produce erratic and dangerous handling.

The rear swing arms used on the various models differ in construction and design. While bearing alignment differs between the various models, replacement is the same for all models.

Removal/Installation

1. Remove the bolts securing the seat and remove it.
2. Remove both number/side panels.
3. Remove the rear wheel and drive chain as described in this chapter.
4. Remove the lower vertical link pivot bolt and nut (**Figure 58**) at the swing arm.
5. Grasp the swing arm as shown in **Figure 59** and try to rock it back and forth, pulling the top and pushing the bottom, then reversing. If you feel any more than a very slight movement of the swing arm, and the pivot bolt is correctly tightened, the bearings should be replaced.
6. Remove the swing arm pivot nut and bolt (**Figure 60**). If you have to knock the bolt out with a rod, take care not to damage the bearings or the end of the pivot bolt.
7. Remove the swing arm along with any external washers, shims or seals. See **Figure 61** (1983-1984), **Figure 62** (1985) or **Figure 63** (1986-on).
8. Inspect the bearings (**Figure 64**). If necessary, replace them as described in this chapter.
9. Inspect the chain guards and plates for wear or damage. See **Figure 65** and **Figure 66**. Replace worn parts before the drive chain starts to wear into the swing arm.
10. Clean the old grease from all parts. After the parts have been cleaned and dry, apply a liberal amount of lithium waterproof wheel bearing grease to the bearings, sleeves and pivot shaft.
11. Installation is the reverse of these steps. Note the following:
   a. Tighten the swing arm pivot shaft nut to the torque specification in **Table 2** (1983-1985) or **Table 3** (1986-on).
   b. Tighten the vertical link pivot bolt to the torque specifications in **Table 2** (1983-1985) or **Table 3** (1986-on).
   c. Adjust the drive chain as described in Chapter Three.

SWING ARM BEARING REPLACEMENT

Refer to **Figure 61** (1983-1984), **Figure 62** (1985) or **Figure 63** (1986-on) when performing this procedure.

1. Remove the swing arm as described in this chapter.
2. Secure the swing arm in a vise with soft jaws.

CAUTION
Do not remove the bearings just for inspection as they are usually damaged during removal.

3. Carefully tap out the bearing. Use a suitable size drift or socket and extension and carefully drive the bearing out from the opposite end.

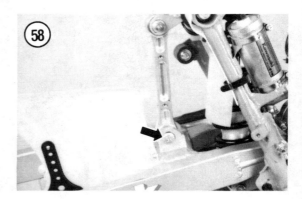

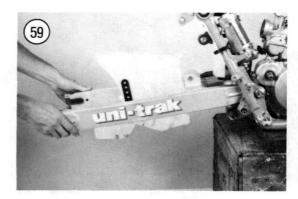

REAR SUSPENSION

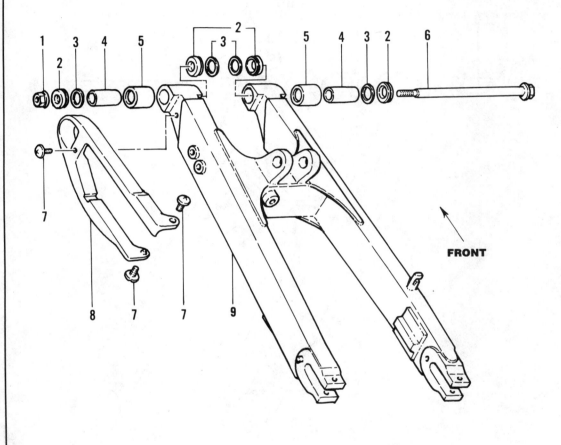

**REAR SWING ARM
(1983-1984)**

1. Nut
2. Dust cap
3. Shim
4. Sleeve
5. Needle bearing
6. Pivot shaft
7. Screw
8. Chain guard
9. Swing arm

CHAPTER ELEVEN

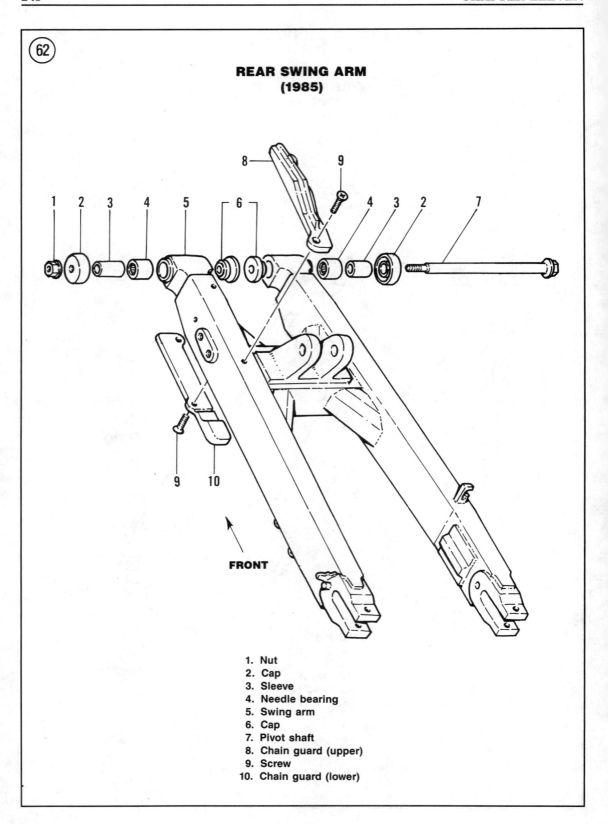

⑥² REAR SWING ARM
(1985)

1. Nut
2. Cap
3. Sleeve
4. Needle bearing
5. Swing arm
6. Cap
7. Pivot shaft
8. Chain guard (upper)
9. Screw
10. Chain guard (lower)

REAR SUSPENSION

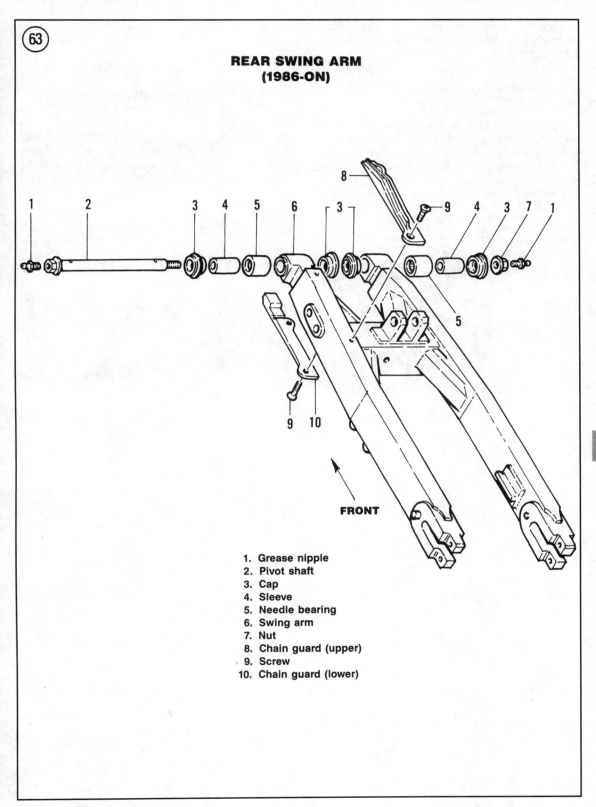

REAR SWING ARM (1986-ON)

1. Grease nipple
2. Pivot shaft
3. Cap
4. Sleeve
5. Needle bearing
6. Swing arm
7. Nut
8. Chain guard (upper)
9. Screw
10. Chain guard (lower)

4. Clean the swing arm thoroughly in solvent. Check the bearing mounting areas for cracks, wear or other damage.

NOTE
A press will be required to accurately and safely install the bearings.

5. Apply a light coat of lithium waterproof wheel bearing grease to all parts before installation.
6. Using a press, install the new bearings.
7. After installing the bearings, liberally coat them with lithium waterproof wheel bearing grease.
8. Install the swing arm as described in this chapter.

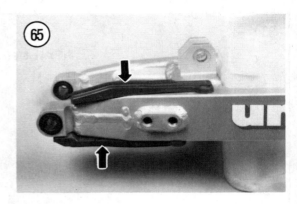

REAR SUSPENSION

Table 1 REAR SUSPENSION SPECIFICATIONS

Rear wheel travel	
1983-1985	280 mm (11.02 in.)
1986-on	290 mm (11.4 in.)
Rear tire size	
1983-1985	4.00 × 18 (4PR)
1986-on	100/100 × 18 59M
Uni-trak spherical bearing wear limit	0.7 mm (0.028 in.)
Rear shock spring free length	
Standard	
1983-1985	270 mm (10.63 in.)
1986-on	280 mm (11.0 in.)
Wear limit	
1983-1985	264.6 mm (10.42 in.)
1986-on	274 mm (10.8 in.)
Uni-trak sleeve diameter	
1983-1985	
Standard	23.987-23.000 mm (0.9444-0.9449 in.)
Wear limit	23.95 mm (0.943 in.)
1986-on	—
Rim runout	
Axial	
Standard	0.5 mm (0.02 in.)
Limit	2.0 mm (0.08 in.)
Radial	
Standard	0.8 mm (0.032 in.)
Limit	2.0 mm (0.08 in.)

Table 2 REAR SUSPENSION TIGHTENING TORQUES (1983-1985)

	N·m	ft.-lb.
Swing arm pivot shaft nut	78	58
Rear axle shaft nut	98	72
Rear sprocket bolts	29	22
Rear shock hose bolt	18	13
Rear shock ring nut		
1983	54	40
1984-1985	—	—
Rear shock bolts	69	51
Uni-trak		
Rocking arm center bolt	108	80
Vertical link bolts	69	51

Table 3 REAR SUSPENSION TIGHTENING TORQUES (1986-ON)

	N·m	ft.-lb.
Swing arm pivot shaft nut	78	58
Rear axle shaft nut	98	72
Rear sprocket nuts	25	19
Rear shock absorber bolts	57	42
Rear shock absorber bracket bolts	37	27.5
Uni-trak bolts	78	58

CHAPTER TWELVE

BRAKES

All models are equipped with drum brakes at the rear. On 1983-1985 models, drum brakes were also installed at the front. Starting with 1986 models, disc brakes are used on the front.

Brake specifications are listed in **Tables 1-3** at the end of this chapter.

DRUM BRAKES

Figure 1 illustrates the major components of a typical drum brake assembly. Activating the brake lever or pedal pulls the cable or rod which in turn rotates the camshaft. This forces the brake shoes out into contact with the brake drum.

Lever and pedal free play must be maintained on both brakes to minimize brake drag and premature brake wear, and maximize braking effectiveness. Refer to *Front Brake Lever Adjustment* and *Rear Brake Pedal Free Play* in Chapter Three, for complete adjustment procedures.

Glaze buildup on the brake shoes reduces braking effectiveness. The brake shoes should be removed and cleaned regularly to assure maximum brake shoe contact.

The front brake cable must be inspected and replaced periodically as it will stretch with use and can no longer be properly adjusted.

Disassembly

Refer to the illustration for your model when performing this procedure:
Figure 2: Front drum brake (1983-1985).
Figure 3: Rear drum brake (1983-1985).
Figure 4: Rear drum brake (1986-on).

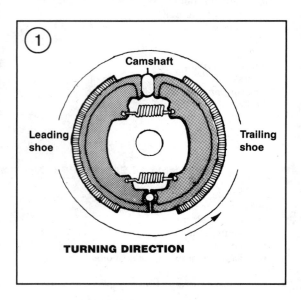

BRAKES

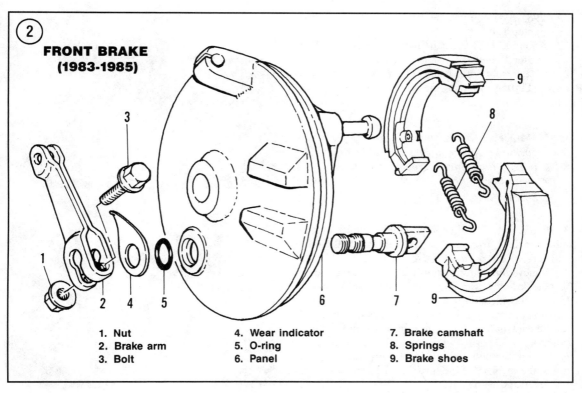

FRONT BRAKE (1983-1985)

1. Nut
2. Brake arm
3. Bolt
4. Wear indicator
5. O-ring
6. Panel
7. Brake camshaft
8. Springs
9. Brake shoes

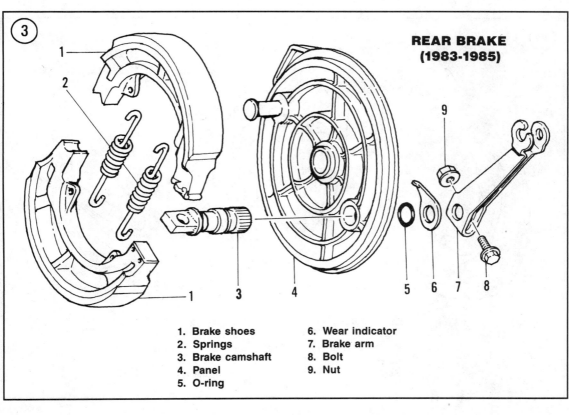

REAR BRAKE (1983-1985)

1. Brake shoes
2. Springs
3. Brake camshaft
4. Panel
5. O-ring
6. Wear indicator
7. Brake arm
8. Bolt
9. Nut

1A. *1983-1985:* Remove the front wheel as described in Chapter Ten.
1B. *All models:* Remove the rear wheel as described in Chapter Eleven.
2. Pull the front brake panel (**Figure 5**) or rear brake panel (**Figure 6**) out of the wheel.

NOTE
*Mark each brake shoe (**Figure 7**) for position before removing them in Step 3. In addition, place a clean shop rag on the linings to protect them from oil and grease during removal.*

3. Remove the brake shoe assembly, including the return springs, from the brake panel. Pull both brake shoes from the panel (**Figure 8**).
4. Remove the return springs and separate the shoes.
5. Check for factory alignment marks on the brake lever and camshaft. If they aren't visible, mark the position of the brake lever (**Figure 9**) as it is installed on the camshaft so it can be reinstalled in the same position.
6. Loosen the bolt and nut (A, **Figure 10**) securing the brake lever (B, **Figure 10**) to the cam. Remove the lever and camshaft.

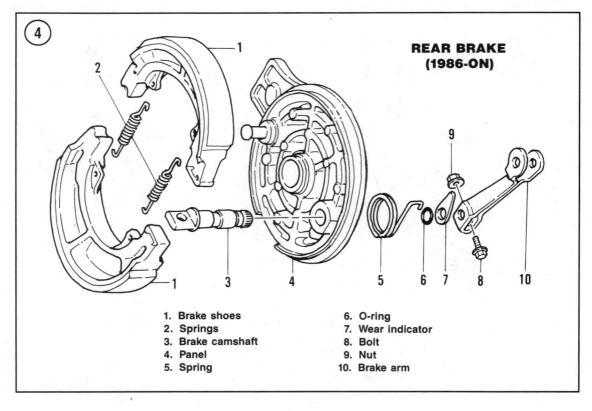

REAR BRAKE (1986-ON)

1. Brake shoes
2. Springs
3. Brake camshaft
4. Panel
5. Spring
6. O-ring
7. Wear indicator
8. Bolt
9. Nut
10. Brake arm

BRAKES

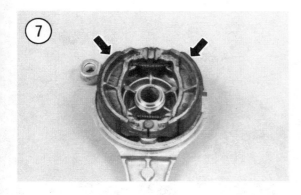

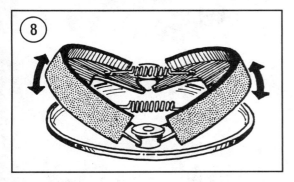

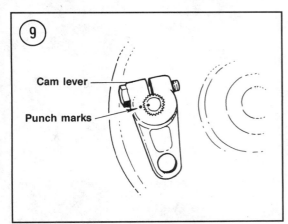

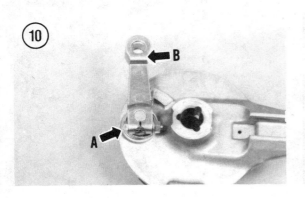

Inspection

1. Thoroughly clean and dry all parts except the linings.
2. Check the contact surface of the drum (A, **Figure 11**) for scoring. If there are deep grooves or the drum surface is severely damaged, the hub will have to be replaced. This type of wear can be avoided to a great extent if the brakes are disassembled and thoroughly cleaned after the bike has been ridden in mud or deep sand, or after each race.

NOTE
If oil or grease is on the drum surface, clean it off with spray brake cleaner— do not use any solvent that may leave an oily residue.

3. Use vernier calipers (**Figure 12**) and check the inside diameter of the drum for out-of-round or excessive wear. Refer to **Table 1** for brake specifications.
4. Inspect the linings for embedded foreign material. Dirt can be removed with a stiff wire brush. Check for traces of oil or grease. If the linings are contaminated, they must be replaced.

CHAPTER TWELVE

5. Measure the brake lining thickness (**Figure 13**) with a vernier caliper as shown in **Figure 14**. Replace the linings if worn to the wear limits in **Table 1**.

NOTE
Do not include the metal shoe thickness when measuring lining thickness.

6. Inspect the cam lobe and the pivot pin area of the shaft for wear and corrosion. Minor roughness can be removed with fine emery cloth.
7. Measure the length of the brake shoe spring with a vernier caliper as shown in **Figure 15**. Replace the springs if they exceed the wear limit specifications in **Table 1**. If the brake shoe springs are stretched, they will not fully retract the brake shoes resulting in a power-robbing drag on the drums and premature wear of the linings and drum.
8. Check the sealed bearing (**Figure 16**) or the oil seal (B, **Figure 11**) on the brake drum side for damage that would allow grease to enter the brake drum and contaminate the drum and brake shoes. Replace the bearing or seal as described in Chapter Ten (front wheel) or Chapter Eleven (rear wheel).

Assembly

Refer to illustration for your model when performing this procedure:
Figure 2: Front drum brake (1983-1985).
Figure 3: Rear drum brake (1983-1985).
Figure 4: Rear drum brake (1986-on).
1. Grease the shaft, cam, and pivot post with a light coat of brake grease. Avoid getting any grease on the brake plate where the linings come in contact with it.
2. Install the brake lever onto the brake cam. Make sure to align the 2 marks (**Figure 9**) made during disassembly.
3. Hold the brake shoes in a V-formation with the return springs attached (**Figure 8**) and snap them in place on the brake panel. Make sure they are firmly seated (**Figure 7**).

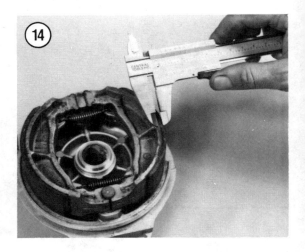

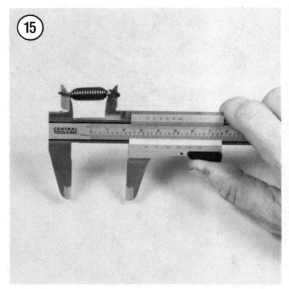

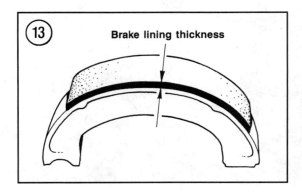

BRAKES

⑰

⑱

⑲

⑳

4. Install the brake panel assembly into the brake drum. See **Figure 5** or **Figure 6**.
5A. *1983-1985:* Install the front wheel as described in Chapter Ten.
5B. Install the rear wheel as described in Chapter Eleven.
6A. *1983-1985:* Adjust the front brake as described in Chapter Three.
6B. Adjust the rear brake as described in Chapter Three.

FRONT BRAKE CABLE

Brake cable adjustment should be checked periodically as the cable stretches with use and increases brake lever free play. Free play is the distance that the brake lever travels between the released position and the point when the brake shoes come in contact with the drum.

If the brake adjustment, as described in Chapter Three, can no longer be achieved the cable must be replaced.

Replacement

1. At the hand lever, loosen the locknut (A, **Figure 17**) and turn the adjusting barrel (B, **Figure 17**) all the way toward the cable sheath.
2. Disconnect the front brake cable at the wheel as follows:
   a. Remove the cotter pin from the clevis pin (**Figure 18**).
   b. Remove the washer (**Figure 19**).
   c. Remove the clevis pin (**Figure 20**).
   d. Loosen the brake cable adjuster (**Figure 21**) at the front hub and disconnect the cable from the hub.
3. Disconnect the cable from the cable guide on the left-hand fork slider (**Figure 22**).
4. Pull the hand lever all the way to the grip, remove the cable nipple from the lever and remove the cable.

㉑

5. Withdraw the cable from the plastic holders on the front fork clamps (**Figure 23**).

NOTE
Prior to removing the cable, make a drawing (or take a Polaroid picture) of the cable routing through the frame. It is very easy to forget how it was once it has been removed. Replace it exactly as it was, avoiding any sharp turns.

6. Install by reversing these removal steps.
7. Adjust the brake as described under *Front Brake Lever Adjustment* in Chapter Three.

FRONT DISC BRAKE (1986-ON)

The front disc brake is actuated by hydraulic fluid and controlled by a hand lever on the master cylinder. As the brake pads wear, the caliper piston moves out to automatically adjust for wear.

When working on hydraulic brake systems, it is necessary that the work area and all tools be absolutely clean. Any tiny particles of foreign matter and grit in the caliper assembly or master cylinder can damage the components.

Consider the following when servicing the front disc brake.

1. Use only DOT 3 brake fluid from a sealed container.
2. Do not allow disc brake fluid to contact any plastic parts or painted surfaces as damage will result.
3. Always keep the master cylinder reservoir and spare cans of brake fluid closed to prevent dust or moisture from entering. This would result in brake fluid contamination and brake problems.
4. Use only disc brake fluid (DOT 3) to wash parts. Never clean any internal brake components with solvent or any other petroleum base cleaners.
5. Whenever *any* component has been removed from the brake system the system is considered "opened" and must be bled to remove air bubbles. Also, if the brake feels "spongy," this usually means there are air bubbles in the system and it must be bled. For safe brake operation, refer to *Bleeding the System* in this chapter for complete details.

CAUTION
Disc brake components rarely require disassembly, so do not disassemble unless absolutely necessary. Do not use solvents of any kind on the brake system's internal components. Solvents will cause the seals to swell and distort. When disassembling and cleaning brake

components (except brake pads) use new DOT 3 brake fluid.

FRONT BRAKE PAD REPLACEMENT

There is no recommended time interval for changing the friction pads in the front disc brake. Pad wear depends greatly on riding habits and conditions.

To maintain an even brake pressure on the disc, always replace both pads in the caliper at the same time.

Refer to **Figure 24** for this procedure.

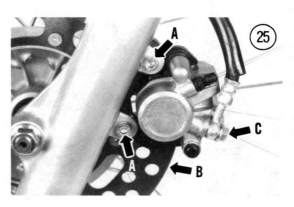

BRAKES

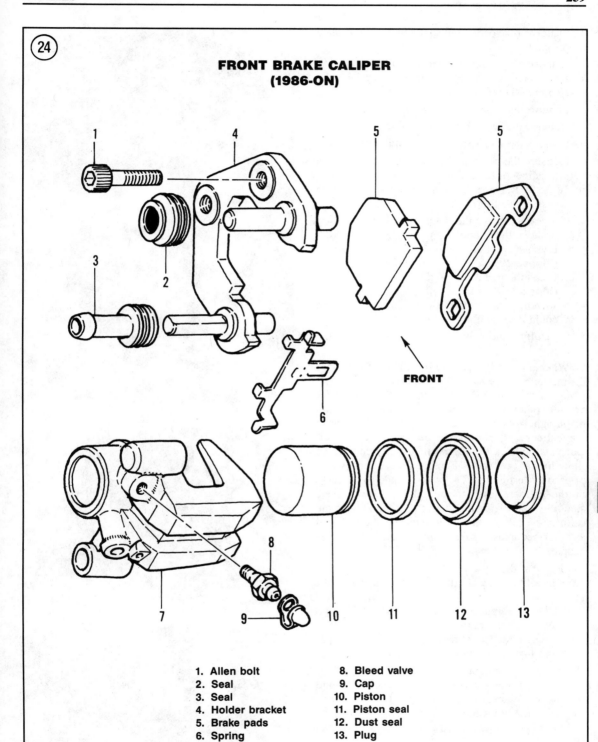

FRONT BRAKE CALIPER (1986-ON)

1. Allen bolt
2. Seal
3. Seal
4. Holder bracket
5. Brake pads
6. Spring
7. Housing
8. Bleed valve
9. Cap
10. Piston
11. Piston seal
12. Dust seal
13. Plug

1. Place the bike on a stand so the front wheel clears the ground.
2. Remove the brake caliper mounting bolts (A, **Figure 25**) and pull the brake caliper off of the brake disc (B, **Figure 25**).
3. Remove the inner brake pad (**Figure 26**).
4. Remove the outer brake pad (**Figure 27**).
5. Remove the pad spring (A, **Figure 28**).
6. Measure the brake pad friction thickness with a vernier caliper or ruler. Compare to the specifications in **Table 2**. Replace the brake pads if the friction thickness is too thin.
7. If necessary, check the piston assembly as follows:
    a. Remove the support bracket (B, **Figure 28**).
    b. Remove the plug from the end of the piston (**Figure 29**).
    c. Clean the pad recess and the end of the piston (**Figure 30**) with a soft brush. Do not use solvent, a wire brush or any hard tool which could damage the cylinder and/or piston.
8. Carefully remove any rust or corrosion from the disc.
9. When new brake pads are installed in the caliper the master cylinder brake fluid will rise as the caliper piston is repositioned. Clean the top of the master cylinder of all dirt. Remove the cap (**Figure 31**) and diaphragm from the master cylinder and slowly push the caliper piston (**Figure 30**) into the caliper. Constantly check the reservoir to make sure brake fluid does not overflow. Remove fluid, if necessary, prior to it overflowing. The piston should move freely in the caliper bore. If the piston doesn't move smoothly and there is evidence of it sticking in the caliper, the caliper should be removed and serviced as described under *Front Caliper Rebuilding* in this chapter.
10. Perform the following:
    a. Install the plug (**Figure 29**) into the end of the piston.
    b. Coat the support bracket pivot rods with high temperature grease.
    c. Align the support bracket arms with the caliper and install the support (B, **Figure 28**).
11. Install the pad spring (A, **Figure 28**).
12. Install the outer brake pad into the caliper behind the support bracket (**Figure 27**).
13. Align the holes in the inner brake pad with the caliper support bracket arms and install the brake pad (**Figure 26**).
14. Align the brake caliper with the brake disc. The brake shoes should be on each side of the brake disc with the brake friction material facing against the disc. See B, **Figure 25**.

BRAKES

15. Install the brake caliper mounting bolts (A, **Figure 25**) and tighten them to the torque specification in **Table 3**.

16. Spin the front wheel and activate the brake lever as many times as necessary as it takes to refill the cylinder in the caliper and correctly locate the pads.

17. Refill the master cylinder reservoir, if necessary, to maintain the correct brake fluid level. Install the diaphragm and top cover (**Figure 31**).

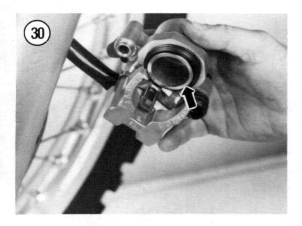

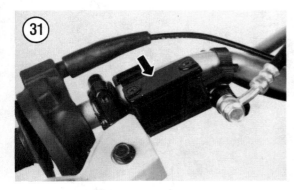

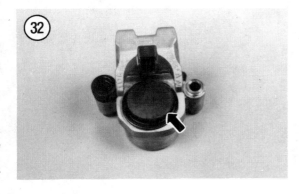

WARNING
Use brake fluid clearly marked DOT 3 from a sealed container. Other types may vaporize and cause brake failure. Always use the same brand name; do not intermix as many brands are not compatible.

WARNING
Do not ride the motorcycle until you are sure the brake is operating correctly with full hydraulic advantage. If necessary, bleed the brake system as described in this chapter.

FRONT CALIPER

Removal/Installation

1. Place the bike on a stand so the front wheel clears the ground.
2. Disconnect the caliper brake hose and washers. See C, **Figure 25**.
3. Place the end of the brake hose in a clean container. Operate the front brake lever to drain the master cylinder and brake hose of all brake fluid. Dispose of this brake fluid—never reuse brake fluid. To prevent the entry of moisture and dirt, cap the end of the brake line and tie the loose end up to the forks.
4. Remove the brake pads as described in this chapter. Remove the brake caliper.
5. Install by reversing these removal steps, noting the following.
6. Install the bracket and the 2 mounting bolts. Tighten the bolts to the torque specification in **Table 3**.
7. Install the brake hose, with a sealing washer on each side of the fitting, onto the caliper (**Figure 24**). Install the banjo bolt and tighten to the torque specification in **Table 3**.
8. Install the brake pads and tighten the caliper bolt as described in this chapter.
9. Bleed the brake as described in this chapter.

WARNING
Do not ride the motorcycle until you are sure the brake is operating properly.

Disassembly/Inspection/Reassembly

Refer to **Figure 24** for this procedure.
1. Remove the plug (**Figure 32**) from the piston if you have not previously done so.

2. Remove the dust seal from around the piston (**Figure 33**).

3. Cushion the caliper pistons with a shop rag. Then apply compressed air (**Figure 34**) through the brake line port to remove the piston (**Figure 35**).

WARNING
Cushion the piston with a shop rag. Do not try to cushion the piston with your fingers, as injury could result.

4. Remove the piston seal (**Figure 36**) from the piston bore.

5. Check the piston (**Figure 37**) and the caliper bore (A, **Figure 38**) for deep scratches or other obvious wear marks. If either part is less than perfect, replace it.

6. Check the caliper housing for damage; replace if needed.

7. Remove the bleed screw and check it for wear or damage.

8. Check the banjo bolt threads in the caliper. Check thread condition by screwing the bolt into the caliper.

9. Check the caliper bushing (B, **Figure 38**) for wear or damage; replace the bushing by pulling it out of the caliper. Reverse to install.

10. Check the support bracket bushing (A, **Figure 39**) for wear or damage; replace the bushing if necessary by pulling it out of the bracket. Check the rod (B, **Figure 39**) for cracks, scoring or damage; replace the support bracket assembly if necessary.

11. Check the pad spring for cracks or damage. Replace if necessary.

12. Measure the brake pad friction thickness (**Figure 40**) with a vernier caliper or ruler. Compare to the specifications in **Table 2**. Replace the brake pads if the friction material is too thin.

13. Replace the piston seal (A, **Figure 41**) and dust seal (B, **Figure 41**).

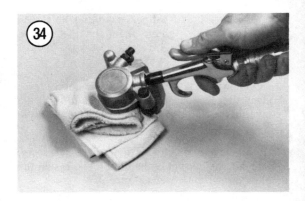

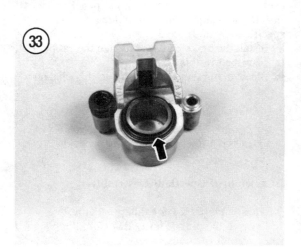

BRAKES

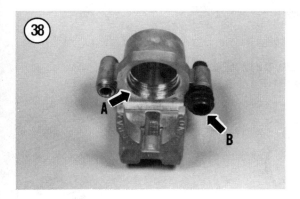

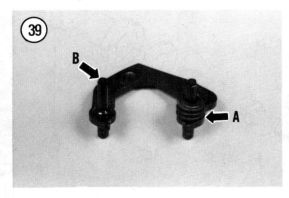

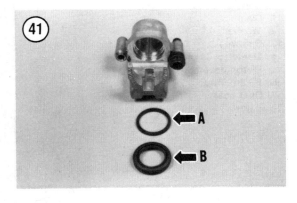

14. Measure the piston outside diameter (**Figure 37**) and the brake caliper piston bore (A, **Figure 38**) inside diameter. Compare the service wear limits in **Table 2**. Replace the piston and caliper housing as a set if any one part is worn excessively.

15. Clean all parts (except brake pads) with DOT 3 brake fluid.

16. Soak the new piston seal in fresh brake fluid. Coat the inside of the cylinder with fresh brake fluid prior to the assembly of parts.

17. Install a piston seal (A, **Figure 41**) into the second groove in the cylinder bore. See **Figure 36**.

NOTE
Check that the seal fits squarely in the cylinder bore groove. If the seal is not installed properly, the caliper assembly will leak and braking performance will be reduced.

18. The piston (**Figure 42**) has one open and one closed end. Insert the piston into the cylinder so that the open end faces out (**Figure 35**). Push the piston in all the way.

19. Install the dust seal around the piston (**Figure 33**). Make sure the dust seal fits into the groove completely.

20. Install the brake caliper assembly as described in this chapter.

FRONT MASTER CYLINDER

Removal/Disassembly

Refer to **Figure 43**.

1. Place the bike on a stand so the front wheel clears the ground.

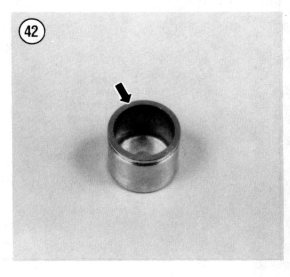

CHAPTER TWELVE

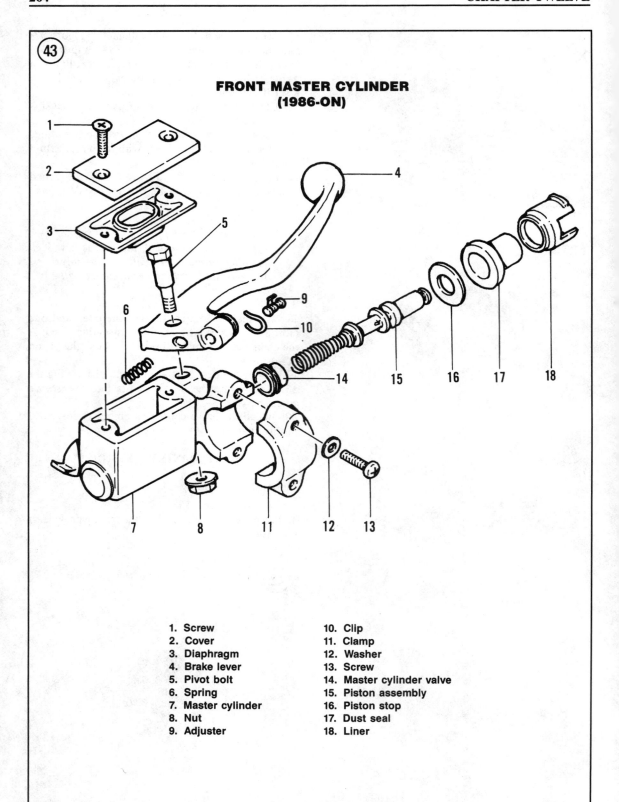

FRONT MASTER CYLINDER (1986-ON)

1. Screw
2. Cover
3. Diaphragm
4. Brake lever
5. Pivot bolt
6. Spring
7. Master cylinder
8. Nut
9. Adjuster
10. Clip
11. Clamp
12. Washer
13. Screw
14. Master cylinder valve
15. Piston assembly
16. Piston stop
17. Dust seal
18. Liner

BRAKES

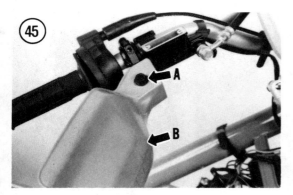

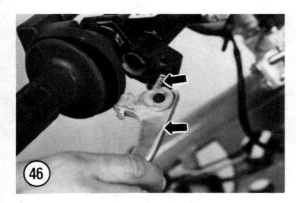

2. Remove the caliper banjo bolt and washers (**Figure 44**) and disconnect the brake hose at the caliper.

3. Place the end of the brake hose in a clean container. Operate the front brake lever to drain the master cylinder and brake hose of all brake fluid. Dispose of this brake fluid—never reuse brake fluid. To prevent the entry of moisture and dirt, cap the end of the brake line and tie the loose end up to the forks.

4. Remove the brake lever pivot bolt (A, **Figure 45**) and nut and remove the hand guard (B, **Figure 45**).

5. Remove the brake lever and spring (**Figure 46**).

6. Loosen the brake hose banjo bolt (**Figure 47**) at the master cylinder. Remove the bolt and washers (**Figure 48**).

7. Remove the bolts securing the master cylinder housing (**Figure 49**) and remove it.

NOTE
*Wrap the end of the brake hose in a plastic bag to prevent brake fluid from dripping onto other parts (**Figure 50**).*

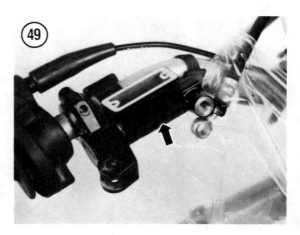

8. Using a small tipped screwdriver (**Figure 51**), press the plastic liner tabs out of the master cylinder housing grooves and remove the liner (**Figure 52**).
9. Remove the piston assembly (**Figure 53**).

Inspection

Refer to **Figure 43** for this procedure.
1. Clean all parts in fresh DOT 3 brake fluid.
2. The piston assembly is identified in **Figure 54**:
   a. Valve.
   b. Spring.
   c. Piston/primary cup.
   d. O-ring.
   e. Piston stop.
   f. Dust seal.

> *CAUTION*
> *Do not attempt to remove the primary cup (C, Figure 54) from the piston. The primary cup will be damaged and the piston assembly must be replaced.*

3. Remove the dust seal and piston stop from the piston assembly. Replace the dust seal if worn or damaged.
4. Check the piston assembly for wear or damage. The piston assembly must be replaced as a set if any one part is worn or damaged. Individual replacement parts are not available from Kawasaki.
5. Inspect the cylinder bore (A, **Figure 55**) and piston contact (C, **Figure 54**) surfaces for scratches, pitting or rust. If either part is less than perfect, replace it.

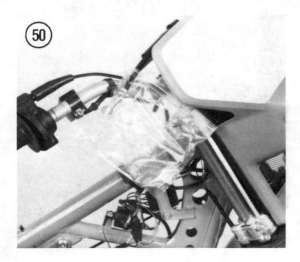

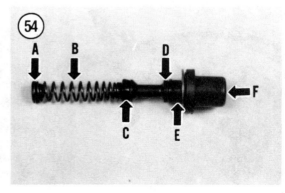

BRAKES

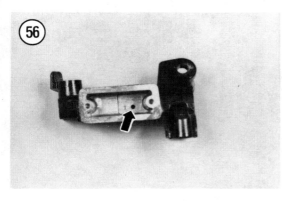

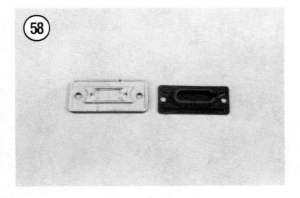

6. Check the spring (B, **Figure 54**) for cracks or damage. If the spring appears okay, measure its length with a vernier caliper and compare to the wear limit in **Table 2**. Replace the piston assembly if the spring is too short.

7. Check the primary cup (C, **Figure 54**) and O-ring (D, **Figure 54**) on the piston. Replace the piston assembly if these parts are worn, softened, swollen or damaged.

8. Measure the primary cup with a micrometer or vernier caliper and compare to the dimensions listed in **Table 2**. Replace the piston assembly if the primary cup outside diameter is too small.

9. Measure the piston outside diameter and the master cylinder bore inside diameter and compare to the specifications in **Table 2**. Replace both parts if any one part is worn excessively.

10. Check the piston stop (E, **Figure 54**) for cracks. Replace it if necessary.

11. Inspect the pivot hole in the hand lever and master cylinder (B, **Figure 55**). If worn or elongated it must be replaced.

12. Make sure the passages in the bottom of the brake fluid reservoir are clear (**Figure 56**). A plugged relief port will cause the pads to drag on the disc.

13. Check the banjo bolt threads in the master cylinder housing (**Figure 57**). Repair the threads with a tap if necessary.

14. Check the reservoir cap and diaphragm (**Figure 58**) for damage and deterioration and replace as necessary.

15. Check the liner for cracks or other damage that would allow the piston assembly to unseat during operation.

Assembly/Installation

Refer to **Figure 43**.

1. Soak the piston assembly in fresh DOT 3 brake fluid. Coat the inside of the cylinder with fresh brake fluid before assembling parts.

2. Assemble the piston assembly as shown in **Figure 54**.

3. Insert the piston assembly into the bore in the direction shown in **Figure 53**.

CAUTION
*Make sure the primary cup (C, **Figure** 54) does not turn inside out when installing the piston.*

4. Compress the piston assembly (**Figure 59**) and install the liner around the dust seal (**Figure 52**). Push the liner into the bore until it snaps into position. Check that the piston cannot fly out of the bore.
5. Mount the master cylinder housing (**Figure 49**) onto the handlebar assembly.
6. Remove the end of the brake hose from the plastic bag (discard the bag).
7. Insert the banjo bolt and the 2 sealing washers through the brake hose (**Figure 48**). Install the banjo bolt (**Figure 47**) and tighten to the torque specification in **Table 3**.
8. Insert the spring (**Figure 46**) into the brake lever. Then align the brake lever with the master cylinder pivot hole and install the lever (**Figure 60**).
9. See **Figure 45**. Align the hand guard (B) with the brake lever and install the pivot bolt (A) and nut. Tighten the nut securely. Operate the lever to make sure the pivot bolt is not too tight.
10. Refill the master cylinder and bleed the brake as described in this chapter.

WARNING
Do not ride the bike until the front brake is working properly.

FRONT BRAKE HOSE REPLACEMENT

Under racing conditions, the brake hose should be replaced once a year or whenever it shows signs of wear or damage.
1. Place a container under the brake line at the caliper. Remove the banjo bolt and sealing washers at the caliper assembly (**Figure 44**).
2. Place the end of the brake hose in a clean container. Operate the front brake lever to drain the master cylinder and brake hose of all brake fluid. Dispose of this brake fluid—never reuse brake fluid.
3. Remove the banjo bolt and sealing washers at the master cylinder (**Figure 47**). See **Figure 48**.
4. Disconnect the brake hose at the front fork (**Figure 61**).
5. Install a new brake hose in the reverse order of removal. Install new sealing washers and banjo bolts if necessary.
6. Tighten the banjo bolts to torque specification listed in **Table 3**.
7. Refill the master cylinder with fresh brake fluid clearly marked DOT 3. Bleed the brake as described in this chapter.

WARNING
Do not ride the motorcycle until you are sure that the brakes are operating properly.

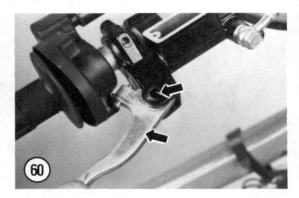

BRAKES

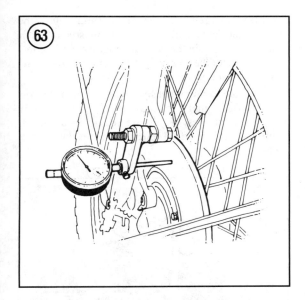

FRONT BRAKE DISC

Inspection

It is not necessary to remove the disc from the wheel to inspect it. Small marks on the disc are not important, but radial scratches deep enough to snag a fingernail reduce braking effectiveness and increase brake pad wear. If these grooves are found, the disc should be resurfaced or replaced.

1. Measure the thickness around the disc at several locations with vernier calipers or a micrometer (**Figure 62**). The disc must be replaced if the thickness at any point is less than specified in **Table 2**.
2. Make sure the disc bolts are tight prior to performing this check. Check the disc runout with a dial indicator as shown in **Figure 63**. Slowly rotate the wheel and watch the dial indicator. If the runout exceeds the limit in **Table 2**, the disc must be replaced.
3. Clean the disc of any rust or corrosion and wipe clean with lacquer thinner. Never use an oil-based solvent that may leave an oil residue on the disc.

Removal/Installation

1. Remove the front wheel as described in Chapter Ten.

NOTE
Place a piece of wood in the caliper in place of the disc. This way, if the brake lever is inadvertently squeezed, the piston will not be forced out of the cylinder. If this does happen, the caliper might have to be disassembled to reseat the piston and the system will have to be bled.

2. Remove the screws securing the disc to the wheel. See **Figure 64**.
3. Install by reversing these removal steps. Tighten the screws to the torque specification in **Table 3**.

BLEEDING THE SYSTEM

This procedure is necessary only when the brakes feel spongy, there is a leak in the hydraulic system, a component has been replaced or the brake fluid has been replaced.

1. Flip off the dust cap from the brake bleeder valve (**Figure 65**).

2. Connect a length of clear tubing to the bleeder valve on the caliper (**Figure 66**). Place the other end of the tube into a clean container. Fill the container with enough fresh brake fluid to keep the end submerged. The tube should be long enough so that a loop can be made higher than the bleeder valve to prevent air from being drawn into the caliper during bleeding.

CAUTION
Cover the front wheel, fender and fuel tank with a heavy cloth or plastic tarp to protect it from the accidental spilling of brake fluid. Wash any spilled brake fluid off of any surface immediately, as it will destroy the finish. Use soapy water and rinse completely.

3. Clean the top of the master cylinder of all dirt and foreign matter. Remove the cap and diaphragm (**Figure 67**). Fill the reservoir to about 10 mm (3/8 in.) from the top. Insert the diaphragm to prevent the entry of dirt and moisture.
4. If the master cylinder was disassembled or is dry, it must be bled. Remove the banjo bolt and hose from the master cylinder.
5. While holding your thumb over the banjo bolt hole, pump the brake lever three or four times. Hold the lever in, then slightly release thumb pressure. Some air bubbles and fluid will ooze out. Repeat this procedure until you feel some resistance when pumping the brake lever. Top off the master cylinder with brake fluid.
6. Reinstall the banjo bolt and tighten it. Again, pump the lever three or four times and hold the lever in. Now, loosen the banjo bolt about 1/4 turn. Some air bubbles and fluid will ooze out. Repeat this procedure until no more air comes out of the banjo joint. Tighten the banjo bolt to the torque specification in **Table 3**. Top off the master cylinder with brake fluid.

WARNING
Use brake fluid clearly marked DOT 3 only. Others may vaporize and cause brake failure. Always use the same brand name; do not intermix the brake fluids, as many brands are not compatible.

7. Slowly apply the brake lever several times. Hold the lever in the applied position and open the bleeder valve about 1/2 turn (**Figure 66**). Allow the lever to travel to its limit. When this limit is reached, tighten the bleeder screw. As the brake fluid enters the system, the level will drop in the master cylinder reservoir. Maintain the level at about 10 mm (3/8 in.) from the top of the reservoir to prevent air from being drawn into the system.
8. Continue to pump the lever and fill the reservoir until the fluid emerging from the hose is completely free of air bubbles. If you are replacing the fluid, continue until the fluid emerging from the hose is clean.

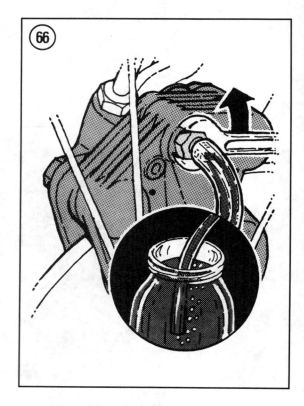

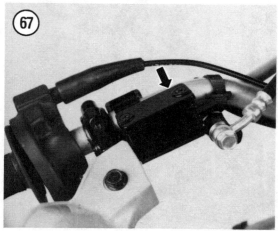

BRAKES

NOTE
If bleeding is difficult, it may be necessary to allow the fluid to stabilize for a few hours. Repeat the bleeding procedure when the tiny bubbles in the system settle out.

9. Hold the lever in the applied position and tighten the bleeder valve. Remove the bleeder tube and install the bleeder valve dust cap (**Figure 65**).
10. If necessary, add fluid to correct the level in the master cylinder reservoir. It must be above the level line.
11. Install the cap and tighten the screws. See **Figure 67**.
12. Test the feel of the brake lever. It should feel firm and should offer the same resistance each time it's operated. If it feels spongy, it is likely that air is still in the system and it must be bled again. When all air has been bled from the system and the brake fluid level is correct in the reservoir, double-check for leaks and tighten all fittings and connections.

WARNING
Before riding the motorcycle, make certain that the front brake is working correctly by operating the lever several times. Then make the test ride a slow one at first to make sure the brake is working correctly.

Tables are on the next page.

Table 1 FRONT AND REAR DRUM BRAKE SPECIFICATIONS

	Standard mm (in.)	Wear limit mm (in.)
Brake shoe lining thickness	4.0 (0.16)	2.0 (0.08)
Brake drum inside diameter		
Front (1983-1985)	120.00-120.16 (4.724-4.731)	120.75 (4.754)
Rear (all models)	110.00-110.16 (4.331-4.337)	110.75 (4.360)
Brake shoe spring free length		
Short spring	30.8-31.2 (1.21-1.23)	32.4 (1.28)
Long spring	44.5-45.5 (1.75-1.79)	47.0 (1.85)

Table 2 FRONT DISC BRAKE SPECIFICATIONS (1986-ON)

	Standard mm (in.)	Wear limit mm (in.)
Brake pad friction material thickness	4 (0.16)	2 (0.08)
Brake disc thickness	3.1-3.3 (0.12-0.13)	2.5 (0.10)
Disc runout	0-0.15 (0-0.006)	0.3 (0.01)
Brake caliper		
Cylinder inside diameter	33.94-33.98 (1.336-1.338)	34.00 (1.339)
Piston outside diameter	33.887-33.900 (1.3341-1.3346)	33.85 (1.333)
Master cylinder		
Cylinder inside diameter	11.000-11.063 (0.4331-0.4356)	11.08 (0.436)
Piston outside diameter	10.823-10.850 (0.4261-0.4272)	10.80 (0.425)
Primary cup diameter	11.3-11.7 (0.445-0.461)	11.2 (0.441)
Spring free length	38.3-42.3 (1.51-1.67)	36.4 (1.43)

Table 3 FRONT DISC BRAKE TIGHTENING TORQUES (1986-ON)

	N·m	ft.-lb.
Brake hose banjo bolts	29	21.7
Caliper mounting bolts	25	16.5
Disc mounting screws	10	7

INDEX

A

Air cleaner 161

B

Brakes
    bleeding the system 269-271
    cable 257-258
    caliper 261-263
    disc (1986-on) 258
    disc, front 269
    drum 252-257
    hose replacement 268
    master cylinder 263-268
    pad replacement 258-261
    troubleshooting 31-33
Break-in procedure 91

C

Caliper 261-263
Capacitor discharge ignition 187-188
Capacitor discharge unit 190-191
Carburetor
    fuel level adjustment 178-183
    operation 161-162
    service (1983-1987) 162-178
Cleaning solvent 38
Clutch 27
    cable 138-139
    clutch release mechanism 139
    cover (1983-1985) 122-123
    cover (1986-on) 123-130
    removal/disassembly 130-137

Crankcase and crankshaft 101-120
Cylinder 78-85
Cylinder head 75-77

D

Disc brakes
    1986-on 258
    front 269
Drive chain 230-231
Drive sprocket 230
Drum brakes 252-257

E

Electrical system
    capacitor discharge ignition 187-188
    capacitor discharge unit 190-191
    enduro timer case 194
    engine kill switch 192
    ignition coil 191
    lighting system 192-193
    magneto 188-190
    spark plug 192
Enduro timer case 194
Engine kill switch 192
Engine, lower end
    crankcase and crankshaft 101-120
    engine sprocket 101
    removal/installation 96-100
    servicing engine in frame 96
Engine lubrication 38-39
Engine noises 25
Engine performance 24-25

Engine starting troubles 23-24
Engine, top end
   break-in procedure 91
   cleanliness 75
   cooling 73-75
   cylinder 78-85
   cylinder head 75-77
   lubrication 73
   piston, wrist pin and
     piston rings 85-91
   principles 73
   servicing engine in frame 75
   valve assembly 92-93
Engine tune-up 57-64
Excessive vibration 25
Exhaust system 183-184
   decarbonizing 184
   repair 185
External shift mechanism 143-146

Lubrication
   cleaning solvent 38
   engine 38-39
   periodic 39-45

M

Magneto 188-190
Maintenance
   periodic 45-57
   pre-checks 35-36
   storage 66-67
   suspension adjustment 64-66
   tires and wheels 36-38
Master cylinder 263-268
Mechanic's tips 17

F

Fasteners 5-9
Forks, front 213-222
Front suspension and steering 31
Fuel system
   air cleaner 161
   shutoff valve 183
   tank 183

P

Pad replacement 258-261
Parts replacement 10
Periodic lubrication 39-45
Periodic maintenance 45-57
Piston, wrist pin and
   piston rings 85-91
Pre-checks 35-36
Primary drive gear 137-138

H

Handlebar, front 206-207
Hose replacement 268
Hub
   front 200-202
   rear 226-230

S

Safety first 2
Service hints 2-4
Shock absorbers, rear,
   1983-1985 232-236
Spark plug 192
Starting difficulties 23
Starting the engine 22-23
Steering head, front 207-213
Storage 66-67
Suspension adjustment 64-66
Suspension and steering, front 31
   forks 213-222
   handlebar 206-207
   hub 200-202
   steering head 207-213
   tire changing 203-204
   tire repairs 204-206
   wheels 196-200

I

Ignition coil 191
Ignition system, troubleshooting 28
Instruments 22

K

Kickstarter 139-143

L

Lighting system 192-193
Lubricants 9-10, 38

INDEX

Suspension, rear
   drive chain 230-231
   drive sprocket 230
   hub.................................226-230
   shock absorbers (1983-1985) 232-236
   swing arm 245-246
   swing arm bearing
     replacment........................246-250
   tire changing and tire repairs 231
   uni-trak linkage 240-245
   uni-trak shock absorber
     (1986-on) 236-240
   uni-trak suspension 231
   wheel.............................224-226
Swing arm bearing
   replacement 246-250
Swing arm, rear 245-246

T

Test equipment 15-17
Tires and wheels 36-38
Tires, front
   changing 203-204
   repairs 204-206
Tires, rear
   changing 231
   repairs 231
Torque specifications 5
Transmission 28
   internal shift mechanism 156
   operation 148-149
   overhaul 149-155

Troubleshooting
   brakes..............................31-33
   clutch 27
   engine noises 25
   engine performance 25
   engine starting troubles 23-24
   excessive vibration 25
   front suspension and steering 31
   ignition system.........................28
   instruments 22
   operating requirements 21-22
   starting difficulties 23
   starting the engine 22-23
   transmission 28
   two-stroke pressure testing 25-27
Tune-up..............................57-64
Two-stroke pressure testing 25-27

U

Uni-trak
   linkage............................240-245
   shock absorber, 1986-on 236-240
   suspension 231

V

Valve assembly 92-93

W

Washing the bike 4-5

WIRING DIAGRAMS

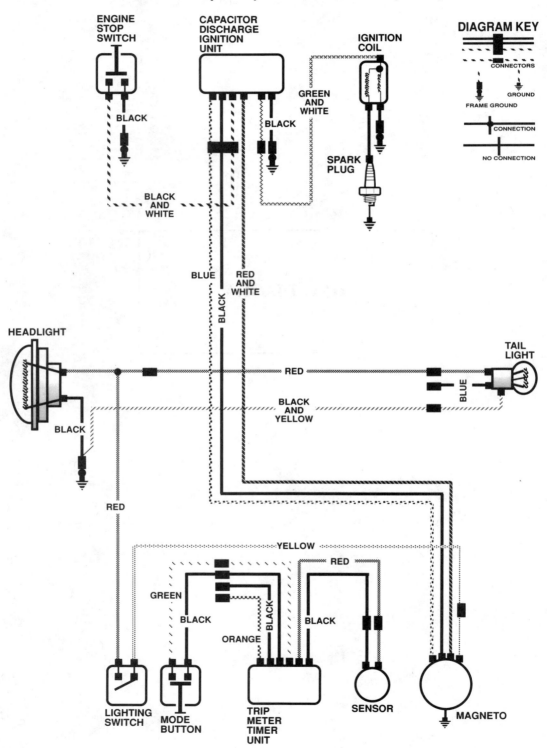

WIRING DIAGRAMS

279

KAWASAKI KDX200-C2 (1987) & KDX200-C3 (1988)

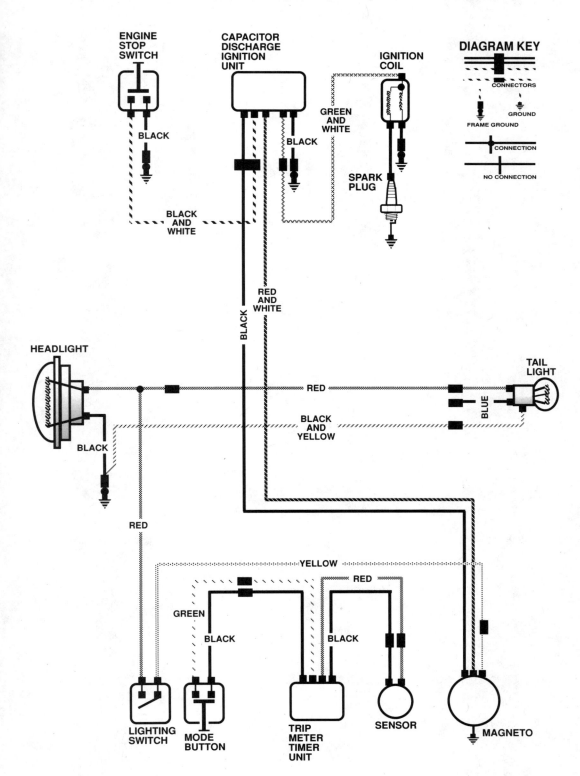

NOTES

MAINTENANCE LOG

Date	Miles	Type of Service

Check out clymer.com for our full line of powersport repair manuals.

BMW
M308	500 & 600 CC Twins, 55-69	
M309	F650, 1994-2000	
M500-3	BMW K-Series, 85-97	
M501	K1200RS, GT & LT, 98-05	
M502-3	BMW R50/5-R100 GSPD, 70-96	
M503-3	R850, R1100, R1150 and R1200C, 93-05	

HARLEY-DAVIDSON
M419	Sportsters, 59-85
M428	Sportster Evolution, 86-90
M429-4	XL/XLH Sportster, 91-03
M427-1	Sportster, 04-06
M418	Panheads, 48-65
M420	Shovelheads,66-84
M421-3	FLS/FXS Evolution,84-99
M423-2	FLS/FXS Twin Cam, 00-05
M422-3	FLH/FLT/FXR Evolution, 84-99
M430-4	FLH/FLT Twin Cam, 99-05
M424-2	FXD Evolution, 91-98
M425-3	FXD Twin Cam, 99-05

HONDA
ATVs
M316	Odyssey FL250, 77-84
M311	ATC, TRX & Fourtrax 70-125, 70-87
M433	Fourtrax 90 ATV, 93-00
M326	ATC185 & 200, 80-86
M347	ATC200X & Fourtrax 200SX, 86-88
M455	ATC250 & Fourtrax 200/250, 84-87
M342	ATC250R, 81-84
M348	TRX250R/Fourtrax 250R & ATC250R, 85-89
M456-3	TRX250X 87-92; TRX300EX 93-04
M215	TRX250EX, 01-05
M446-2	TRX250 Recon & ES, 97-04
M346-3	TRX300/Fourtrax 300 & TRX300FW/Fourtrax 4x4, 88-00
M200-2	TRX350 Rancher, 00-06
M459-3	TRX400 Foreman 95-03
M454-3	TRX400EX 99-05
M205	TRX450 Foreman, 98-04
M210	TRX500 Rubicon, 98-04

Singles
M310-13	50-110cc OHC Singles, 65-99
M319-2	XR50R, CRF50F, XR70R & CRF70F, 97-05
M315	100-350cc OHC, 69-82
M317	Elsinore, 125-250cc, 73-80
M442	CR60-125R Pro-Link, 81-88
M431-2	CR80R, 89-95, CR125R, 89-91
M435	CR80, 96-02
M457-2	CR125R & CR250R, 92-97
M464	CR125R, 1998-2002
M443	CR250R-500R Pro-Link, 81-87
M432-3	CR250R, 88-91 & CR500R, 88-01
M437	CR250R, 97-01
M352	CRF250, CRF250X & CRF450R, CRF450X, 02-05
M312-13	XL/XR75-100, 75-03
M318-4	XL/XR/TLR 125-200, 79-03
M328-4	XL/XR250, 78-00; XL/XR350R 83-85; XR200R, 84-85; XR250L, 91-96
M320-2	XR400R, 96-04
M339-7	XL/XR 500-650, 79-03

Twins
M321	125-200cc, 65-78
M322	250-350cc, 64-74
M323	250-360cc Twins, 74-77
M324-5	Twinstar, Rebel 250 & Nighthawk 250, 78-03
M334	400-450cc, 78-87
M333	450 & 500cc, 65-76
M335	CX & GL500/650 Twins, 78-83
M344	VT500, 83-88
M313	VT700 & 750, 83-87
M314-2	VT750 Shadow (chain drive), 98-05
M440	VT1100C Shadow , 85-96
M460-3	VT1100C Series, 95-04

Fours
M332	CB350-550cc, SOHC, 71-78
M345	CB550 & 650, 83-85
M336	CB650,79-82
M341	CB750 SOHC, 69-78
M337	CB750 DOHC, 79-82
M436	CB750 Nighthawk, 91-93 & 95-99
M325	CB900, 1000 & 1100, 80-83
M439	Hurricane 600, 87-90
M441-2	CBR600F2 & F3, 91-98
M445-2	CBR600F4, 99-06
M434-2	CBR900RR Fireblade, 93-99
M329	500cc V-Fours, 84-86
M438	Honda VFR800, 98-00
M349	700-1000 Interceptor, 83-85
M458-2	VFR700F-750F, 86-97
M327	700-1100cc V-Fours, 82-88
M340	GL1000 & 1100, 75-83
M504	GL1200, 84-87
M508	ST1100/PAN European, 90-02

Sixes
M505	GL1500 Gold Wing, 88-92
M506-2	GL1500 Gold Wing, 93-00
M507-2	GL1800 Gold Wing, 01-05
M462-2	GL1500C Valkyrie, 97-03

KAWASAKI
ATVs
M465-2	KLF220 & KLF250 Bayou, 88-03
M466-4	KLF300 Bayou, 86-04
M467	KLF400 Bayou, 93-99
M470	KEF300 Lakota, 95-99
M385	KSF250 Mojave, 87-00

Singles
M350-9	Rotary Valve 80-350cc, 66-01
M444-2	KX60, 83-02; KX80 83-90
M448	KX80/85/100, 89-03
M351	KDX200, 83-88
M447-3	KX125 & KX250, 82-91 KX500, 83-04
M472-2	KX125, 92-00
M473-2	KX250, 92-00
M474-2	KLR650, 87-06

Twins
M355	KZ400, KZ/Z440, EN450 & EN500, 74-95
M360-3	EX500, GPZ500S, Ninja R, 87-02
M356-4	Vulcan 700 & 750, 85-04
M354-2	Vulcan 800 & Vulcan 800 Classic, 95-04
M357-2	Vulcan 1500, 87-99
M471-2	Vulcan Classic 1500, 96-04

Fours
M449	KZ500/550 & ZX550, 79-85
M450	KZ, Z & ZX750, 80-85
M358	KZ650, 77-83
M359-3	900-1000cc Fours, 73-81
M451-3	1000 &1100cc Fours, 81-02
M452-3	ZX500 & 600 Ninja, 85-97
M453-3	Ninja ZX900-1100 84-01
M468-2	Ninja ZX-6, 90-04
M469	ZX7 Ninja, 91-98
M453-3	Ninja ZX900, ZX1000 & ZX1100, 84-01
M409	Concours, 86-04

POLARIS
ATVs
M496	Polaris ATV, 85-95
M362	Polaris Magnum ATV, 96-98
M363	Scrambler 500, 4X4 97-00
M365-2	Sportsman/Xplorer, 96-03

SUZUKI
ATVs
M381	ALT/LT 125 & 185, 83-87
M475	LT230 & LT250, 85-90
M380-2	LT250R Quad Racer, 85-92
M343	LTF500F Quadrunner, 98-00
M483-2	Suzuki King Quad/ Quad Runner 250, 87-98

Singles
M371	RM50-400 Twin Shock, 75-81
M369	125-400cc 64-81
M379	RM125-500 Single Shock, 81-88
M476	DR250-350, 90-94
M384-3	LS650 Savage, 86-04
M386	RM80-250, 89-95
M400	RM125, 96-00
M401	RM250, 96-02

Twins
M372	GS400-450 Twins, 77-87
M481-4	VS700-800 Intruder, 85-04
M482-2	VS1400 Intruder, 87-01
M484-3	GS500E Twins, 89-02
M361	SV650, 1999-2002

Triple
M368	380-750cc, 72-77

Fours
M373	GS550, 77-86
M364	GS650, 81-83
M370	GS750 Fours, 77-82
M376	GS850-1100 Shaft Drive, 79-84
M378	GS1100 Chain Drive, 80-81
M383-3	Katana 600, 88-96 GSX-R750-1100, 86-87
M331	GSX-R600, 97-00
M478-2	GSX-R750, 88-92 GSX750F Katana, 89-96
M485	GSX-R750, 96-99
M377	GSX-R1000, 01-04
M338	GSF600 Bandit, 95-00
M353	GSF1200 Bandit, 96-03

YAMAHA
ATVs
M499	YFM80 Badger, 85-01
M394	YTM/YFM200 & 225, 83-86
M488-5	Blaster, 88-05
M489-2	Timberwolf, 89-00
M487-5	Warrior, 87-04
M486-5	Banshee, 87-04
M490-3	Moto-4 & Big Bear, 87-04
M493	YFM400FW Kodiak, 93-98
M280-2	Raptor 660R, 01-05

Singles
M492-2	PW50 & PW80, BW80 Big Wheel 80, 81-02
M410	80-175 Piston Port, 68-76
M415	250-400cc Piston Port, 68-76
M412	DT & MX 100-400, 77-83
M414	IT125-490, 76-86
M393	YZ50-80 Monoshock, 78-90
M413	YZ100-490 Monoshock, 76-84
M390	YZ125-250, 85-87 YZ490, 85-90
M391	YZ125-250, 88-93 WR250Z, 91-93
M497-2	YZ125, 94-01
M498	YZ250, 94-98 and WR250Z, 94-97
M406	YZ250F & WR250F, 01-03
M491-2	YZ400F, YZ426F, WR400F WR426F, 98-02
M417	XT125-250, 80-84
M480-3	XT/TT 350, 85-00
M405	XT500 & TT500, 76-81
M416	XT/TT 600, 83-89

Twins
M403	650cc, 70-82
M395-10	XV535-1100 Virago, 81-03
M495-4	V-Star 650, 98-05
M281-2	V-Star 1100, 99-05
M282	Road Star, 99-05

Triple
M404	XS750 & 850, 77-81

Fours
M387	XJ550, XJ600 & FJ600, 81-92
M494	XJ600 Seca II, 92-98
M388	YX600 Radian & FZ600, 86-90
M396	FZR600, 89-93
M392	FZ700-750 & Fazer, 85-87
M411	XS1100 Fours, 78-81
M397	FJ1100 & 1200, 84-93
M375	V-Max, 85-03
M374	Royal Star, 96-03
M461	YZF-R6, 99-04
M398	YZF-R1, 98-03
M399	FZ1, 01-05

VINTAGE MOTORCYCLES
Clymer® Collection Series
M330	Vintage British Street Bikes, BSA, 500–650cc Unit Twins; Norton, 750 & 850cc Commandos; Triumph, 500-750cc Twins
M300	Vintage Dirt Bikes, V. 1 Bultaco, 125-370cc Singles; Montesa, 123-360cc Singles; Ossa, 125-250cc Singles
M301	Vintage Dirt Bikes, V. 2 CZ, 125-400cc Singles; Husqvarna, 125-400cc Singles; Maico, 250-501cc Singles; Hodaka, 90-125cc Singles
M305	Vintage Japanese Street Bikes, Honda, 250 & 305cc Twins; Kawasaki, 250-750cc Triples; Kawasaki, 900 & 1000cc Fours